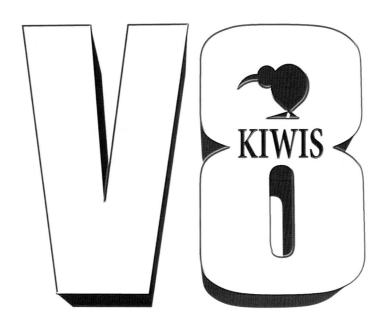

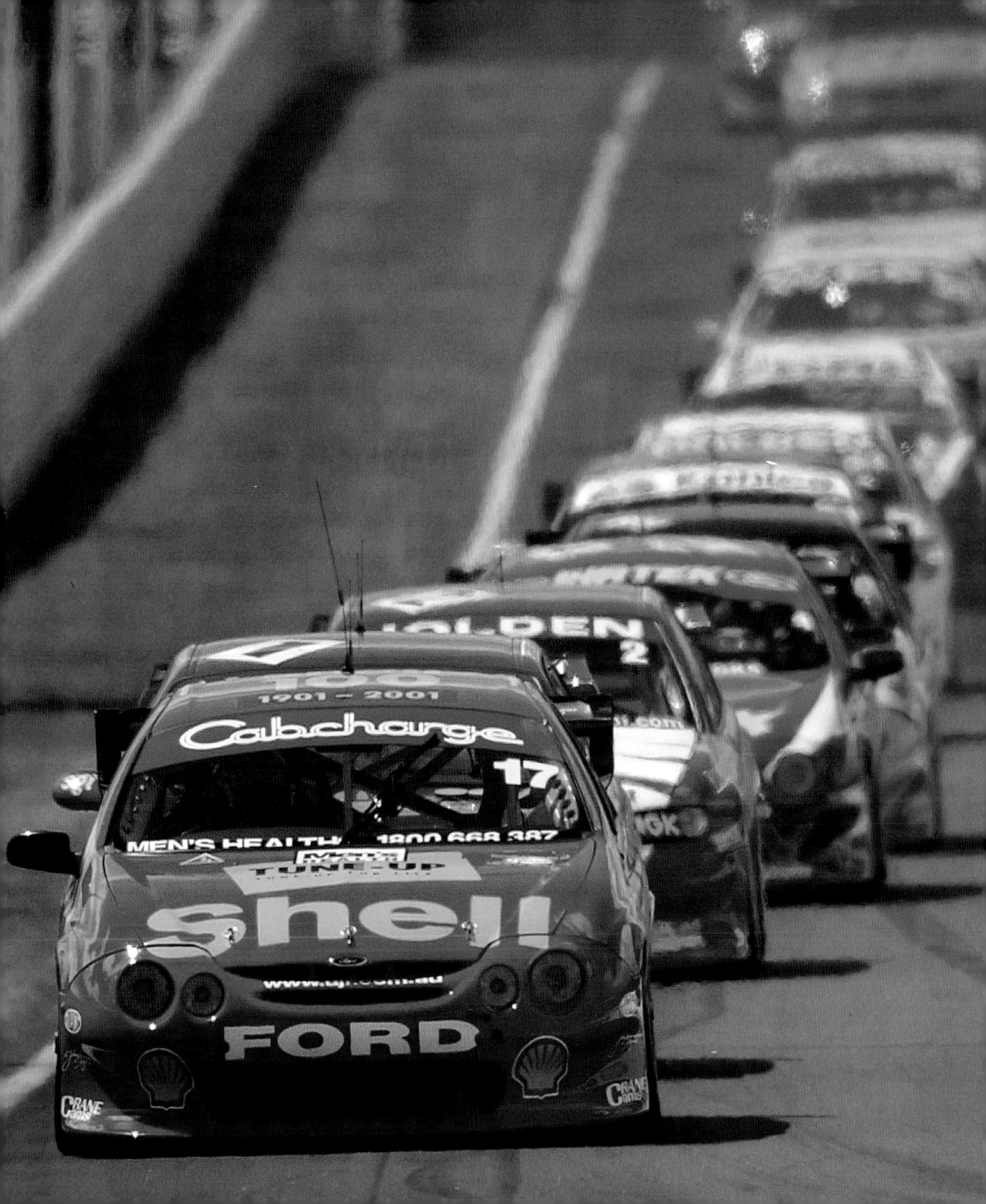
1901 - 2001
Cabcharge
17
MEN'S HEALTH
1800 668 387
shell
FORD
2

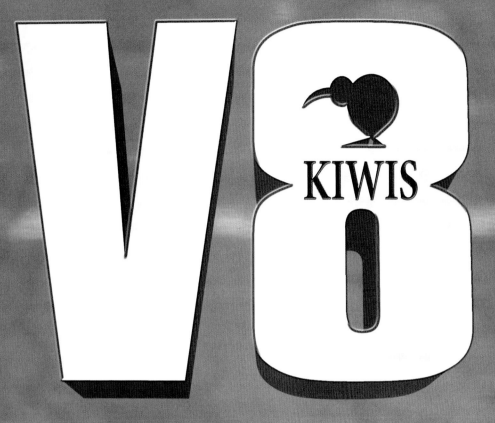

V8 KIWIS

NEW ZEALANDERS MAKING IT BIG IN TOURING CARS

Peter Bidwell

Hodder Moa

Credits — chapter opening pages:

Ch. 1, pp 12–13: Spectacular action at Bathurst, 2004 — Getty Images
Ch. 2, pp 38–39: Peter Brock in practice for the Bathurst 1000 km, 2004 — Getty Images
Ch. 3, pp 54–55: Marcos Ambrose's Ford during practice at Bathurst, 2005 — Getty Images
Ch. 4, pp 74–75: Jason Richards of TKR at Winton circuit, Victoria — Dirk Klynsmith/Graphic Dak Photography
Ch. 5, pp 92–93: Jim Richards and Mark Skaife in action at Bathurst, 2002 — Getty Images
Ch. 6, pp 122–123: Greg Murphy practises at Bathurst, 2005 — Getty Images
Ch. 7, pp 154–155: Paul Radisich in a practice lap at Pukekohe, 2004 — Getty Images
Ch. 8, pp 168–169: The Richards/Whincup Holden at Bathurst, 2005 — Getty Images
Ch. 9, pp 186–187: Simon Wills in action during the Big Pond 300 km, 2003 — Getty Images
Ch. 10, pp 196–197: Team Brock's 05 practising at Bathurst, 2002 — Getty Images
Ch. 11, pp 208–209: Greg Murphy practises at Pukekohe, 2004 — Getty Images

National Library of New Zealand Cataloguing-in-Publication Data

Bidwell, Peter.
V8 Kiwis : New Zealanders making it big in touring cars / Peter Bidwell.
Includes bibliographical references.
ISBN-13: 978-1-86971-060-6
ISBN-10: 1-86971-060-6
1. Automobile racing drivers—New Zealand. 2. Automobiles,
Racing—Australia. I. Title.
796.720922—dc 22

A Hodder Moa Book

Published in 2006 by Hachette Livre NZ Ltd
4 Whetu Place, Mairangi Bay
Auckland, New Zealand

Designed and produced by Hachette Livre NZ Ltd
Printed by Tien Wah Press Ltd, Singapore

Front cover: Russell Ingall, Stone Brothers Racing (left); Greg Murphy, Super Cheap Auto Racing (right) — Getty Images
Back cover: The New Zealand drivers shortly before competing in one of the touring car endurance rounds, 2002. Back row (from
              left): John McIntyre, Mark Porter, Jim Richards, Greg Murphy, Craig Baird, John Faulkner. Front row (from left): Steven
              Richards, Jason Richards, Simon Wills, Paul Radisich — Dirk Klynsmith/Graphic Dak Photography

To Sue, for allowing me to follow my dreams, and Hamish, Kirsty and Guy for

putting up with my many absences.

Contents

Acknowledgements

This book would not have been completed without the co-operation of numerous people. I would like to particularly thank the following:

Jim Richards, whose passion for motor racing, even at the age of 58, is an inspiration to us all.

Greg Murphy, for being just as forthright out of the car as in it, and whose exploits provided a lot of the impetus for this project.

Ross Stone, for being happy to tell the Stone brothers' remarkable story, after initial uncertainty.

Craig Baird, whose honesty, insight, and support were of great help.

David John, for not giving up on his dream despite the many hurdles.

Jason Richards, for his willingness to share it all.

Paul Radisich, for his patience and professionalism.

Robbie Francevic, for whetting my appetite for saloon car racing when I was a teenager.

Kevin Murphy, for reminding us that you can still have a high-powered new career in your 50s.

Simon Wills, for being prepared to talk about the hard times.

Nigel Greenway, for his painstaking research and statistical information.

Tony Cochrane, for his support of the book.

Cole Hitchcock, Supercars' hard-working media manager, who answered my many requests for assistance.

Hachette Livre NZ, especially Warren Adler, for sharing my enthusiasm for V8 Supercars, and Caroline List and designer Craig Violich for their help and expertise.

Foreword

It's been great to see the development of V8 Supercars into one of the premier sporting championships in Australia. Touring car racing used to be largely for the diehard fans, with much of the focus centred on the legendary Bathurst 1000 km. What happens at Mount Panorama is almost as big as Melbourne Cup day but now the other Supercar rounds attract huge attention too.

When I left Auckland for Australia in 1975 it was good to be paid a few dollars to race at national level. But even with a little sponsorship times were pretty hard. The growth of professionalism has allowed V8 drivers to be full-time. They have long since left the cars to their mechanics and engineers, and some of them are being paid an absolute fortune compared to the pittance I used to get. I'm not complaining though. In recent years I have been paid well for doing something I would have done for nothing anyway. I've had a lifetime of enjoyment out of the sport, and I now derive pleasure out of watching my elder son, Steven, footing it with the best Supercar drivers. I'm enjoying my racing as much as, if not more than, ever. At the age of 58, I feel blessed that I'm still competing at the top level, driving my Porsches in the Carrera Cup and various road rallies, including the New Zealand Targa Rally. And I'm still being invited to drive for the Holden Racing Team in the two big V8 endurance rounds. I still set high standards for myself, and being a V8 part-timer these days it has made some of my recent Bathurst appearances so special.

In 2002 I partnered probably the most complete driver I've raced against, Mark Skaife, to victory there. The year after I was third fastest in the top 10 shootout, and in 2005 I was still competitive enough to be in the shootout. Going to Bathurst has always been a great experience for me, and I've had a number of my most memorable sporting moments there. Over the years since the late Rod Coppins and I first appeared at Bathurst in 1974, other Kiwi drivers have also come to Australia to race. I never saw myself as a trailblazer when I moved to Australia in 1975. Though I often raced as a lone Kiwi, I was just a driver proud to be representing New Zealand. Not that Australians made life hard for me. In fact it's been the opposite. They recognised my ability, and treated me as one of their own. It's good for New Zealand that there are more Kiwi drivers, mechanics, and team owners than ever before in Supercars. Among the pluses has been the development of New Zealand's own increasingly successful V8 series.

My most satisfying period came between 1989 and 1995 when I raced alongside Mark Skaife in Fred Gibson's team. There was a terrific atmosphere. Mark, Fred and I were such good friends, and for a lot of that time Mark and I were often unbeatable. It also allowed me to be around for the first three years of the V8 formula. There were some hard times, but it was soon evident that the 'Ford v Holden' concept would be a winner. New Zealanders are just about as passionate about it as their trans-Tasman cousins, which has helped make it a much bigger thing than any of the original planners ever thought possible.

Jim Richards, December 2005

Introduction

Australia's V8 Supercars championship has captured the imagination of New Zealand sporting fans. It is reflected in the thousands who have attended each of the rounds at Pukekohe for the first five years, the big groups who cross the Tasman each year to witness rounds in Adelaide, Surfers Paradise, Melbourne and Bathurst, and the consistently strong ratings for the Sunday afternoon coverage provided by Television New Zealand. Over the years they have revelled in the classic Holden versus Ford battles, exhibiting a fervour similar to that of the Australian fans, and have been enraptured by the deeds of the legendary drivers: charismatic Peter Brock, Holden's No. 1 pin-up boy for so long; Ford's Dick Johnson; fellow Australian Larry Perkins; expat Canadian Allan Moffat; and New Zealand's own seven-times winner of the Bathurst 1000 km, Jim Richards.

Today's crowds have been enthralled by the brilliance of another New Zealander, Greg Murphy, competing more than favourably against Australia's elite of Mark Skaife, Marcos Ambrose, Russell Ingall, and Greg Lowndes — who horrified the legions of Holden fans in 2001 by crossing over to the enemy, Ford. Murphy has been the one New Zealand driver able to win Supercar rounds in the three years to 2005. Four other New Zealanders, Paul Radisich, Craig Baird, Jason Richards and Simon Wills, have joined Murphy full-time on the grid in recent years with varying degrees of success, and a fifth driver, Auckland-born Steven Richards, is often identified as a Kiwi though he thinks of himself as more of an Australian.

Eleven New Zealanders competed in the series in 2005, the five regulars being joined for the Sandown and Bathurst endurance races by veterans Jim Richards and John Faulkner, and the younger Mark Porter (who also contested the V8 development championship), Kayne Scott (who will feature in the development championship in 2006), Matthew Halliday and Fabian Coulthard (who will also have greater Supercar opportunities in 2006).

A number of other New Zealand drivers have competed in the championship since the start of the V8 formula in 1993, and those who have contested earlier Australian touring car events include the extroverted Robbie Francevic; New Zealand's only Formula One world champion, Denny Hulme; and former motorcycle ace Graeme Crosby.

The top team in the series, Stone Brothers Racing, is owned by brothers Jimmy and Ross Stone, formerly of Pukekohe, whose drivers Ambrose and Ingall have won the individual touring car championship from 2003–2005. Three other 2005 teams had strong New Zealand connections: perennial battlers Team Kiwi Racing, which is still based in Auckland; Tasman Motorsport, whose managing director is Greg Murphy's father, Kevin Murphy; and Team Dynamik, owned by a former national champion Kieran Wills. An interesting newcomer for 2006 is Paul Cruickshank Racing's one-car team, which has graduated from the development series. Cruickshank, formerly of Ashburton, has strong engineering and team management credentials, and a crew largely made up of New Zealanders.

V8 Supercars Australia boss, Tony Cochrane, estimated that there were 120 New Zealanders involved in a variety of tasks among the 19 teams who started in 2005, and despite having reservations about the facilities at Pukekohe, he recognised the importance of continuing to have a round of the Supercar series in New Zealand. Cochrane was bewildered when New Zealand's daunting Resource Management Act torpedoed attempts to have a street race round in Auckland or Wellington. With the outdated Pukekohe still the only option for a Supercar round in the country, a frustrated Cochrane threatened to drop New Zealand from the series, before reason and strong talking from several influential Kiwis brought a reprieve for two years — from 2006 — while a better option was found. Critically, Pukekohe's crowds are the third largest in the series, behind Adelaide and Bathurst, (excluding Surfers Paradise), with an estimated 85,000 attending over the three days in 2005, all seemingly happy to gloss over the shabby facilities, even though they are light years behind the Formula One-standard set-up at China's Shanghai circuit, a series newcomer in the same year.

Despite the drama and white-hot competition, motor racing has yet to be fully embraced by sections of the New Zealand media, and the Supercar competition is no exception in this regard. The media is happy to give the poorly performing New Zealand Breakers basketballers and Knights soccer players, and the wobbly rugby league New Zealand Warriors, extensive weekly coverage in their Australian competitions, while the equally worthy Kiwis in the V8s receive patchy coverage for weeks on end, only getting some attention when it's time for Pukekohe or Bathurst. Such relative neglect has failed to hold back the enterprising Murphy. He is an astute self-promoter and with his four wins in the Bathurst 1000 km since 1996 — which makes him one of the biggest names in the event's history — and an uncanny knack for winning at Pukekohe, he enjoys a high profile.

In the V8 era Holden's drivers shade Ford's by seven titles to six in the battle for the touring car championship, and there is no room for complacency. Ford has closed the gap on Holden with victories from 2003–2005. New Zealanders have won the title just five times: Jim Richards, who has lived in Melbourne since 1975, on four occasions, and Francevic once, though never when it was just Ford against Holden. In recent years, Murphy's seconds in 2002 and 2003 have led the way for New Zealand drivers.

This book looks at the New Zealand drivers and teams lured to Australia in search of glory and a full-time motor racing lifestyle driving the heavy, hairy-handling, flame-belching V8 touring cars.

Getty Images

Cars about to be loaded, two by two, on to a Boeing 747 — a mode of transport now also used to get cars to Pukekohe — for the long flight to Shanghai, 2005.

THE SUPERCAR CHAMPIONSHIP

How It Evolved

A hastily arranged meeting in early 2000 in Adelaide provided the springboard to New Zealand being awarded a round of the Australian V8 Supercar championship, the first time the series had ventured outside Australia. Motorsport New Zealand president Steven Kennedy, vice-president Martin Fine, and Kerry Cooper, who succeeded the highly respected Ian Snellgrove as general manager, were in Adelaide to sample the delights of the superbly staged Clipsal 500 km V8 street race. While they were also looking for anything they might be able to incorporate into their own racing categories, it was supposed to be a leisurely weekend. Motorsport New Zealand had acknowledged the huge appeal of the Supercars, and had even looked at having its own series, till it had become apparent that the costs were prohibitive, just as they had been for the United States-styled TransAm competition, which had been dropped as a national championship category.

Early in the weekend the trio's presence became known to officials of their Australian equivalent, the Confederation of Australian Motorsport (CAMS). A phone call or two later and the executives were soon in the presence of the hard-talking chairman of the Australian Vee Eight Supercar Company (AVESCO), Tony Cochrane, and the director of promoters, from the International Management Group (IMG) in Australia, Geoff Jones.

They met in a room behind the pits for about an hour to talk about how New Zealand might become involved in the Supercar competition. Though the parties had differing views, and Kennedy remembers it being 'fiery at times', there was enough common ground for the parties to go away with every hope a New Zealand round would become a reality. 'Suddenly the whole tone of the weekend changed,' Kennedy recalled. 'We realised that what we were seeking, to give our track racing the profile that would

. . . there was enough common ground for the parties to go away with every hope a New Zealand round would become a reality.

The field poised to leave the grid at the Clipsal 500 km in Adelaide in 2002, where, two years earlier, New Zealand officials had first met their Supercar opposites, leading to the 2001 round at Pukekohe.

attract the big corporates, was now a possibility. AVESCO already had thoughts on taking the V8s to New Zealand, which on reflection was probably not surprising. A lot of New Zealanders were involved with the teams in various capacities. Holdens and Fords are two of the bigger-selling cars in New Zealand, and the fans had been going to Australia in big numbers for years to watch the V8 races.'

Kennedy said that Jones was a straight shooter, and 'we hit it off straight away'. Cochrane had a reputation for being confrontational, and for getting his own way, but Kennedy said he was undaunted as they sifted through the issues. 'I respected Tony's views,' Kennedy said. 'I can't stress enough that we have an excellent working relationship with him. Tony makes positive progress in Australia with his forthright approach. It tends to rub some people up the wrong way here. He's very good at using the media to deliver his message. You can't underestimate what he has to sell. It's been proven to be a damn good package. The V8s is getting bigger every year. It's one of the best touring car series in the world.'

Despite having successfully staged the international Nissan-Mobil series in Auckland and Wellington, between 1985 and 1996 motor racing in New Zealand was in the doldrums much of the time. It was a period of financial difficulty and it led to Motorsport New Zealand pruning its categories, so that by 2000 the national TransAm, super touring and Mini Seven championships had all been terminated. Motor racing had been invigorated, however, by the development of New Zealand's own V8 series, a much cheaper version of the Australian format, but with the cars looking and sounding strikingly similar. And the fields were big and the racing intense as well. Strengthening the case for New Zealand's inclusion in the Australian Supercar championship was the infrastructure and expertise that had been amassed from hosting the annual international two-round series and an annual round of the world rally championship.

By the time a round of the V8 Supercars first appeared at the Pukekohe circuit in November 2001 the series was already a huge hit in Australia,

and the competition organisers were ready to test the water offshore. The formula was introduced in 1993, as Australia strove to find a touring car category to replace the increasingly controversial international group A, and with the formation of AVESCO (which became V8 Supercars Australia in 2005) in time for the 1997 season, the competition rapidly gathered momentum.

Tony Cochrane, often painted as a bully boy, had revolutionised Supercars. He had been the prime driving force in converting it from a popular branch of Australian motor sport into one of the more watched events in Australia. And the expansion continues. From 2006 the schedule has a third overseas round with Bahrain, in the Middle East, joining China's Shanghai and Auckland's Pukekohe on a five-year deal. Going offshore is a massive operation, requiring two giant Boeing 747 freighters to transport 32 cars and all the equipment required by the teams, who themselves number around 500 people. Despite this, a fourth overseas round, in Malaysia from 2008, is a strong possibility.

Cochrane is very much a 'what you see is what you get' individual, who will admit to being something of a dictator. He's been compared to both motor racing's ultimate dictator, Bernie Ecclestone, who, though raising the Formula One world championship to new levels, has sometimes used methods that have upset the teams, sponsors and fans, and Bill France, who heads the hugely popular NASCAR series in the United States.

For months Cochrane almost became the angry face of Supercars to New Zealanders, particularly Aucklanders, as the Queen City street race debate became a major issue. Cochrane was at odds with those who opposed it, and he regarded the Resource Management Act, which eventually killed the street race, as unnecessarily inhibiting. With his desire for a street race and dislike of Pukekohe, he talked of New Zealand being dropped from the Supercar series. But the fast-talking Cochrane is no petrol-head. Though passionate about Supercars he is an entrepreneur, an ideas man with vision, eager to express his philosophies and turn a profit. He is first and foremost in the entertainment business,

Dirk Klynsmith/Graphic Dak Photography

The usually animated Supercars boss Tony Cochrane in uncharacteristic reflective pose.
His readiness to speak out and act decisively has not always endeared him to people.

involved in booking international acts for events such as Hawke's Bay's annual Mission Estate concert. Cochrane never finished high school in Adelaide, where he was born. He formed his own production company, doing lighting and audio producing, which developed into sports and concert management. Nowadays he is a director of Sports and Entertainment Limited (SEL), which has a 25 per cent holding in Supercars Australia. The other 75 per cent belongs to the Supercar teams, known as the Touring Car Entrants Group of Australia (TEGA). SEL is responsible for capturing and maintaining the broadcasting rights, sponsorship, licensing and sanction agreements, and TEGA manages the teams, the rules, technical management, and the supply of cars and drivers.

After starting with a staff of two, Supercars Australia now employs more than 20, and has taken over a lot of the work previously undertaken by IMG. Cochrane's background is in marketing. He was well prepared to launch the new company, having received an ideal grounding working for IMG in Australia, where he was senior vice-president. He was running the CART Indycar round at Surfers Paradise, but in 1995 he could see the outstanding potential of the V8s. 'I wrote a white paper in my own time, and in May 1996 I got the teams together, and I painted a brave new world for them,' Cochrane said. 'In September they came back to me, and said they were prepared to go ahead, and I committed $A50,000 for IMG to set it up.'

Like many Australians, Cochrane grew up with the traditions associated with the Bathurst 1000 km race. 'I offered a completely different fresh exterior view of the formula when I came along,' Cochrane said. 'What's happened is beyond my wildest dreams. Supercars has such a head of steam now, being seen on television in 110 countries, it's at the leading edge of touring cars around the world. . . . I don't get offended at being labelled a dictator. I tend to operate on the philosophy it's my way or the highway. When we were starting it needed strong direction and decisions, and I provided them. . . . You (I) have a go. I lead with my chin sometimes and it gets battered and bruised.'

Though Australia's touring car tradition had been built around the fierce rivalry between Holden and Ford, as exemplified by the battles in the late 1960s between Holden's Peter Brock and Ford's Allan Moffat, and later Dick Johnson, overseas marques increasingly made an impact. In the 1980s the Australian touring car title was won by a Japanese Mazda, twice by a German BMW with New Zealander Jim Richards at the wheel, by a Swedish Volvo driven by another Kiwi, Robbie Francevic, and twice by a European Ford Sierra. And the first three titles of the 1990s went to a Japanese Nissan. The biggest event on the touring car calendar, the Bathurst 1000 km, was won five times in the eight years till the end of 1992 by cars other than Australian-built Holdens and Ford Falcons, including a British Jaguar XJS in 1985.

The greater variety of machinery had a lot to do with Australia's decision to embrace the international group A category, which attracted welcome overseas exposure for the country when the Bathurst race became a round of the short-lived world touring

car championship in 1987. However, it came at the cost of growing displeasure from Holden and Ford. By the time the twin-turbo, four-wheel drive Nissan GTR was cleaning up pretty well everything in the early 1990s, Ford and Holden had had enough. Unable to keep up and lacking resources, they were considering withdrawing and venturing into other forms of racing.

The Confederation of Australian Motorsport (CAMS) was concerned about the economic downturn and the increasing costs of running a group A car with turbos. The Nissans were said to cost more than $A400,000 each (not far from the $A500,000 for a new V8 now). CAMS moved to develop a new formula, aiming to provide close racing at a substantially cheaper cost.

At the time Australia lacked the technology to develop two-litre engines like those in the British

. . . the fierce rivalry between Holden and Ford, as exemplified by the battles in the late 1960s . . .

Fairfax Sunday Newspapers: *NZ Truth* Collection

Long-time adversaries Alan Moffat (left) and Peter Brock after one of their two Wellington street race wins in the mid-1980s, driving a Holden Commodore.

Ford-driving great Dick Johnson looks a little glum at Bathurst in 1999, his farewell season racing Supercars. Seven years earlier, his provocative comments there on the podium helped trigger Jim Richards' 'arsehole' outburst.

The comment was completely out of character for a man universally known in Australasian motor racing as 'Gentleman Jim'. There were extenuating circumstances, however. That same day New Zealand's only Formula One champion, Denny Hulme, had died of a heart attack at the wheel of his BMW on Mountain Straight, and on the podium the second-placed Dick Johnson fired up the crowd, saying that, unlike Richards, who had crashed, his Ford Sierra RS500 turbo was still running when the race ended. 'Denny was a good friend, and a master on the track. We'd got to know each other pretty well,' Richards recalled. 'I was naturally upset. I shed a tear. We didn't mind all the crap that we got over the GTR. It didn't get to us. We laughed at the fans most of the time. But something got to me for a moment on the podium.'

With all the flak Richards and Skaife attracted, they certainly needed a sense of humour. To try and slow them down, their Nissans were repeatedly loaded with extra weight and their turbo boosts limited. But their mechanics at the Fred Gibson

An upset Richards uttered perhaps the most infamous words in Australian motor racing . . . 'you're a pack of arseholes'.

touring car championship. The normally-aspirated V8 engine was the cheapest option to develop and race in Australia, and Ford and Holden and their fiercely patriotic supporters were more than happy to be left to run head to head. The Nissan GTR's second successive Bathurst win in 1992 was unpopular with a large section of the crowd and the car was dubbed 'Godzilla' (King of the Monsters). The barrage of fury reached a crescendo at the presentations after that 1992 win, which involved Jim Richards, arguably New Zealand's best touring car racer. Amid a chorus of boos, Richards and fellow driver Mark Skaife were declared the winners when the race was stopped after heavy rain had created chaos on the track. An upset Richards uttered perhaps the most infamous words in Australian motor racing, and among the best remembered in Australian sport, when he said 'you're a pack of arseholes'.

Motorsport team were undaunted, and continued to develop the cars so successfully that they still managed to stay at the head of the pack.

'The attitude of the other drivers was still good,' Richards recalled. 'We'd still have a beer with them afterwards. It's not like that now. The drivers of the various teams don't mingle socially any more, which is a pity. They have their upsets on the track, and a few words are exchanged, which doesn't always make for good relations.'

Richards attributes this change to growing competition and increased professionalism, saying that drivers are now required to spend more time with their sponsors, and to 'protect' their results. If a driver is seen mixing with another team, it is likely he would be asked to explain himself.

'There's the risk a driver might drop his guard, and say something that gives a competitor an advantage,'

Richards explained. 'It's more professional than when I was in the championship full-time [till the end of 1995]. We were still pros though. When I was with Fred Gibson, Winfield [the cigarette company] had fantastic budgets to go racing.'

Richards said the Nissan was the fastest car he had driven till then. 'It had a similar top speed to the V8s now [around 300 kmh] and as much horsepower, but with the regulations we were required to run under, the Nissan was heavier,' he said. 'With the weight we went through brakes, and for increased safety we needed stronger wheels. The Nissans were not quite as expensive as the V8s, but were just about double the price of anything else because of their complex nature and upkeep.' Contrary to his friend Mark Skaife's opinion, Richards said the Nissan was not hard to drive. It had nice traits even when made heavier, he said, and it was very reliable. Skaife, on the other hand, commented that, 'the GTR was one of the hardest cars I've driven. It was big and heavy and had small tyres and no aerodynamics.' New Zealanders witnessed 'Godzilla's' awesome might in the 1991 Nissan-Mobil series. Wellington's bumpy Cable Street caused the Nissan to suffer drive train damage when leading in the first leg, and Richards and Skaife eventually finished third. The GTR came into its own, however, the following weekend at Pukekohe, when Richards claimed the lap record in setting up victory.

Jim Richards was unhappy when the Nissans were squeezed out in 1992. But he came to realise that CAMS had acted in the best long-term interests of the touring car championship. Instead of Skaife and Richards continuing to blow away their opposition, the new category allowed the growling Fords and Holdens full expression, and with more drivers and cars becoming competitive the championship battle became more engrossing.

It was not suddenly all a bed of roses though. CAMS initially hedged its bets by allowing the two-litre super tourers to run alongside the V8s in the new formula. It certainly helped to boost numbers on the grid. Richards remembered the V8s being a bit thin to start with. But for the 1994 season the classes were split. No longer directly competing on the racetrack, the V8 and super tourer formulas were now

Jim Richards in his days racing for Fred Gibson's team between 1989 and 1995, a period when he was at the peak of his powers and enjoying huge success.

in competition. In 1997 and 1998 this rivalry led to the ridiculous situation of each formula having 1000 km events of their own at Bathurst within a few weeks of each other. The super tourers took the traditional October date, leaving the V8s to tag along behind.

The five-litre, pushrod, two-valve, V8-engined Commodores and Falcons were initially more popular. However, by 1996 the super tourers had claimed the high ground. The V8s, yet to be marketed as Supercars, had lost momentum, and this was attributed to mediocre television coverage, particularly in the states where Australian Rules football dominated television sports for months. Incredibly, the traditions established by racing icons Brock, Moffat, Johnson, Richards and Larry Perkins were in danger of suffering a lingering death. The V8s were still popular with the faithful, but had largely dropped off the radar for the general public. Unkind references to the V8s being dinosaurs compared to the nimble super touring thoroughbreds, which had a proven international reputation, were becoming increasingly accurate. The V8 teams also found sponsorship hard to come by when the big-spending cigarette companies were banned in 1995.

With the loss of Winfield sponsorship, Fred Gibson's team, now running Holdens, became a one-car operation, and the younger, more-involved Skaife stayed while Richards departed.

In 1996, fearing for their investment, CAMS and the V8 team owners made a decision that saved the category and was the start of its phenomenal growth. They handed over the marketing to IMG. It provided Tony Cochrane, then a senior IMG employee, with the opportunity of leading the V8s out of the wilderness. Among the first priorities was to raise the television profile of V8 racing. This meant coming up with a new name, and it was decided that in future the Commodores and Falcons would simply be marketed as V8 Supercars. Cochrane's loud, brash style upset a lot of people. A number of them were very conservative and suspicious, and all they really knew was motor racing. They did not always appreciate being told what they needed to do by someone with no background in the sport.

IMG still had a key battle to win, though, before it could press on with complete confidence — and that was the matter of television coverage. The Seven Network, a joint promoter of the Bathurst 1000 km, had televised it since it had first been raced over 500 miles in 1963, and wanted to retain it in 1997. However, Seven showed little interest in covering the rest of the V8 season. This was untenable for the new company. Network Ten was keen to broadcast the entire championship, but only if it included the centrepiece Bathurst 1000 km. The only solution was to establish a rival event for the V8s two weeks after the super tourer race which would be covered by the Seven Network.

It became a test of which formula Australian, and to some extent New Zealand, motor sport fans would support. The V8s and Network Ten won handsomely, confirming once and for all what form of touring car racing was preferred. The spectator and television numbers comfortably outstripped those for the super tourers, and Network Ten and V8 Supercars established a partnership of continued

Photosport

Jim Richards' Nissan being harassed by a couple of nimble little BMWs at the Wellington street race in 1991. He and Mark Skaife drove a Nissan GTR to victory at Pukekohe in the same year.

excellence. Ten's coverage of Bathurst in 2004 won it a Logie award for the second year running, for the best coverage of a sporting event by an Australian channel, surpassing, among others, the presentation of the Athens Olympics.

After one more attempt at including two-litre cars in 1998, the Bathurst 1000 km became the exclusive preserve of the Supercars. The twin winners in 1997 and 1998 are still recognised in the official Bathurst records — the 1998 super touring victory being Jim Richards' sixth there when, driving a Volvo, he was hard pressed to head off the attentions of his son, Steven Richards, in a Nissan Primera.

The Holden Racing Team (HRT) was the fastest to embrace the new era. HRT had suffered hard times, much to the despair of its many supporters. Bathurst in 1995 was a particularly dark time, with both cars being eliminated inside the first 90 minutes. The picture changed dramatically the following year, though, and over the following seasons HRT set a benchmark for excellence that was not seriously challenged till Stone Brothers Racing (SBR) and their Ford drivers, Marcos Ambrose and Russell Ingall, further raised the bar in 2003.

🏁

In 1996 HRT's 'Kick-ass Kids', Craig Lowndes and New Zealander Greg Murphy, secured the Sandown 500 km-Bathurst 1000 km double, and Lowndes became the youngest driver to win the Australian touring car title at 21 years, 11 months and 11 days. Lowndes became Supercars' No. 1 poster boy, filling huge shoes in taking over from

Lowndes became Supercars' No. 1 poster boy, filling huge shoes in taking over from fellow HRT driver Peter Brock . . .

Alastair Ritchie

The Holden Commodore of Greg Murphy and Craig Lowndes, which carried the 'Kick-ass Kids' to victory at Bathurst in 1996.

fellow HRT driver Peter Brock, who ended his full-time involvement in 1997. It was a changing of the guard, which became even more pointed two years later when Dick Johnson joined Brock on the sidelines. The charismatic Lowndes helped trigger a growing culture of 'personalities' within the formula that saw some drivers gaining higher profiles among the big names in other Australian sports, and, as a consequence, also taking some of the emphasis away from the traditional Holden v Ford scrap.

Lowndes, and Brock's replacement Mark Skaife, made HRT almost invincible, as the team won six touring car championships in seven years between 1996 and 2002. Three of these went to Lowndes before his controversial departure to Ford in early 2001, and three went to Skaife, a welcome addition to the two he earned at Fred Gibson Motorsport.

It seemed incomprehensible that Lowndes would feel the need to leave HRT given his standing in Supercars, his success with the team, and the team's proven superiority over its opponents. This is not to mention the shock waves a move to Ford would create. Unless Lowndes went to the Stone brothers, any move would probably be to an inferior team. It seemed that his decision to move must have come from some deep dissatisfaction with aspects of HRT, even though the team appeared to have his best interests at heart by signing him to a long-term contract. On the other hand it appeared that Ford Motorsport was guaranteeing his financial future with the lure of big bucks.

HRT manager Jeff Grech was devastated by Lowndes's departure. He had taken a punt on Lowndes, first giving the fresh-faced kid an opportunity in 1994. At the time HRT was in the doldrums, and Grech's future was under threat, and he had seen Lowndes as the team's saviour when others were not yet convinced of his ability. Grech's insistence that Lowndes was their man had proved a masterstroke.

Lowndes said he left simply because he was unhappy at HRT; the team was going in one

Craig Lowndes holding sway in the Queensland 500 km at Ipswich in 2000. He and Mark Skaife carved out yet another victory for the Holden Racing Team.

Getty Images

A scene that became all too common in V8 Supercars, Holden team-mates Mark Skaife (left) and Craig Lowndes revelling in yet another victory.

Lowndes, and Brock's replacement Mark Skaife, made HRT almost invincible . . .

direction, and he wanted to go in another. He had some regrets that HRT's owner before Mark Skaife, Tom Walkinshaw Racing, did not allow him more than one season to prove himself in European Formula 3000 open-wheelers in 1997, before sending him back to Australia. He was still dealing with Walkinshaw in negotiations with HRT, which dragged on for almost a year, before he decided to walk away. 'I was still winning races but I wasn't happy,' Lowndes said. 'My wife [Natalie] and I made the decision to make the change. We tried to find another Holden team, which we weren't able to achieve, so we looked at Ford. Geoff Polites (Ford Australia president) transformed the way Ford looked at motor sport after they'd dropped out for a while and suffered accordingly. He came up with a plan we were happy with. I hoped that the fans would understand. It was very complex, but in the end I had to do what was right for me.'

Ford's decision to lift its game by investing heavily in motor racing came from years of being heartily sick of continually finishing behind Holden. Polites redirected sponsorship money that had previously been invested in the Australian Open tennis competition. Confirmation that Ford was paying huge money to its elite drivers, Lowndes, Marcos Ambrose, Russell Ingall and Jason Bright, came during a Supreme Court hearing in 2005 when it was revealed that Lowndes would earn $A780,000 plus whatever his Irish bosses, Triple Eight Race Engineering, paid him, and any other deals he might make.

However, Lowndes was disappointed that his reputation for being one of the very best Supercar drivers evaporated following his departure from HRT. He had four lean years racing AU and BA Falcons for three different teams, and was often lumbered with cars that did not allow him to perform consistently. In that time he earned just one round victory, and it was a lucky one, at Victoria's Phillip Island in 2003 when he was leading behind the safety car when the event was called off. The move to Triple Eight's Team Betta Electrical in 2005, in place of New Zealand's Paul Radisich, revived his stuttering career and silenced those who wondered whether he would ever recapture his former brilliance. It also allowed him a reprieve from being continually asked whether he had any regrets about the way his fortunes had plummeted since he traded in the superior stability and professionalism offered by HRT for something a lot less structured and more erratic. Though Lowndes was second in the championship, 57 points behind winner Russell Ingall, he enjoyed superior results, if not quite the same overall consistency, in winning four rounds and 12 races to Ingall's one round and two races. Lowndes climbed 18 places in the championship on his previous year's effort, but his blunder at Bathurst might have cost him the title. He tagged a wall in The Cutting when in the

Getty Images

Craig Lowndes's BA Ford loses a little traction as it slides off the track at Bathurst in 2005, a year in which he revived his career.

lead, and after an errant wheel later destroyed his windscreen he limped home in 15th position.

Lowndes's impact and the esteem in which he is held was reflected in the series annual awards for 2005. He collected three awards: the Barry Sheene Medal for his outstanding leadership, personality, fan appeal and sportsmanship; the people's choice award as the most popular driver; and the Champion Pole award for starting on pole position five times.

■■■■■■■■■■

One of Supercars' most spectacular developments has been Adelaide's Clipsal 500 km street race, which arose out of the ashes created by the loss of the Australian Grand Prix to Melbourne. Disappointment at the Grand Prix's departure was soon replaced by the excitement generated by the V8s in the inaugural race in 1999. Adelaide has made the Clipsal the most happening round of the

having been a non-championship round for a long time, Surfers now enjoys equal billing with the Indycars, and with the rising popularity of Supercar racing looks set to attract as many spectators as the rival formula.

Despite being the biggest race on the V8 programme, known both for its tradition and frequent drama, the Bathurst 1000 km did not become a part of the touring car championship till 1999. Not until the advent of AVESCO did an organising body realise the importance of having Bathurst in the championship. It is the one V8 race on the calendar that many casual fans watch. Now that it is part of the championship many of the part-time observers who tune in to watch 'The Great Race' have been swept up in the race for the title, and become more regular followers of the series.

There is a strong belief that the series champion should have to perform well on Bathurst's Mount Panorama circuit to earn the title. It is the toughest race to win, and in which to secure a good result. Just

. . . the series champion should have to perform well on Bathurst's Mount Panorama circuit to earn the title.

championship, attracting huge crowds to what has been promoted as a four-day carnival. In 2005 a record 255,600 people attended over the weekend. It has won a number of accolades, including best major festival at the Australian Tourism Awards, and is a multiple winner of a Supercar award as Australia's best national motor sport event. Its success helped spawn the Canberra 400 km street race, which lasted three years before becoming one of the series' few failures. The ACT Government blamed the city's bitterly cold June climate for the dwindling crowds and subsequently spiralling costs when it terminated the contract two years early.

The V8s first became involved with Indycar open-wheelers on the streets of Surfers Paradise in 1994. In those days the V8s were very much second billing, but with CART being increasingly overshadowed in the United States by the rival Indy Racing League — in which New Zealand's Scott Dixon drives — the standing of the V8 Supercars has improved. After

ask Marcos Ambrose, who, despite his spectacular success, continues to draw a blank there with a best placing of fourth in five starts.

Not only have exciting new rounds been developed in recent years, but other aspects of the series have also evolved over time. The inclusion of a shootout for all rounds, when it used to be the sole preserve of Bathurst, came from a desire to entertain on what might otherwise be a slow Saturday at some rounds. It has worked well, and hardly detracted from the excitement generated in the pursuit of pole at Bathurst. Compulsory pit stops have added to the drama, making teams more professional, and giving fans more value for their money with a greater number of longer races. They have also added a greater tactical element, and been invaluable in teams gaining an advantage when passing has been difficult, particularly in the tight street circuits. Races have been won and lost on the ability of pit crews, and the timing of the stops.

There has also been a sweeping revision of pit lane safety after some scary moments and a few injuries. Since 2001 there has been a pit lane speed limit of 40 kmh. A number of drivers have been penalised for exceeding it, and there is a requirement that all pit crew wear protective clothing.

Each team is limited to six test days annually, a restriction aimed at ensuring the bigger-budget outfits do not gain an unfair advantage, and consequently the two-hour practice session at each round has been welcomed. The teams are restricted to a certain number of laps depending on the length of the circuit but the extended period allows for better preparation than the previous short, sharp

He called the decision 'a despicable act' and wondered if there was malice in the decision.

sessions with periods in between when the track and weather conditions might change significantly. A Dunlop control tyre has been successfully introduced, which not only helps reduce costs but also promotes a more even playing field. Previously, an open-tyre policy had created quite significant inequalities between the cars.

Tim Schenken, who has the thankless and often highly unpopular job of Supercars' race director, says the success of the formula has been demonstrated by how even the two marques have been in terms of performance. The closeness of the competition has been repeatedly illustrated by the mere fractions of a second covering most of the 30-plus cars in the qualifying rounds, and this has heightened the belief in Australia that it has the best touring car series in the world. The cars are a minimum weight of 1355 kg, develop more than 600 bhp at 7500 rpm, have Australian-made six-speed manual Holinger gearboxes, and can accelerate to 100 kmh in around four seconds. The Holdens and Fords are built to almost identical specifications, and among their few differences are their body silhouettes.

Schenken said the development of the formula

had exceeded his expectations after CAMS and television partner Network Seven started the rescue operation in the early 1990s. 'Tony Cochrane has done extremely well, picking up a lot on the management and promotion of Formula One, and building a national version of that,' Schenken said. 'He's had the vision to look further than his own back yard. I really believe that Supercars will become more popular than Formula One. It is becoming a proper international series with three overseas rounds in 2006, and the prospects of another.'

Schenken considered four offshore rounds was probably enough, and that CART had lost its way when it had more than that. He thought the V8s' greater international profile would also attract high-calibre overseas drivers and create greater competition for positions in teams. However, it is well accepted that no matter how good they are overseas, drivers take some time to master the skills required to be confident when fully extending a Supercar. It has resulted in fewer teams being inclined to hire an overseas hotshot to be a co-driver at Bathurst. A lot of international rules have been adopted, particularly in ensuring the circuits meet high safety standards, and the cars are built so strongly that the drivers have a good chance of surviving a nasty accident. All drivers are required to wear a HANS (head and neck safety) device, which is attached behind the helmet. The device helped ensure Tasman Motorsport's New Zealand driver Jason Richards was not seriously hurt in a frightening, airborne crash at Queensland's Ipswich circuit in 2005.

In the early 1970s, Schenken was a skilful Formula One racer alongside New Zealanders Denny Hulme, Chris Amon, and friend and business partner Howden Ganley. Schenken's best finish was third in the Austrian Grand Prix of 1971, in a Brabham, when he was a team-mate of a former world champion, Graham Hill.

On race day Schenken is kept busy controlling the action at the start, as well as making decisions as

Jim Richards under pressure at Bathurst in 2002 in the Holden he and great friend Mark Skaife guided to victory. This was Richards' seventh win there and the third partnering Skaife.

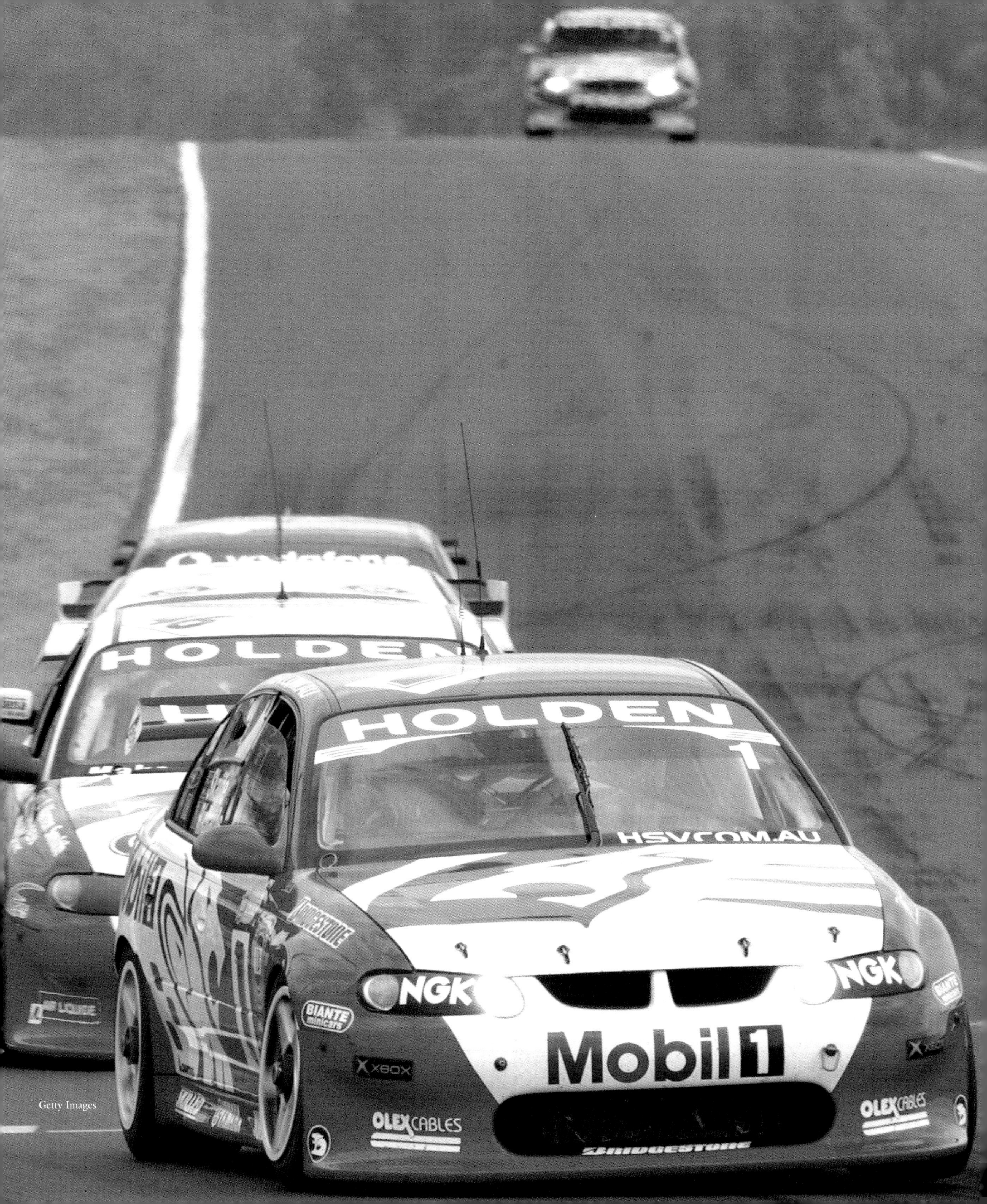

Getty Images

Getty Images

Legendary New Zealand driver and constructor Bruce McLaren, pictured in 1970, sitting on a wheel of one of the distinctive orange cars that bore his name.

to when to bring out the safety car or black flag to signal a driver to pit. He is also there to help ensure the drivers maintain the highest standards, and in the heat of battle the picture can become decidedly testy. 'There's a fine line between close and exciting racing, when the cars are rubbing up against each other, and when cars are being unfairly pushed off the track,' Schenken says. 'You never get it right all the time. At the end of the day only the drivers know what truly happened. When you get them in a room they have different stories. CAMS has to make a decision with the help of such people as driving standards observer Colin Bond.'

Understandably, not all the decisions please everybody. New Zealand's Greg Murphy, for example, was enraged by his five-minute stop-go penalty at Bathurst in 2002, for driving off with the fuel hose still connected. He called the decision 'a despicable act' and wondered if there was malice in the decision. Schenken responded by saying: 'That's a silly thing to say. Each incident is judged on merit by the stewards of the race, not by me. The penalty was pretty severe but there could have been a very serious incident.'

Jim Richards has the honour of being the first New Zealander to win the Australian tour title, which he managed in a BMW 635 in 1985, and repeated in a BMW M3 two years later, the only occasions on which a BMW has been successful. Then followed those all-conquering Nissan Skylines, which Richards drove to the 1990 and 1991 championships. His four titles have been bettered by just three others, and they are all Australians: Ian Geoghegan, Dick Johnson and Mark Skaife, who each have five titles. No Kiwi has won the championship since Richards' victory in 1991, the best efforts being Richards' second to Skaife, his Nissan team-mate, in 1992, and Greg Murphy's seconds in 2002 and 2003.

Ian Snellgrove, long a leading New Zealand motor sport official and technical expert, considers Richards to be among New Zealand's best drivers. In his opinion, only 1967 Formula One champion Denny Hulme is further up the totem pole than Richards, and Snellgrove puts Richards on a similar level to two other Formula One racers, Bruce McLaren and Chris Amon. 'I'd put Jim on a pedestal. He's one of New Zealand's real greats,' Snellgrove said. 'As a young kid with a limited budget, he was dicking people. He could jump into anything and make it competitive. He was so talented then.'

Neal Lowe, like Richards a Kiwi racer who has lived in Australia for many years, is also in no doubt about Richards' contribution. Lowe was good enough to win the Pukekohe round of the Nissan-Mobil series in 1986, driving for Brock's Holden Dealer Team (HDT). He was second in the Bathurst 1000 km the same year, and he went on to be a successful development engineer and manager for Dick Johnson, and to manage HRT. 'Jim's got to be the best all-rounder I've come across,' Lowe said. 'He does a brilliant job no matter how you set-up a car, and he does it cheerfully. He's totally free with his information too. He's probably New Zealand's best motor sport export. Jim's still as competitive as ever, and he's just loving it.'

Though a sizeable number of New Zealanders have appeared in the Australian touring car championship since Paul Fahey, Rod Coppins and Red Dawson tested the water, even if only fleetingly, in the 1960s, colourful Aucklander Robbie Francevic became New Zealand's only other champion when he won the title in 1986. Francevic's feat was even more meritorious as he is the oldest driver to win the championship, doing so at 44 years, eight months and 25 days.

Even among his forthright opposition, Francevic was regarded as loud and brash. He was never slow at talking up his chances of winning the championship, which earned him a number of nicknames including 'Cassius' (as in the outrageously bragging former heavyweight boxing champion Cassius Clay, who later became Muhammad Ali) and 'motormouth'. However, in 1986, despite the late surge of George Fury in a Nissan Skyline turbo, Francevic was able to match his boastful words with the necessary results in a Swedish Volvo 240 turbo.

In what many people would regard as typical of Francevic, his win was not without its off-track drama,

which he said detracted from the satisfaction of his achievement. When Francevic first started racing the Volvo in the Australian touring car championship during 1985 it belonged to long-time Auckland racer and team manager, Mark Petch. Petch was unsure of his involvement in 1986, and soon after Francevic's victories in the opening two rounds, Volvo Australia bought the car and equipment from Petch, and formed the Volvo Dealer Team. Francevic says he and Petch had a 'love-hate' relationship, and Francevic and his new engineer and manager John Sheppard eventually fell out. Francevic says his Volvo did not improve during the year after its promising start, and he blames Sheppard for this. The bad blood resulted in Francevic leaving the team before the year was out. Instead he returned to Petch's team for the Bathurst 1000 km, driving a Ford Sierra turbo with another New Zealander, Leo Leonard. 'John built beautiful cars but he wasn't a developer,' Francevic says now. 'As the season went on I wasn't able to win any races. I had to rely on the points I'd built up

New Zealander Neal Lowe (left) and his Australian driving partner John Harvey after winning the Pukekohe round of the Nissan-Mobil series in 1986, in a Holden Commodore.

Fairfax Sunday Newspapers: *Auckland Star Collection*

early on, and keep finishing as well up as I could. I wanted to win races. In the end I could only do my best with the equipment I was given. To me it was a poor way to win the championship. I was left with mixed feelings. I don't believe I was treated with the respect I was due. It left a sour taste.'

Francevic found himself having to bow to Sheppard's wishes. Instead of feeling the team revolved around him, he became just a driver. He said he was not permitted to do any development, and team-mate John Bowe, who went on to twice win the Bathurst 1000 km, and be touring car champion in 1995, increasingly became a rival. Sheppard was quoted as saying he had not previously worked with someone as difficult as Francevic.

In 1986 the Kiwi hit the ground running, securing three victories in the first four rounds,

and although a blown head gasket in round seven at Victoria's Calder track was a setback, he cobbled together sufficient points to retain his lead in the championship – five points ahead of Fury. Come the 10th and final round, at Oran Park, near Sydney, Francevic needed to finish no higher than ninth to be the overall winner and his sixth to Fury's victory was sufficient to give him the championship. He signalled his elation with a clenched-fist salute as he crossed the finish line. Making it even more commendable, Francevic won without living in Australia. He would cross the Tasman a few days before each round. 'I'm the only outsider to win the Australian touring car championship,' Francevic says proudly.

He tends to think the racing in the mid-1980s was better than it is now. 'It's too difficult to pass

'In my time it was easier to pass people. Someone might have the speed on the straight, but not in the corners.'

Fairfax Sunday Newspapers

Robbie Francevic's Volvo out in front in the early stages of a Wellington street race in the mid-1980s. He and the Belgian driver Michel Delacourt won the first street race in 1985.

someone, which detracts from the competition,' Francevic says. 'In my time it was easier to pass people. Someone might have the speed on the straight, but not in the corners.'

His name is invariably mentioned in any discussion about New Zealand's better drivers over the years, and his 1986 effort is among his most prized. His turbo, like Fury's, was invariably a cut above the opposition, which included Jim Richards and Tony Longhurst in BMWs, the Holden Commodore of Peter Brock, Dick Johnson in a Ford Mustang, and another Kiwi, Graeme Crosby. Though Francevic's performances that year dwarfed those of Brock, Francevic has no hesitation in nominating Brock as the best driver he had come across 'by a country mile because of his natural skill and knack of selling himself'. 'Everyone knows how good Jim Richards is but Peter had the complete package,' Francevic says. 'He's the ultimate Australian, he achieved so much, and he has the X factor.'

Francevic tells an amusing story about his racing at that time. He overheard a father telling his son that he used to watch Francevic's father racing till Robbie pointed out, 'I'm the same bloke'.

Francevic described Petch's purchase of the Volvo as a 'fluke'. 'Mark was looking to get a Rover. He just happened to ring Volvo one day, and caught them at a weak moment,' Francevic said. 'I understand it was the only one to be sold to an outsider.' Petch bought it with the intention of running it in the New Zealand Nissan-Mobil series, which started in 1985. Francevic said it was to be driven by experienced Belgian racer Michel Delcourt and the guy who had built it in Sweden. Francevic was going to be helping the team, till it was decided he and Delcourt should pair up, and they had instant success in winning the first Wellington street race. 'Mark really believed in me, and he was a very resourceful chap,' Francevic says. 'He was good at finding ways of getting things we needed. But our relationship was a very fiery one because of our natures and egos.'

Petch said for all his natural ability Francevic was an enigma. 'He was a difficult guy to work with,' Petch recalled. 'He had colossal mood swings. He was either on top of the world or down in the dumps.

Fairfax Sunday Newspapers

Robbie Francevic never quite cracked it in several attempts at Bathurst.

Robbie could be like a child at times. We were seen as upstarts when we first went to Australia, and the locals made it difficult for us. I got sick of their tactics in the end.'

In his younger days Francevic formed a winning partnership with an Auckland neighbour, mechanical engineer Tony Kriletech. He built the highly modified Ford Customline, famously known as the 'Custaxie', which won 25 of its races in the mid-1960s. The young pair went to the United States in 1967 to buy a Ford Fairlane to replace the 'Custaxie', and they ended up staying for months. Francevic raced 'stock cars' in a semi-professional league just below NASCAR, driving similar cars on the same oval tracks. 'I was promoted as the New Zealand champion,' Francevic remembers. 'I didn't always have the right gear or much backup. The oval racing was a bit woolly. I was never involved in a major crash but I caused a couple.'

He did so well he was named rookie of the year, and he was offered the opportunity to gain

Peter Brock back at Bathurst for his 32nd and most recent time in 2004, which ended dismally when the car he shared was damaged before he got to race.

further experience the following year in the same competition and contest some full NASCAR events. He opted to stay at home, but as he says, 'I made some dreadful decisions in my career'. A Dalmatian, he has had his own garages and dealerships over the years but these days a tall, lean Francevic is a sales executive for Jerry Clayton BMW at Takapuna.

⬛⬜⬛⬜⬛⬜⬛⬜⬛⬜⬛⬜⬛

Peter Brock sat behind the wheel of his first racing car, an Austin A30, at Winton Raceway in 1967. It was reportedly 'a terrifyingly quick and ill-handling beast'. Almost 40 years later, Brock's fame and popularity on both sides of the Tasman stretches far beyond motor racing. He has become one of Australia's most revered sports stars, and despite his retirement from full-time racing in 1997 at Bathurst, he has remained in the public eye, and is still very much in demand.

Like Francevic, Neal Lowe holds Peter Brock in particularly high regard, though he is among those who did not understand Brock's controversial polariser device, which Brock insisted would enhance a car's performance and which led to his heartbreaking split with Holden in 1987. 'I really admire Peter. He's a top bloke, and he had an uncanny feel for a car,' Lowe said. 'It was almost as though you could take a wheel off a car, and he would do just as well. He has a remarkable relationship with the fans, which crosses the generations. They saw him as this all-Australian hero. He still has that aura about him. Every man is entitled to his beliefs but nobody could understand his polariser theory. There were stories of it coming loose in his cars, and the drivers throwing it out the window. In a lot of ways the polariser was the undoing of him. He's had a battle ever since.'

The last of Brock's record nine Bathurst 1000 km victories occurred in 1987. But it only came after the first two finishers, Swiss Ruedi Eggenberger's Ford Sierra turbos, were disqualified because their front guards were over the permitted width on the one occasion the event was a round of the world touring car championship. In the following decade Brock strived for that elusive 10th win, even coming out of Supercar retirement in 2002 and 2004 in attempts to achieve it. His team raced BMWs in 1988, and Ford Sierra turbos for the following two years, but Brock was back in a Holden from 1991 till the end of his full-time V8 days in 1997, at the age of 52. In his 12 appearances at Bathurst since 1987 his best finish was fourth in a Sierra with Englishman Andy Rouse in 1990. The last of Brock's three touring car titles came in 1980, and he was second 10 years later. However, Brock remained the consummate professional right till the end, finishing third in the championship in 1994 and 1995, fourth in 1996 and sixth in 1997.

Brock, still fit-looking into his 60s, has been ranked the second best touring car driver of all time by respected British magazine, *Motor Sport* — a considerable achievement given that he raced very little in Europe. Editor Paul Fearnley wrote: 'Before you dismiss Brock as a big fish in a small pool, remember that ranged against him were Jim Richards, Dick Johnson, Colin Bond, Allan Moffat, Larry Perkins and Mark Skaife, all of whom, it could be argued, deserved a place on the list. Yes his European visits were rare but the distances and logistics involved, and the strengths of his brand and the scene at home, made such campaigns unnecessary. Had he offered his services in Europe he would have been snapped up, and been successful. Of that there is no question. In a country that measures itself in increments of sporting excellence Brock is mentioned in the same breath as [cricketer Sir Donald] Bradman and [world Formula One champion driver and constructor Sir Jack] Brabham. No other saloon car driver comes close in the household name stakes.'

No other retired driver enjoys the following Brock still attracts. But the articulate Brock is no bighead despite the adulation. He is comfortable with his place in history, satisfied that his battles with Moffat at Bathurst from 1969, driving a Holden against Moffat's Ford, and later Johnson, provided a legacy which helped ensure that Australia's touring car formula would eventually return to the traditional

rivalry between Holden and Ford. 'We enjoyed enormous public support,' Brock said. 'It created a special culture, folklore, tribal approach that has continued through to today. I'm forever signing stuff from those earlier days. There's an awful lot of public goodwill for memorabilia of those times. The foundation was already there for the Supercar era.'

He counts himself among those who, in the early 1990s, worked toward the introduction of the present formula, which outlawed the turbo-powered Nissan Skylines and Ford Sierras, in 1993. 'The big players were Mike Raymond from Channel Seven, Dick Johnson, Larry Perkins, Allan Moffat, [team owner] Fred Gibson, [motor racing director] Alan Gow and myself,' Brock said. 'We had to create fast reliable cars, and the basic specifications we helped develop have remained in place since 1993.'

Brock is understandably very proud of his driving skills and accomplishments, and while reluctant to make comparisons between the drivers from his time and the present, as the quality of machinery,

Alastair Ritchie

Peter Brock at Bathurst in the latter days of his full-time touring car career. He and Tomas Mezera drove together there three times for a best finish of fifth in 1996, in a Holden Commodore VR.

tracks and the teams have improved, Brock is not about to concede that today's drivers are any better. Brock noted that the drivers of his day faced different challenges, with the cars having enormous power but lacking the refinements and perhaps the reliability of today's machines. In addition, the tracks were less forgiving on the cars and driver error, and with safety much less of an issue than it is now, the risks were greater, though that was something, he says, the drivers didn't dwell on.

He says one of his co-drivers, New Zealander Jim Richards, is a 'good example' of a racer who has continued to enhance the standing of those who competed in previous eras. Though Richards, three years younger than Brock, finished full-time racing in V8s in 1995, two years before Brock, he was still good enough to win the Bathurst 1000 km for a seventh time in 2002, partnering Mark Skaife. He also qualified third on the grid the following year, and ninth in 2005, despite only racing the cars twice a year at the endurance rounds of Sandown and Bathurst. 'Jim's done a fantastic job over the years,' Brock said. 'He's a naturally gifted driver, and with his versatility was always going to be successful. His talent is only matched by his good nature.'

Brock regards a former Holden Racing Team team-mate, Craig Lowndes, as the benchmark for today's drivers — ahead of the most dominant performer in recent years, Marcos Ambrose. 'Craig has not been in the right team at times. They have often struggled, but Craig can still get a good result in a car that's not so good,' Brock said. 'Marcos has had a great two or three years. He's been in the right team at the right time [Stone Brothers Racing]. Unlike some people, I can understand why he's opted to leave and try his luck in NASCAR racing. You start looking for new challenges when you're winning most of the races.'

Brock described New Zealand's best performer in recent years, Greg Murphy, as a 'terrific' driver.

Greg Murphy, in an unfamiliar No. 15 car, guns his Holden over the 'mountain' at Bathurst in 2004. On this occasion Murphy shared Rick Kelly's car rather than use his own distinctive No. 51 machine when they secured a repeat victory.

'He's right up there, with his wonderful record at Bathurst and Pukekohe,' Brock said. 'Greg needs a greater level of consistency, which might have a lot to do with his approach.'

He says the push to race overseas has merit, as long as it is not detrimental to the best interests of the many fans in Australia. Brock is happy with a round in New Zealand, saying it is perfectly logical given the many Ford and Holden drivers there, and the high level of interest. The willowy, grey-haired Brock continues to be touched by his 'fantastic' following among Kiwis. He still comes to New Zealand to make personal appearances, and further his business interests. One of his pet projects is the Melbourne-based Peter Brock Foundation, established in 1997, which offers financial help to the disadvantaged and struggling, making many donations in Australia annually.

Brock described New Zealand's best performer in recent years, Greg Murphy, as a 'terrific' driver.

A number of New Zealanders have the distinction of having driven with Brock or raced in his teams. At the top of the list is Jim Richards, who secured a hat-trick of Bathurst 1000 km victories with Brock between 1978 and 1980. David Oxton was his co-driver at Sandown and Bathurst in 1985, only for the car to drop out on each occasion; Paul Radisich suffered the same fate at Sandown four years later; and Craig Baird was 23rd with Brock at Bathurst in 2002. Kent Baigent and Graeme Bowkett were in Brock's team at the Spa 24-hour race in Belgium in 1986, sharing a car with Neal Lowe, which finished 18th, four places better than Brock.

In 2005, Brock's legions of fans were saddened by news that he and his partner of 28 years, Beverley, had split. Though she called herself Bev Brock they never married. In his younger days Brock had a reputation for being a bit wild, but in latter years he had undergone a transformation, which included becoming environmentally conscious, a teetotaller and a vegetarian.

As 2005 drew to a close there were a couple of developments for the new year: one was positive for New Zealanders, with Paul Cruickshank to make his debut as a team owner; and the other was disturbing for most of the Supercar teams, with a decision to implement reverse grids for the second race of every three-heat round.

Cruickshank bought a level two, one-car licence toward the end of 2005 from Australian Rod Nash, whose Autobarn Racing team had run Alex Davison in a Holden. The Decina Bathware-sponsored Paul Cruickshank Racing was set up in time for him to start in the 2003 development series, and in 2005 his two drivers, Warren Luff and Phil Scifleet, were second and sixth respectively in Ford Falcons.

Young Queenslander Marcus Marshall, who has Supercar experience at Sandown and Bathurst, and success in British Formula Three and the World Champ Car Series, was signed in January to race full-time in 2006 in a Falcon. The car would be a combination of a 2003 Ford chassis bought from Triple Eight Engineering, and an engine supplied by the Stone brothers, with whom Cruicksank has had a long and successful relationship since he was a mechanic alongside Ross Stone at Team Nissan New Zealand in Australia in 1987.

Cruickshank's workshop is in a building he leases from the Stones next to their engine shop at Yatala on Queensland's Gold Coast. His is the first team to graduate from the development series. He also ran two cars in the Carrera Cup for Porsches in 2005, which was notable for Jonathon Webb's excellent third behind New Zealanders Fabian Coulthard and Jim Richards. Cruickshank has a long-standing Ashburton friend and accomplished racer, Andy McElrea, as his team manager.

Cruickshank says he was a 'young larrikin' when he first worked with Ross Stone, but he has a strong pedigree. He had three years working for the legendary Dick Johnson before moving to England in the early 1990s to spend more than four years working as a mechanic for distinguished Kiwi expatriate Dick

Edge Photographics

Marcos Ambrose's crumbled Ford is carted off on the back of a truck at Bathurst in 2005 after the controversial collision with Greg Murphy's Holden ended their hopes of a podium finish.

Bennetts. There was also a spell with Supercar driver Craig Baird, when he won the New Zealand Grand Prix; he set-up a Formula Ford team in Australia with a Formula One world champion, Alan Jones; and he spent three years with Fred Gibson's Holden team as workshop manager and crew chief when Jim Richards was still racing V8s full-time.

In the early 2000s he was general manager for Prancing Horse Racing team in Melbourne, which ran numerous Ferraris and other cars for various customers, and had a staff of 38. However, Cruickshank wanted to run his own V8 team, and he and his Australian wife, Sophia, sold their Melbourne home to help finance their move to the Gold Coast.

The full reverse grid decision was sprung on the V8 teams at the final round at Phillip Island at a media conference on the Sunday morning, and it was greeted with immediate dismay. The Supercar board, which included representatives of the teams, kept the decision to themselves for six weeks, justifying the decision as an attempt to provide more entertainment by shaking up the front order and encouraging more passing. The grid for the third race would be determined on the aggregate results of races one and two, but the points on offer in the second race would be fewer than in races one and three – something, it has been argued, which devalues the point of a reverse grid. As it is, the overall points structure, which has existed for some time, can discourage attacking driving when the margins between finishing positions are so narrow.

The teams argued that the reverse grid would penalise those drivers who did well in heat one, turn racing into more of a lottery, and create more accidents, with the resultant damage to the cars increasing the costs when the board was supposedly trying to reduce them. The reverse grid has been unpopular in the Australian development series, and drivers in the New Zealand V8 championship did not like their partial reverse grid either. After Greg Murphy's collision with Marcos Ambrose at Bathurst in 2005 blocked the track and 11 other cars were involved in the resulting pile-up, one team owner, Mark Larkham, said he could not afford the repair

Australian touring car champions in the V8 era

1993, Glenn Seton		(Ford)
1994, Mark Skaife		(Holden)
1995, John Bowe		(Ford)
1996, Craig Lowndes		(Holden)
1997, Glenn Seton		(Ford)
1998, Craig Lowndes		(Holden)
1999, Craig Lowndes		(Holden)
2000, Mark Skaife		(Holden)
2001, Mark Skaife		(Holden)
2002, Mark Skaife		(Holden)
2003, Marcos Ambrose		(Ford)
2004, Marcos Ambrose		(Ford)
2005, Russell Ingall		(Ford)

bill and that Murphy should pay. With that in mind, Murphy found it difficult to fathom why Larkham, as a team representative on the Supercars board, should support the reverse grid when costs would inevitably escalate. Teams were making submissions to have the decision overturned at a special general meeting, and there were even calls for a vote of no confidence in their representatives on the board. Unless there is a change, however, round two at Pukekohe on 21–23 April 2006 is scheduled to be the first time the reverse grid is used.

And it's not as though the racing in 2005 was mundane. Far from it. Though 2005 was very much a Ford year, with Stone brothers' drivers securing their third straight touring car title, Ford drivers filling the first three places in the championship, and Ford being the leading manufacturer by seven round victories to Holden's six, Murphy still referred to it as a 'stellar year' with nine different round winners appearing on the podium, and little between the rival makes.

Note: As this book was about to go to press, it was revealed that the Shanghai round would not go ahead in June 2006 and would be replaced by racing at Victoria's Winton circuit.

THE FASCINATION
OF BATHURST

Bathurst's demanding Mount Panorama layout is by general consensus ranked among the superior circuits in world motor sport. It was recognised as such in 1987 when it staged a round of the short-lived world touring car championship, which was undeservedly scrapped, and was only revived in 2005. It is no surprise then that the lure and challenge of the 'mountain' have continued to fascinate New Zealanders whether they are participants or spectators. They have ventured there in increasing numbers in the pursuit of glory or simply to witness one of the truly memorable motor racing occasions on the planet. Even if the fans have little or no interest in the Australian touring car championship, which belatedly included the Bathurst 1000 km from 1999, they are stirred by the drama and history of the Bathurst race itself. They may not know who has won the touring car title, but the victors at Bathurst live on as part of sporting folklore on both sides of the Tasman.

Scores of Kiwi drivers have acquitted themselves with distinction there but two drivers stand out from the crowd: Jim Richards, one of New Zealand motor racing's greats, has, incredibly, been a winner seven times, and Greg Murphy has tasted victory four times. For many drivers though, it is an achievement simply to gain a starting place in the race. To finish, particularly in the top 10, has almost been akin to winning.

A number of drivers who have made their way to Bathurst have not been good enough to be members of full-time professional teams, as most of the field are these days. Over the years they have come, almost on a pilgrimage, to this setting — tranquil and picturesque for all but a week or two each year — to race as privateers on what are normally private roads. It has offered them a once-in-a-lifetime opportunity to match their skills against the household names in racing — foremost among them the record nine-times winner, Peter Brock,

A youngster steers a motorised cart pulling a couple of trailers carrying a few passengers and a couple of chilly bins in the camping area at Bathurst.

who will forever be linked to Bathurst. It has cost them money to be there, perhaps considerable sums to bring their car and pit crew from New Zealand, or they may have had to pay a team owner for the honour and pleasure of participating. They have lacked the resources of the big teams, and have driven cars of inferior quality, on a track that can be intimidating, renowned as it is for its difficulty and ability to penalise a driver whose focus wavers for just an instant. But, in a typical, practical Kiwi way, they have often risen above their limitations to record a result they will take pride in for the rest of their lives.

The weather can be a telling factor at Bathurst, where it can sometimes be a case of having four seasons in one day. It can be raining on the hill and dry down by the start-finish pit area, and this can be unnerving for even an experienced driver and his frazzled pit crew. They might have to decide whether to change to grooved wet-weather tyres and sacrifice speed, or stick to slick, dry-weather tyres and run the risk of sliding off the track. With 161 laps and more than six hours of racing, Bathurst is a searching examination of a car's durability and speed, the efficiency and calm of the pit crews, and the driver's stamina, skill and concentration. Driving around it, one quickly realises how steep it is to the top of the hill, how narrow the circuit is in places, and how very little margin there is for error.

The legendary, six-and-a-bit kilometre, anti-clockwise circuit commands the hill behind Bathurst, a New South Wales country university town of 35,000 on the edge of the Blue Mountains, 210 km west of Sydney. The words 'Mount Panorama Australia' have been plastered on the town side of the hill, and they can be seen for some distance, guiding spectators to the Mecca of Australian touring car racing like a beacon. The track started life as a scenic tourist drive, offering stunning views of the plains from the top of the hill. However, its potential as a motor sport circuit soon caught the imagination of enthusiasts. In the depressed years of the 1930s the Bathurst City Council fostered the idea of a scenic road to the crest of Bald Hills as an unemployment relief project to be funded by a State

Getty Images

The throaty engine note of the winning Holden of Mark Skaife and Todd Kelly at Bathurst in 2005 is in stark contrast to the quiet rural setting that surrounds the Mount Panorama circuit.

Bathurst 1000 km winners in the V8 era

1993,	Larry Perkins/Gregg Hansford	(Holden Commodore)
1994,	Dick Johnson/John Bowe	(Ford Falcon)
1995,	Larry Perkins/Russell Ingall	(Holden Commodore)
1996,	Craig Lowndes/Greg Murphy	(Holden Commodore)
1997,	Larry Perkins/Russell Ingall	(Holden Commodore)
1998,	Steven Richards/Jason Bright	(Ford Falcon)
1999,	Greg Murphy/Steven Richards	(Holden Commodore)
2000,	Garth Tander/Jason Bargwanna	(Holden Commodore)
2001,	Mark Skaife/Tony Longhurst	(Holden Commodore)
2002,	Mark Skaife/Jim Richards	(Holden Commodore)
2003,	Greg Murphy/Rick Kelly	(Holden Commodore)
2004,	Greg Murphy/Rick Kelly	(Holden Commodore)
2005,	Mark Skaife/Todd Kelly	(Holden Commodore)

Government grant. It was also seen as a possible replacement for the old Vale circuit, and a grant from a local resident, Walter McPhillamy, provided the council with a large area of parkland, now used as the track's camping ground.

The Bathurst Light Car Club recognised the road's wide corners and two escape options as ideal for its members, and the track was first used on 18 April 1938, and was sealed the following year. The first meeting was organised by the New South Wales Light Car Club and the Auto Cycle Union as a joint car/motorcycle race. On that sunny April day a staggering 35,000 spectators watched the speeding machines, a crowd comparable in size to those of today. Over the years the four-wheelers have achieved greater fame than the two-wheelers on the Bathurst track. The Australian Grand Prix has been raced there four times: in 1938, 1947, 1952 and 1958. However, Bathurst has since become synonymous

Fairfax Sunday Newspapers

Accomplished single-seater racer Jim Palmer, seen here driving a Cooper, was New Zealand's first racer to shine in a touring car at Bathurst, with a second in 1968.

with the running of the annual 1000 km race, now for the V8 Supercars, traditionally held in October.

The event was originally conceived as the ultimate endurance test for production cars, and started life at Victoria's Phillip Island track in 1960. When the Phillip Island track was resurfaced in 1963, the event was transferred to Bathurst, and such was its impact, the race never returned south. As at Phillip Island, the race was contested over 500 miles and each car had two drivers to share the task. The first Bathurst event was won by Australians Bob Jane and Harry Firth in a Ford Cortina GT. They became big names in Australian motor sport, and Jane established the T Mart empire, which later became the Bathurst sponsor for three years from 2002 to 2004.

Bathurst was originally thought to be best suited to small cars as, it was argued, the big V8s would struggle with excessive wear to tyres and brakes. But the Mini Cooper S victory of Finnish rallying ace Rauno Aaltonen and Australian Bob Holden in 1966 proved to be an anomaly. The following year a V8 finally won, the Ford Falcon XR GT of Firth and Fred Gibson. For a brief period in the early 1970s it was not compulsory to have a co-driver, and Allan Moffat (twice) and Brock won on their own. Then, in 1973 the distance was increased to its present 1000 km, and each car had to have two drivers, neither of whom could be continuously at the wheel for more than three and a half hours, and neither of whom could drive for more than two-thirds of the distance, 107 laps.

Hamilton garage owner Jim Palmer was the first Kiwi to make his presence felt when he secured a podium finish in 1968. He and an Australian Phil West combined to pilot a Holden Monaro GT 327 to second place. It was a significant milestone. He helped provide the inspiration for a string of his countrymen to make the crossing to Bathurst, as well as establishing a level of excellence eventually only bettered by Jim Richards, New Zealand's best performer in Australian touring cars, and Greg Murphy.

Palmer made his reputation in single-seaters, twice finishing third in the New Zealand Grand Prix at Ardmore at a time when the race attracted the

Before the Holden-Ford V8 Supercar era was ushered in from 1993, Bathurst was won by a variety of other machines, including the controversial turbo-powered Nissans and Ford Sierras, a massive Jaguar XJS V12, a BMW 320i, and a Volvo S40. The latter two won the two-litre 1000 km races in 1997 and 1998, but the superior popularity of the separate V8 1000 km events in the same years, only a few weeks later, spelled the demise of the smaller cars.

Holdens have been victorious on 25 occasions, including a record seven years in a row from 1999 to 2005, well ahead of Ford's 14 wins.

Jim Richards and Swede Rickard Rydell on their way to a hard-earned victory driving a Volvo S40 in the final of two separate two-litre races at Bathurst. It was the sixth of Richards' seven 1000 km wins there.

Bathurst was originally thought to be best suited to small cars . . .

biggest names in Formula One. He had previously raced a Brabham and Cooper Climax at Mount Panorama. At Easter in 1966 he was good enough to win the Australian Racing Drivers' Club Gold Cup race, and at one time held the lap record there in a two-and-a-half-litre Brabham. The Monaro he drove in 1968 was 'stock standard', said Palmer, unlike the V8 Supercars, which apart from the silhouette bear little resemblance to the Holden and Ford cars on our roads. The Monaro had radial tyres and a four-speed gearbox, disc brakes on the front, and Michelin tyres on steel wheels. It was, in fact, highly similar to the car of 1968 winners Bruce McPhee and Barry Mulholland, who scored Holden's first win that year and started a run that has made the marque easily the greatest performer at Bathurst.

Palmer was invited to Bathurst to drive for David McKay's three-car team on the strength of his single-seater deeds there, which included competing alongside fellow New Zealanders Ross Jensen, who raced a classic 250F Maserati, and Tom Clark in a Ferrari. 'I suppose we were Kiwi trailblazers when we raced at Bathurst,' Palmer said. 'We'd read about the successes there of guys like Leo and Ian Geoghegan and Bob Jane. They were legends and we wanted to find out for ourselves what it was like. Races at Bathurst attracted a huge following in Australia straight away. It was exciting, but it was bloody dangerous, especially over Skyline. There wasn't much in the way of safety features as we know it today. In the Brabham I reached speeds of 170 miles

Long-time Queensland resident Neal Lowe was second in 1986 in Peter Brock's HDT second car after an encouraging fifth on debut the year previously. Lowe, who went on to fashion a strong career in Australia as a racing engineer, showed early promise in New Zealand when he became national karting and Mini Seven champion, built a winning two-litre Ford Cortina, and had success in long-distance saloon car races with Kent Baigent. Lowe and Baigent turned their attention to the Australian touring car championship in 1985; Baigent racing a BMW 635 CSi bought from the powerful Schnitzer team, which was often formidable in the Wellington street race leg of the Nissan-Mobil series. Lowe prepared the car, and they were driving partners at Bathurst that year. 'I'd always wanted to race at Bathurst, and first time down the mountain was too fast for me,' Lowe remembered. 'The car was becoming airborne a couple of times on the incredibly long Conrod Straight. It was before they built the chase. It was an

Races at Bathurst attracted a huge following in Australia . . . but it was bloody dangerous, especially over Skyline.

an hour down Conrod Straight, and the car would come off the ground going over the hump, which isn't there now. There was just a wire fence at the top of the mountain [Skyline], and we had no seatbelts or the fireproof suits they're all required to wear now. The guys didn't kick up. They accepted the risks involved.'

In 1968 the race was still over 500 miles. 'It was hard work,' Palmer said. 'We had two driver changes, the car had no brakes at the end, and we'd had a change of brakes. There wasn't much in the way of prize money for finishing second, but we didn't complain. I think we got $A100 or $A200, and a pair of sunglasses.'

Other New Zealanders to shine at Mount Panorama include Team Kiwi Racing's Paul Radisich, who has been second twice; in 1990 when still racing in the British touring car championship, and in 2000. He was also poised to win in 1999 only for an error made when passing a slower car forced his withdrawal.

extremely exciting track. We hung around fifth most of the time. We had a problem with a slipping clutch in the last hour after breaking an oil seal. Without it we could have finished higher.'

Lowe's prospects of a return to Bathurst were dealt a severe blow when Baigent wrote off the BMW in a crash at Manfeild. But then, in an abrupt change of fortune, he had a call from Peter Brock who invited him to share his second HDT car with past Bathurst victor John Harvey, for the Nissan-Mobil races in early 1986. 'It came right out of the blue, and of course it only took a fraction of a second to say "yes",' Lowe said. 'Peter must have known I didn't have a drive, and he would have seen me racing in Australia.'

It was the start of a profitable year both on and off the track, and one that shaped his career.

Paul Radisich at the head of a 'freight train' at Bathurst in 2001 driving a red and yellow Dick Johnson Ford. It didn't last. Radisich and his co-driver Steven Johnson failed to finish.

He and Harvey were third in their first outing at the Wellington street race, won by Brock and Allan Moffat in the No. 1 Commodore, the latter now comfortable as a team-mate of Brock's after having been a huge opponent when racing Fords. Then, when Brock retired from the Pukekohe race with an overheating engine, Lowe and Harvey prevailed. Lowe was also part of the team that competed against the top Europeans in the Spa 24-hour race in Belgium later that year. He drove the second car with Baigent and Graeme Bowkett, and they placed 18th (four places ahead of Brock, Moffat and Harvey) before going on to win the King's Cup teams' prize with another Commodore.

The Lowe-Harvey partnership was revived for the Bathurst 1000 km in 1986, and after leading briefly they finished second, again heading off Brock and Moffat, who were fifth in a car that had been hastily rebuilt after Moffat had crashed it in practice. 'There was a heap more pressure on me at Bathurst that time,' Lowe said. 'I was working for the team as an engineer, and we'd done a lot of development on the cars. I'd even raced Peter's 05 car when he'd been away overseas. At Bathurst people were so tuned in to Peter and his team. Cars were pulling over to let us through.'

Lowe, now 58, never competed at Bathurst again. 'I didn't enjoy racing as much as building and developing cars,' he said. 'I started as a mechanic, and I'd had service stations and built cars before I left New Zealand.'

Graeme Lawrence, of Hamilton, who had an outstanding career in single-seaters, was third at Bathurst in 1978. Lawrence, a member of a high-profile Wanganui motor racing family, made five appearances, the first in 1975 in a little Triumph Dolomite. He made the podium on his fourth attempt, securing third place, with Australian Murray Carter in a Ford Falcon GT, in the same year Jim Richards had the first of his three successive wins alongside Peter Brock.

Fairfax Sunday Newspapers: *Auckland Star* Collection

Celebrated single-seater driver Graeme Lawrence (right) is helped by his father Dougie at a single-seater meeting at the old Levin circuit. Graeme used that experience to finish third at Bathurst in 1978.

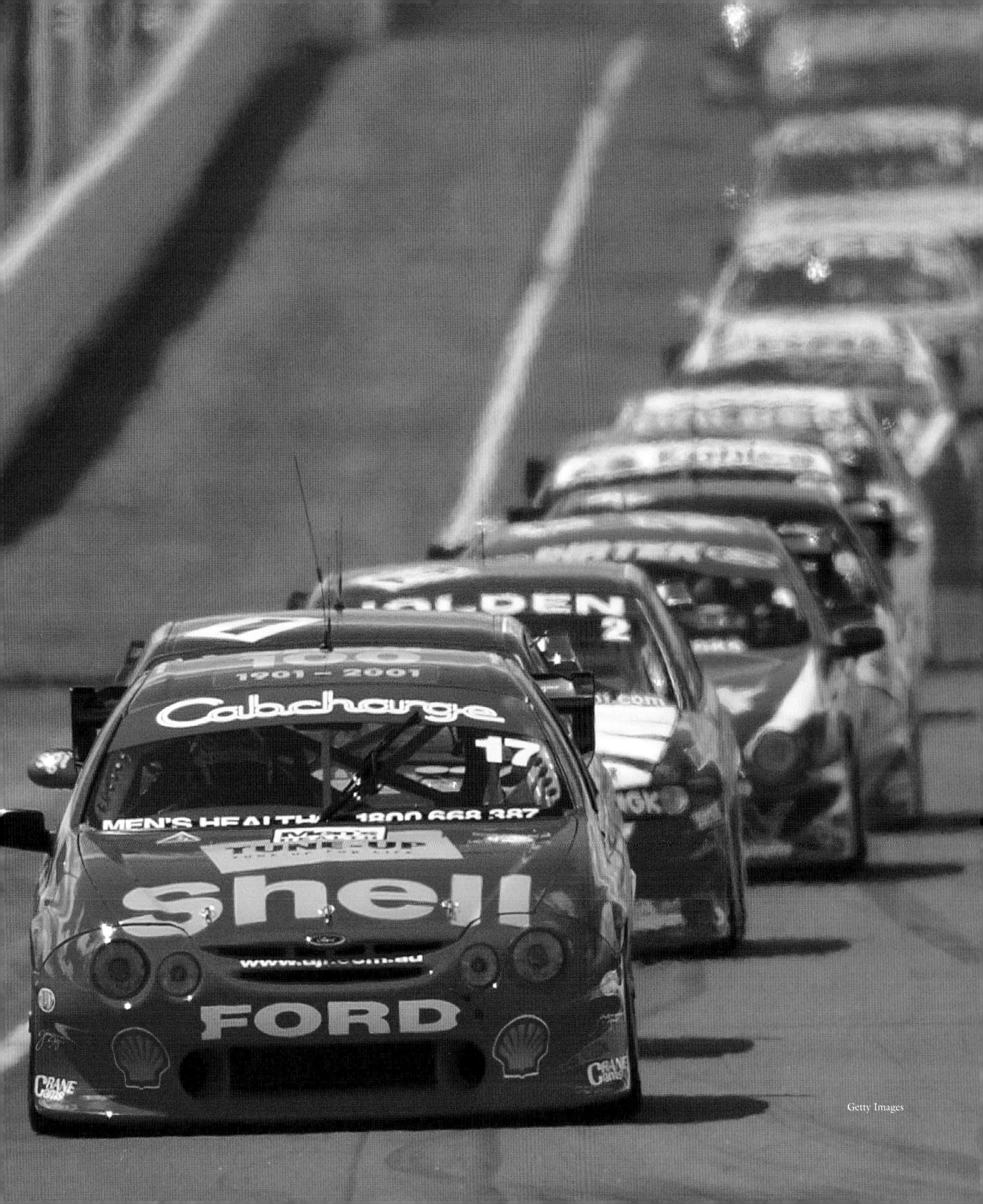

Getty Images

'I loved the circuit. The "up-hill down-dale" nature of it was challenging,' Lawrence recalled. 'It was less of a sprint then and you were more intent on being able to finish. The day we were third we qualified in the top 12 or so, and slowly worked our way through the field. The Falcon was very reliable. We weren't influenced by what was going on around us. We set our own pace. It was a bit hairy on Conrod Straight. We had to drive over a big hump, which was later removed. It was pretty satisfying to finish third, particularly considering I was from single-seaters driving against guys running in touring cars all the time. I raced Fords up there three times and the cars wouldn't handle properly. There was a huge change in driving style, and it was a big test of my stamina.'

Lawrence, now in his mid-60s, had considerable success in the Tasman single-seater series driving a Dino Ferrari formerly raced by Chris Amon, and he

control the car, taking it onto the grass and nudging it into a barrier before it came to a halt.

Williamson was back in Auckland, organising a deal for Hulme with BMW, and watching the Bathurst action on television when his telephone rang. It was race chief Tim Schenken, standing by Hulme's car. He said to Williamson 'it's not good', and then asked about the whereabouts of Hulme's wife, Greta. It transpired that Hulme should probably not have been racing. About a year previously he had been ashen-faced and unable to get out of his car after a race in the United States — and he had been advised to have a check-up. Though Williamson and the gruff Hulme were 'good mates', having known each other since Williamson was a young mechanic trying to impress Hulme at Ray Archibald's Jaguar garage in Christchurch in the early 1960s, he had not known that all was not well.

There was a huge contingent of Kiwis camping nearby, and there were 30 of us in dormitory-style accommodation . . .

also tested for the McLaren Formula One team. But he has had more difficult times too. He spent months in Middlemore Hospital after a bad accident in a Lola, in the New Zealand Grand Prix at Pukekohe, resulted in the death of fellow competitor Bryan Falloon. He recovered from that, however, to again excel in the Tasman series, and to win a number of Grands Prix in South-East Asia.

Denny Hulme, New Zealand's only world Formula One champion, was fourth in 1991 driving a BMW M3 with Australian Peter Fitzgerald, a year before he died there. Hulme's death, aged 56, of a heart attack while driving his BMW on Mountain Straight, cast a shadow over the 1992 race. Hulme was not one to talk a lot on the in-car radio, but on this occasion he was complaining of having visibility problems in the wet a few laps before he died. Lyall Williamson, a long-time friend and a business partner of Hulme's, said it was more likely that Hulme was struggling to see as a result of his rapidly deteriorating health. Despite his condition, Hulme still managed to

That day, another good friend of Hulme's, Jim Richards, won at Bathurst in controversial circumstances after a cloudburst ended the race prematurely. Richards, who has lived in Melbourne since 1975, was later among the many mourners who attended Hulme's funeral back in the little Bay of Plenty town of Te Puke.

Jim Richards retains vivid memories of his first Bathurst experience, which was with co-driver Rod Coppins, who tragically died of cancer in the early 1980s in his mid-40s. Richards would hardly have imagined that his distinguished placing of third on debut in Australia in 1974 would one day lead to a record 34 appearances at Bathurst — two more than Peter Brock. The Holden Torana L34 they drove in that first race belonged to Coppins, who had previously raced in Australia driving a Ford Mustang in the touring car championship. Coppins and Richards were good friends, and a proven combination, having won the Benson and Hedges six-hour at Pukekohe in a Chrysler Charger in 1972 and 1973.

Jim Richards' seven wins at Bathurst were spread between 1978 and 2002, and include the 1998 AMP 1000 km for two-litre touring cars. Greg Murphy's successive victories in 2003 and 2004 lifted his tally to four, eclipsed only by the nine of Mount Panorama favourite Peter Brock, Richards' seven, the six of another iconic Australian, Larry Perkins, and the five of Mark Skaife.

New Zealand has claimed another winner in Steven Richards, elder son of Jim, who was successful two years in a row, 1998 and 1999, the latter with Murphy, first in a Ford and then a Holden. However, though born in Auckland, Steven regards himself as more of an Australian, having lived there almost all of his life.

Jim Richards' seven Bathurst 1000 km wins

1978, with Peter Brock	(Holden Torana)
1979, with Peter Brock	(Holden Torana)
1980, with Peter Brock	(Holden Commodore)
1991, with Mark Skaife	(Nissan Skyline)
1992, with Mark Skaife	(Nissan Skyline)
1998, with Rickard Rydell	(Volvo)
2002, with Mark Skaife	(Holden Commodore)

'Rod paid my airfare to Bathurst, and Rod's mechanic Mark "Jandals" Sheehan went over early and prepared the car at Fred Gibson's garage,' Richards recalled. The preparation was still a bit rushed, and they had to scrounge some wet-weather tyres in case it rained. They managed to buy a couple of wet-weather and two intermediate tyres, and it was just as well they did as it poured on race day. 'Bathurst was like being in heaven for me, it was unbelievable,' Richards said. 'A lot of New Zealanders knew about it. Leo Leonard drove there before I did. I didn't know a lot about Australian motor racing but Bathurst had a reputation for being a great track, and here we were racing over 1000 km against all the best drivers in Australia. There was a huge contingent of Kiwis camping nearby, and there were 30 of us in dormitory-style accommodation on Conrod Straight. The dorms were full of Kiwis, who were drunk every night!'

Richards had the last driving stint, and he gave the Australians an immediate demonstration of his mastery in the wet. 'Towards the end I was passing cars like they were going backwards, but we lost our brakes and in the pouring rain we had to coast to third,' he said. 'There were accidents all around us. One guy careered off the track on Conrod when he lost control in a puddle, and he hit a tree. It was staggering that all he got was a cut ear. The floor of the Torana hit the tree, which bent the car in half. The floor was almost level with the roof.'

Richards and Coppins raced at Bathurst on two other occasions without being able to better that performance. They were eighth in the Torana in 1975, and dropped out after 53 laps in 1977 when Richards' Ford Falcon XB GT developed engine trouble. Coppins was the New Zealand champion for the big saloons on one occasion, and on another (1969–70) he shared the title with Red Dawson. Coppins twice tried to qualify without success for the New Zealand Grand Prix in his 4600 cc Chevrolet V8 TecMec, but he was particularly remembered for the hot Chevrolet Corvette V8-powered Mk II Zephyr he drove in the 1960s, which was distinguished by the radical exhaust pipes pointing skywards straight up through the car's bonnet.

It defied belief that Richards was still competitive enough to be a winner at Bathurst in 2002, 28 years after his debut there, a feat no other driver has approached. It prompted Richards to expand on his simple philosophy, which illustrated the great pleasure he was still deriving from the sport. 'Right from when I started I've never gone in to a race with winning the priority,' he says. 'It may sound strange but when I started I couldn't win. I didn't have the equipment. When I've driven for the top teams my philosophy hasn't changed. My priority hasn't been about winning, it's been competing as well as I can. If that's good enough then I'll have a win. I'm not driven by history. I'm not interested in the number of races I've won.'

Christchurch motor dealer Trevor Crowe was fourth in 1988, and it all happened in a bit of a whirlwind for him. He only had three weeks' notice when he was chosen to race for an Australian team that had been unsuccessful in contracting a top European racer to co-drive a BMW M3. Crowe's partner was Melbourne driver Peter Janson. Crowe described him as a 'bit of a character'. Instead of racing in the regulation fireproof suit, Janson managed to get away with wearing a striped outfit, which Crowe said came from famous London tailor in Savile Row.

Though Crowe had finished 10th the year before with fellow New Zealander Inky Tulloch (who was later mayor of Mataura in Southland), only to be disqualified for having an illegal wing on their car, Crowe started with no great expectations given the rushed preparation. Their modest qualifying spot of 32nd certainly never hinted at anything out of the ordinary. 'When we started we thought somewhere in the top 20 would be brilliant,' Crowe said. 'We couldn't believe it when we were fourth. . . . I thought we were 15th, then I saw a leader board and we were 10th. The M3 just kept lapping consistently, and we kept moving up as the big V8s started having trouble with tyres and brakes. It was astonishing really.'

Crowe, who won the Asia-Pacific title in an M3 in 1988, had done a lot of rallying, which he found invaluable given the demands posed by the Bathurst track, especially in the wet. 'Rallying gave me a kind of sixth sense regarding safety, it made me more car sensitive,' he said. 'Some guys in trouble tend not to ease off.' Later that year he was third in the Wellington street race in another M3 with Mark Thatcher, the son of former England Prime Minister Maggie Thatcher.

My priority hasn't been about winning, it's been competing as well as I can. If that's good enough then I'll have a win.

Fairfax Sunday Newspapers: *Auckland Star Collection*

The late Rod Coppins at the wheel of a Holden Torana, a make of car he and Jim Richards raced twice at Bathurst. On the first occasion in 1974, they came third.

Though Robbie Francevic became only the second New Zealander to win the Australian touring car title when he achieved the feat in 1986, success at Bathurst proved elusive. In 1986 broken rockers plagued the Sierra Francevic was sharing with Leo Leonard and they didn't finish — after having been in the top six. In his several other attempts, his best was sixth in 1987 driving a BMW M3 with German, Ludwig Finauer. He was seventh with another New Zealander, Andrew Bagnall, in a Ford Sierra RS 500 three years later.

Mark Petch, who managed a number of Francevic's Australian campaigns, and who now runs his own motor racing team as well as editing the successful monthly motoring magazine *New Zealand Autocar*, recalled Francevic and John Bowe leading in a Volvo in 1985 only for the car to falter. And in 1989 a wheel fell off when Francevic shared a Ford Sierra RS 500 with former Formula One driver Gianfranco Brancatelli. 'Robbie had a lot of natural driving talent,' Petch remembered. 'He could drive

a bad car fast. However, once things became more sophisticated he struggled a bit.'

Francevic considers one of his best chances to have been in 1989. 'We had a good show in 1989 had Brancatelli been a bit more conservative,' Francevic said. 'He was out in front by 30 seconds when he crashed. I think he was more concerned with the television coverage he got from charging up front than winning the race. I'd have sat back and waited in second or third but I think for a lot of the Europeans who have come out to race at Bathurst it's just another race. They don't care. They have another race the next week.'

Wellington driver Andrew Fawcet's Bathurst appearance in 1999 was a classic case of a New Zealander fulfilling the ambition of a lifetime. The 45-year-old property developer paid to be privateer Nathan Pretty's co-driver in a tired Larry Perkins-built yellow Commodore VS. The grids then were much bigger than are permitted today, and after

Linear Photographs

Trevor Crowe racing a BMW 635 CSi, a make of car that brought him much success, including a fourth at Bathurst.

starting almost last — 53rd in a field of 55 — and having completed 134 of the 161 laps, against all expectation they finished a highly creditable 20th. To complicate matters, Pretty had also crashed the car in practice, and it had been a scramble to have the car ready for the start on Sunday morning.

Despite being an accomplished TransAm driver, having won the Liquor King 500 the previous weekend, and having had success in the Hot Chilly Ford Falcon in New Zealand's increasingly competitive V8 touring car championship, Fawcet would have battled to secure a Supercar drive — where the overwhelming emphasis is on full-time professionals — without being prepared to part with a few dollars. 'I've always been a V8 fan, and I'd always wanted to race in the 1000 km at Bathurst. It was a great experience,' Fawcet said. 'The Prettys were very accommodating. I wouldn't get the same chances again. There are still drives around but it's harder to get in now. It's becoming the domain of the professionals. I wouldn't have missed it.'

Earlier in 1999 Fawcet and a Lower Hutt driver Lewis Scott had leased a car from the Pretty family to contest the Auscar V8 one-and-a-half-hour race at Bathurst. It rained, and the race was abandoned with the pair seventh, and poor Scott yet to get a turn behind the wheel. Fawcet declared it an 'appalling weekend', but it had a silver lining when the Prettys rang him a week before the 1000 km race to invite him to drive their Supercar. Till then Nathan's sister Nicole was to be his co-driver. 'It cost me a bit of money to get the ride, and I didn't have much time to make up my mind, but it was an easy decision,' Fawcet said. 'We had a fantastic team of family and volunteers, really good guys. The Prettys are real enthusiasts. There was not a lot of sponsorship. It was all done on a shoestring.'

Fawcet did not see the car till the first practice on the Thursday, when he managed 10 laps as he sought to come to grips with the car and the track, and had only a few laps on the Friday. Pretty was driving well, being near the top of the bottom 50 per cent of qualifiers, and he decided to go out and

One of the most famous, bizarre and far-reaching incidents occurred in 1980 when Dick Johnson's Ford was stopped in its tracks by a rock pushed on to the circuit by spectators. Johnson was exiting The Cutting and was leading by 40 seconds early in the race when he was suddenly confronted by the rock. While able to avoid a tow truck that blocked the road on his left Johnson could not miss the rock on his right. With his path blocked he was cruelly eliminated. The front wheel on his XD Falcon was destroyed, and it took a police investigation to clear Holden fans, initially thought to have deliberately pushed the rock in front of Johnson.

Instead of it being a disaster for the cash-strapped, little-known privateer the heavy chunk of rubble launched his career (which became among the best in Australian touring car history) and now holds pride of place in Johnson's Queensland workshop museum. In his moment of despair, his savings gone, and looking as if he would never return to Bathurst, Johnson caught the imagination of the watching public. They rallied, stumping up $A50,000 in pledges, and with Ford matching the figure, Johnson suddenly had $A100,000 to finance his campaign the following year.

He used it superbly. In a classic tale of rags to riches, Johnson won Bathurst and the Australian touring car title in 1981, both for the first time. He went on to win Bathurst three times and became a legend, particularly among Ford fans, who saw him as very much a working-class battler. His name lives on with Johnson's Ford team the oldest on pit lane, and still a force to be reckoned with. His son, Steven, placed 12th in the 2005 Supercars championship, drives for his father.

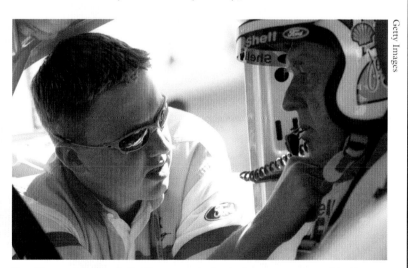

Getty Images

Son Steven Johnson (left) offers some last minute encouragement to his legendary father Dick Johnson before he contests the top 10 shootout in his farewell appearance at Bathurst in 1999. The pair went on to finish fourth.

Mount Panorama came of age in 1987 with the staging of the race as a round of the world touring car championship. Millions of dollars were spent upgrading the circuit and its facilities. The first major track change made at Bathurst since it was opened came when the Caltex Chase was added — a chicane at the braking end of the high-speed downhill Conrod Straight. In theory this made the circuit safer but it also created a whole new spectator viewing area and has led to some spectacular racing.

The 1987 race was a nerve-wracking affair with the Australian scrutineers allegedly applying the international group A regulations more stringently than the European teams and the global organising body. It led to the first two cars across the line, European-entered Ford Sierra turbos, being disqualified for bodywork irregularities months after the event, and the race was awarded to the third-placed Peter Brock, giving him his ninth and last victory. They called him 'Peter Perfect'. For many, an abiding memory of Bathurst has been Peter Brock in his famous numbered 05 Holden — though, much to the consternation of fans, he did drive a BMW and a Ford Sierra (twice) there in the years 1988–1990 when he fell out with Holden Australia. But all nine of his victories came in a Holden, the first in 1972, when he drove by himself, and the last 15 years later with David Parsons and Peter McLeod, when drivers were still allowed to jump into the team's other car if their own had expired or to help improve the position of another of the team's cars.

Peter Brock's nine Bathurst 1000 km wins

1972, on his own	(Holden Torana)
1975, with Brian Sampson	(Holden Torana)
1978, with Jim Richards	(Holden Torana)
1979, with Jim Richards	(Holden Torana)
1980, with Jim Richards	(Holden Commodore)
1982, with Larry Perkins	(Holden Commodore)
1983, with Larry Perkins/John Harvey	(Holden Commodore)
1984, with Larry Perkins	(Holden Commodore)
1987, with David Parsons/Peter McLeod	(Holden Commodore)

attempt to post a time good enough to climb into the bottom of the top 50 per cent. However, on cold tyres, Pretty tried too hard, and he ended up running the car into a wall at McPhillamy Park. They still scraped into the final field, their best lap times being within 107 per cent of the fastest car, as the regulations required.

It required a superhuman effort to be on the grid. The local panel beaters and chassis straighteners laboured through the night to repair the car in time. The Prettys didn't pick it up till 7 a.m. on the Sunday morning. Despite the setback the car ran strongly, being well up in the field till a universal joint on the driveshaft had to be replaced. By the end the power steering had failed, probably the result of something being missed in the rush to repair the car, and the clutch no longer worked, and there was no sixth gear. 'Without the power steering it turned into a wrestling match,' said Fawcet, who drove the second and last stints. 'It was so exhausting trying to steer the car without it. It was a considerable achievement to finish. So many teams have gone up there [to Bathurst] and never finished. It was pretty exciting to drive the last session.'

Fawcet said he was not unnerved by the occasion or put off when he had the frontrunners filling his mirrors and queuing up to pass him. 'I gave guys room when I could,' he said. 'It was bloody tough trying to stay on the track and off the walls, which were on both sides of the track in places. I just tried to stay on the black stuff. I never had a problem with the faster guys. We weren't the slowest on the track. Other privateers were battling too.'

Fawcet said it was all so rushed there wasn't time to mix much with the drivers of the other teams, something he would have enjoyed, although he had met the man himself, Peter Brock, years earlier at Pukekohe. It had been in Fawcet's first season of TransAm racing, when, in his words, 'we didn't have a bloody clue'. 'It was a round of the Nissan-Mobil series,' Fawcet said, 'and Peter Brock happened to notice us, and walked up and said, "What are you doing?" He was so helpful to us in setting up the car properly.'

After the Second World War the New South Wales police were becoming agitated about circuit safety at Bathurst. The infamous Conrod Straight was the most dangerous part of the circuit and, despite its modification with the introduction of the Caltex Chase, it is arguably still dangerous. It's a corner that can still be taken at close to full speed despite the elimination of the two humps that were there and the introduction of a tighter left-hand bend that needs heavy braking.

The two drivers killed most recently were the accountant for the organising club, the Australian Racing Drivers' Club, Mike Burgmann, who died in 1986; and Victorian Don Watson in 1994. Burgmann's Holden Commodore lost control when it became airborne over a Conrod hump. The car slid onto the grass, and slammed into a thick tyre wall at more than 200 kmh. The impact broke Burgmann's safety harness, and he was flung backwards. He died at the scene. That resulted in the creation of the Caltex Chase. Unfortunately, however, the Chase couldn't save Watson. His Commodore shattered a brake disc, which blew out a tyre in the Chase at around 260 kmh, and the car careered in to a tyre barrier.

Among the largest crashes was that which occurred at the top of the hill on the opening lap in 1969 when a pileup claimed a quarter of the 65-car field.

Also synonymous with Bathurst are the diehard fans who spend the week camping on the hill. Some of them can be downright intimidating and they are often a law unto themselves, with their infamous all-night activities that can include letting off 'earth-shattering' fireworks, lighting fires and flaming soccer balls (toilet rolls dipped in kerosene), and using old cars for smash-up derbies in what is called the 'bull pit'. One group of fans wears distinctive Army greatcoats emblazoned with the patches of their favourite cars and teams, while other fans don't travel light, pulling trailers with portaloos and generators behind them. The race organisers also recognise the need to have areas where families and campers intent on a quiet time can enjoy themselves, but if you want to camp on the hill you have to recognise it's not for the faint-hearted.

Then there are the 30 or so locals who live on the circuit, who find their pastoral environment invaded by the thunderous V8s, which travel along Conrod Straight at speeds close to 300 kmh. The locals have to make do with getting in and out during a clear window at lunchtime once the day's activities have started.

Getty Images

Smoke hangs in the air from barbecue fires in a camping ground at Bathurst where a beer is forever close at hand.

STONE BROTHERS RACING

Brothers in Arms

It's an extraordinary story — among the best in V8 Supercars. Two unassuming, middle-aged Kiwi brothers, Jimmy and Ross Stone, head the top team in arguably the world's toughest touring car championship. Stone Brothers Racing (SBR), formed in late 1997, is the team everyone is now trying to emulate or better, after HRT's long domination. It has been based on a typical no-nonsense New Zealand attitude of complete dedication to whatever they are doing, and the pair's tongue and groove-like teamwork.

With Jimmy's engineering expertise leaving Ross free to concentrate on running an increasingly sophisticated business, they have had all the bases covered since the team's earliest days. Their life revolves around the team. Little else matters. They have a reputation for being extremely clever, are quite happy to work for endless days on end to ensure that nothing is left to chance in their quest for even the slightest advantage, and they have staff willing to be just as diligent and thorough. The Stones were highly regarded in Australian touring cars long before they went out on their own, and they have steadily increased the momentum since establishing their Ford team. In the last three years the Stones have fashioned a formidable record with the help of principal sponsors Ford, Caltex and Pirtek Fluid Systems. Their brilliantly prepared Ford Falcon BAs have carried their drivers to the individual title on several occasions: Marcos Ambrose in 2003 and 2004, just the sixth driver to win consecutive championships since the series started in 1960, and Russell Ingall in 2005.

Their deeds also made SBR the champion team for 2004 and 2005, and as further acknowledgement of its standing it supplied engines to two other Ford Supercar teams in 2005, including that of its

It has been based on a typical no-nonsense New Zealand attitude of complete dedication to whatever they are doing . . .

The no-nonsense, workaholic Stone brothers, Ross (left) and Jimmy, who have established new standards of excellence in the sport.

toughest competitor, Triple Eight Race Engineering.

It will be supplying engines to two more teams in 2006, including Kiwi newcomer Paul Cruickshank Racing, and Ross says it makes sound economic sense as teams strive to keep a rein on soaring costs.

Triple Eight driver Craig Lowndes revelled in the increased potency of his car, and posed the biggest threat to Ingall's and Ambrose's chances of winning the individual championship in 2005. After starting on pole at Bathurst he might have pushed them even further but for a moment of sloppiness when his Falcon hit a wall, and he limped home in 15th place. He completed the year in second place overall, just 57 points behind Ingall after starting the last round at Phillip Island, Victoria, trailing by 49. Ambrose was third. Right in Lowndes's corner was his engineer Campbell Little, a foundation staff member with the Stones when they went in to partnership with Alan Jones in late 1995, who defected to Triple Eight in late 2003, just before Ambrose became champion for the first time. Little was technical and racing manager when he left, and

on the Triple Eight website he still lists Jimmy and Ross Stone as among his heroes. Ross said they bear no ill will toward Little despite his close relationship with Lowndes, who, in winning four of the 13 rounds in 2005, was the biggest obstacle to the Stones's continued dominance.

The Stones had actually sought to hire Lowndes for 2001 when he was the hottest young driver in Supercars, having already won three touring car titles at the age of 26, and preparing to turn the series on its head by jumping from Holden to Ford. 'We were the ones originally trying to get him,' Ross recalls. 'We understood Ford was keen but it didn't work out.' It's interesting to ponder the scenarios had Lowndes joined SBR. With Dave Besnard already signed, it would have been at the expense of Ambrose, and Lowndes would not have been in the wilderness as long as he was. He spent four disillusioning years driving for three other Ford teams, all totally inferior to the Stones. Only in 2005 did Lowndes have a package good enough for him to display the sustained brilliance that made him such a hit at the Holden Racing Team.

The Stone brothers' pride and joy in 2005, the BA Falcons of Marcos Ambrose (bottom) and Russell Ingall, about to be loaded on the plane to Shanghai.

The 2005 result was a great one for Ford with the first three in the championship driving BA Falcons, and much of that was due to SBR. The team has given Ford a credibility missing since Glenn Seton won his second championship in 1997 in one of its cars. Ross, aged 53, and Jimmy, 60, have become household names in Australian motor sport, for their ability to build cars and engines, and run a successful operation in two massive warehouse spaces at Yatala, halfway between Brisbane and the Gold Coast. The adulation is almost an embarrassment to them. The generally reticent pair are more than happy to stay out of the spotlight. They much prefer to allow their results to speak for themselves, and leave their highly paid drivers to do the talking.

In Ambrose and Ingall they had a pair more than capable of handling themselves in public, and not afraid to be confrontational, and even controversial,

They have never forgotten why they are in this business. There has been no taking their eyes off the ball or, as a former SBR driver, Craig Baird, said, they don't feel the need to flaunt their superiority by having 'the biggest boat in pit lane'. The Stones's achievements have made an impact in Australia, but they have generally slipped under the radar of the New Zealand sporting public. Only followers of motor sport know the significance of their efforts, yet they are huge even when compared with New Zealand's involvement in other Australian competitions, such as the Breakers in the national basketball league, the Knights soccer team, and the New Zealand Warriors in the National Rugby League. If SBR had been in the NRL, its accomplishments would have earned high praise and wide recognition and would have put it in the running as a finalist in the annual Halberg Awards 'teams' category for 2005,

They are a rarity in this business. They are not ego driven, although they are often surrounded by people who are.

in *and* out of the car. Ambrose's departure for the United States at the end of 2005, just the third Australian behind Dick Johnson and Allan Grice to pursue a career in NASCAR, seems certain to make life an awful lot quieter in the SBR garage.

There are team owners and managers who happily make themselves available to the media, but you won't see the Stones queuing up. They are a rarity in this business. They are not ego driven, although they are often surrounded by people who are. They are motivated by a love of what they do, and the pursuit of excellence. After years of battling, and being persistent and patient, it has brought them success and financial security. And this is after mortgaging their Gold Coast houses to buy themselves out of a partnership with past Formula One world champion, Alan Jones, that allowed them to finally do their own thing.

Two-time Australian touring car champion Marcos Ambrose is surrounded as he celebrates victory at the Clipsal 500 km in Adelaide in 2005.

alongside netball's Silver Ferns, the Kiwis rugby league team, the All Blacks and the world champion rowing crews.

There is a strong Kiwi component in the Stones's full-time team of 52, plus its two drivers, which includes a number of family members. There are three brothers — the eldest, Jimmy, followed by Kevin and Ross, all of whom are steeped in the sport — and two sisters, Anne and Marilyn. They come from the south Auckland town of Onewhero, 20 km from Pukekohe, and not far from Glenbrook where Kevin is now a market gardener. Their father, Jim, was a builder, and as the boys grew up Jimmy showed a liking for pulling things apart and putting them back together. It was a natural progression when Jimmy took up an apprenticeship to become a motor mechanic. Eventually, Kevin and Ross followed him into the trade — one that would eventually provide them with a passport to overseas travel, and the chance to be involved in top-flight motor racing.

It was hardly surprising that the Stone brothers were keen on motor racing with the Pukekohe track nearby. With help from Kevin, Ross and Jimmy built and raced a Formula Ford. Jimmy later raced a twin-cam Ford Escort, and he and Ross built a Formula Pacific car they made from 'bits and pieces' they bought. Jimmy named it a 'Cuda'. He had spent a lot of time in the United States, and he reckoned it sounded American. The Ford-powered Cuda JR3 offered an early indication of the brothers' engineering prowess when Ross drove it to the national Gold Star single-seater championship in the summer of 1977–78 against accomplished opposition, including Kenny Smith, who is still racing well into his 60s, Robbie Francevic, Dave McMillan and Steve Millen.

However, the brothers were more attracted to the less glamorous and more time-consuming challenges of preparing cars for others to race, and they went offshore to sharpen their skills, broaden their experience, and to be paid for doing something that fascinated them. Jimmy, and later Kevin, worked for Bruce McLaren's team in England; Jimmy on the CanAm cars and Kevin the Formula One. Jimmy

was at the Goodwood track in Sussex the day in June 1970 when McLaren — widely regarded as New Zealand's greatest motor racing car builder and engineer — died when testing a new CanAm sports car, nicknamed the 'Batmobile'. McLaren, only 32 at the time of his death, forged a reputation as an outstanding driver, winning four Formula One grand prix races, and finishing second, and twice third, in the drivers' world championship. He was also a gifted engineer and enjoyed the satisfaction of successfully racing Formula One and sports cars of his own design. It is a tribute to McLaren's brilliance that more than 35 years later a car of the same name is still a leader in Formula One. Only Ferrari have been there longer.

Jimmy was with the CanAm team in the United States when their sports cars were in a class of their own, at one stage winning 36 of 42 races. Such experience was priceless for Jimmy, helping to fuel his intention to one day be in a position to have a team of his own.

When Ross came back from overseas he started a workshop business with Kevin. But the interest

Fairfax Sunday Newspapers: *Auckland Star* Collection

Denny Hulme (left) and co-driver Ray Smith won the Benson and Hedges saloon car race at Pukekohe in 1983. Ross Stone became their mechanic when they raced a Holden Commodore in Australia two years later.

in racing was still there, and at one stage Ross and Jimmy built a V8 Vauxhall Victor sports sedan for Jack Nazer, which won national titles. Ross gained an appreciation of Bathurst's magic in 1974 — the year fellow Kiwi Jim Richards made a fine impression on debut by taking out third spot with Rod Coppins in a Holden Torana — when he was 'shouted' a trip to the race. He stayed in a church hostel on Conrod Straight, which was in stark contrast to his weekend spent sampling some of Australia's unique hospitality on the 'hill'.

The workshop business went well, but Ross eventually became disenchanted with simply repairing cars for the general public. He missed being involved in regular racing and started looking around for other opportunities. Finally he hooked up with fellow New Zealander Ray Smith in Australia in 1985. Smith was running a Holden Commodore VK, sponsored by his company, Auckland Coin and Bullion Exchange. He had New Zealand's only Formula One world champion, Denny Hulme, as his senior driver in the Australian endurance touring

car races, and the Nissan-Mobil series back home. Smith, whose business dealings would later result in a criminal conviction and jail sentence, sold his Commodore to another New Zealander, recently retired motorcycle ace, Graeme Crosby, and, in the words of Ross Stone, 'Graeme inherited me'.

Crosby contested the full Australian touring car championship as a privateer in 1986, the year it was won by Aucklander Robbie Francevic. Ross Stone, who drove the car transporter and was one of two mechanics, moved his family to rented accommodation in Melbourne, the first step toward what was to become a permanent shift two years later. In those days Ross and wife Dianne had two pre-school children, Nick (four) and Anna (three months). Their youngest child, Emily, was born in 1988. With Crosby's talent, evidenced by his second placing in the world 500 cc motorcycle championship in 1982, and his zest for life, there were of plenty of laughs.

Crosby made a significant impact, finishing seventh in the championship after best placings of second,

Ross Stone with his pride and joy, a Ford Cobra. He'd always wanted to own one, or a Ford Mustang, but after a year he sold the Cobra, not having the time to really enjoy it.

Australian motor racing great Frank Gardner. Jimmy Stone worked for Gardner and it was also his BMW team that Denny Hulme was racing for in 1992, when he died at Bathurst.

behind Francevic, in round four in Adelaide, a couple of fourths, a sixth and a seventh. On occasions Crosby was faster than Peter Brock's 'official' Commodore, and his spectacular driving style won him many fans. The *Australian Motor Racing Yearbook* of 1986–87 described Crosby as 'perhaps the biggest surprise of the season' and 'probably the most popular driver in the championship'. When Channel Seven installed a camera in his car he became a television celebrity. 'He was one of the most natural guys I've come across,' Ross recalled. 'He could have been anything [in motor racing] if you got him to listen. He laid down a good foundation for the future, but he didn't carry on.' Crosby 'had made a lot of money in motorcycling' Ross said. It enabled him to finance the 1986 venture, which was costly. Crosby was a 'larger than life character', who liked to be the clown, Ross said. 'That year I had some of the funniest times in my life.'

When it didn't last, Ross transferred his attention to two other Kiwis in the Australian championship,

Kent Baigent and Graeme Bowkett, who raced Skylines for Team Nissan New Zealand. In a limited season the pair did well in finishing 11th and 13th respectively in the championship.

In 1988 Ross and Dianne Stone made the decision to move to Australia permanently. They sold their house in New Zealand, and Ross admitted there was an element of risk in selling everything and taking the plunge. Jimmy, his wife Beverley, and their family, went too, and the brothers started their long association with Ford, a move that became one of the most successful in Australian motor sport. The Stones were in Sydney in 1988 running Ford Sierra turbos for Australian Andrew Miedecke and New Zealander Andrew Bagnall, the latter to become a big player in the leisure business in New Zealand as the managing director of Gullivers Travel. That arrangement lasted two years, the second based on the Gold Coast, where the Stones have lived ever since. Though there were some good results, Miedecke sold out, and Ross went to work for privateer Kevin Waldock, a steady racer who had made his money in explosives for the mining business. Waldock was fifth in a Sierra in the Bathurst 1000 km in 1991.

Ross received his best opportunity yet in Australia when he was invited to be Dick Johnson's team manager for 1992. This included looking after the Ford Sierras of Johnson and John Bowe, and Ross was elated. They were two of the biggest names in the business. Johnson had already won the Australian touring car title a record-equalling five times, and he and Bowe were victorious at Bathurst in 1989. It was the strongest indication yet that the Stones were rated among the better engineers and race team bosses in the championship.

Jimmy was at Frank Gardner's factory-backed Benson and Hedges BMW team in the early 1990s before he too had the call to work for Dick Johnson midway through 1992, an arrangement that worked particularly well till the end of 1995 when the Stones were ready to start their partnership with 1980 Formula One world champion, Alan Jones. The Stones will always remember the Sunday of Bathurst in 1992 with mixed emotions. Johnson and Bowe might well have won the 1000 km event. Instead they had to be satisfied with second, after the race was stopped following a cloudburst that turned the track into a skating rink and caused multiple crashes.

The safety car had been used earlier in the day, allowing the cars to circulate, maintaining their race positions, under a cautionary yellow flag until the track had been cleared of crashed cars and normal racing resumed. But the safety car wasn't used when the track was flooded, and the carnage occurred, seemingly because the conditions were still considered too dangerous. The race winners were Jim Richards and his younger co-driver Mark Skaife, even though Richards had been one of the casualties in the rain, unlike Johnson and Bowe, whose Sierra was still running.

Race officials based the final results on the positions held before the carnage occurred, and at

that time Richards led in a Nissan Skyline. Ross Stone was disappointed.

'Dick [Johnson] was superb that day,' he said. 'It was one of his best drives. He and John [Bowe] drove the wheels off the car. They should have won. As the rules were written, the officials had no choice but to declare Jim and Mark the winners. Typically at Bathurst, not long after the race was called off the weather changed for the better.'

It was also the day when New Zealand motor racing great Denny Hulme died of a heart attack at the wheel of a BMW being run by a former Australian racing great Frank Gardner. Hulme was only 56. The Stones were shattered by the tragedy, having enjoyed strong working relationships with Hulme, who was making his mark in Formula One when the brothers were starting out. 'We knew there

It was also the day when New Zealand motor racing great Denny Hulme died of a heart attack at the wheel of a BMW . . .

Two of New Zealand's best all-time racers, Jim Richards (left) and Denny Hulme, at a driver briefing before a Nissan-Mobil race at Pukekohe. They became great friends, and Richards experienced wildly differing emotions at Bathurst in 1992 when Hulme died at the wheel, the same day he won his fifth 1000 km event there.

was something wrong when we heard Denny had crashed on Mountain Straight,' Ross said. 'Jimmy knew straight away what had happened. He was upset.' Ross also perfectly understood when on the podium Jim Richards uttered his infamous words, 'you're a pack of arseholes', to a crowd that booed when he and Skaife were declared the winners, a comment that was completely out of character. 'Jim Richards and Denny were great mates,' Ross said. 'I can understand 100 per cent where he was coming from. It was an emotional time for everyone.'

Jimmy Stone had been hired by Dick Johnson with an eye toward the new V8 era due to start in 1993. With Ford not then having its own operation, Jimmy had the honour of building its first car to the new specifications, and John Bowe drove the car in its debut in the Wellington street race of late 1992. It wasn't an auspicious start: the car failed to finish after an encounter with a concrete wall, and then an

has since made way for houses). Bowe's Shell Falcon won, but it was to be their only victory in 1993. In that first season Glenn Seton's Ford Falcon EB was superior to everyone in winning the touring car title and Bowe could only place third, with Johnson fifth. The following year Mark Skaife's Holden Commodore VP cleaned up the championship, though the Johnson-Bowe partnership reasserted itself in a Falcon EB when they secured the Sandown 500 km and Bathurst 1000 km endurance double. It was the second time the pair had won at Bathurst.

Bowe was the class act of 1995, becoming the driving champion in a Falcon EF after a dominant display in the final round at Oran Park in Sydney. He and Johnson won at Sandown once again, and were on course for a third win together at Bathurst when an incident with Seton's Ford ended their hopes.

The Stones left Dick Johnson Racing after Bathurst that year, and it is fair to say the team has not been quite

There were no half measures. The Stones started with a bare shed, and turned it into a superb engineering workshop.

engine problem prevented it appearing in the other Nissan-Mobil round at Pukekohe.

By now the Stones were key players for Johnson. Ross was team manager and Jimmy was the engineer, an arrangement that suited them so well it has remained in place ever since, whether it be their team or another. Ross puts it this way: 'Jimmy's not interested in anything other than the cars and their engineering. He's unique and so mechanically practical. He moves when he's worked it out. He makes it dead simple. You'd think it would never work.'

Ross did not know what to think when the new formula approached. 'I had no idea how big it was going to be till we brought out the new car at the Lakeside track in Queensland, the one John Bowe would drive in Wellington,' he said. 'I didn't realise how much passion people had for the V8s till then. The car's appearance had been advertised on the radio, and there were people everywhere.'

They were well prepared for the first V8 championship race, at Sydney's Amaroo Park (which

the same since. But having savoured the satisfaction of producing a winning car at Bathurst and the season-long consistency needed to win a championship, the brothers wanted to try life on their own.

They were going to start a small engineering business till a call from Alan Jones changed everything. He had a sponsor, tobacco giant Philip Morris, and wanted to run two cars, one for himself, and the other for promising youngster Paul Romano. The Stones were offered the chance to be equal partners in the new team, later named Pack Leader Racing.

There was no time to waste. Setting up a team from scratch was a huge task, and the Stones worked endless hours from early October 1995 to have two immaculate cars ready for the first championship round at Sydney's Eastern Creek the following February. There were no half measures. The Stones started with a bare shed, and turned it into a superb engineering workshop. They built their own engines. They worked seven days a week, and their staff of 14 only had Sundays off. 'There was a horrendous amount of work to be done. For six weeks in a row Jimmy and I never got home till midnight, and we were back at the workshop at seven o'clock the next morning,' Ross said.

That was typical of the commitment required for teams to simply be competitive. In race teams, the engineers, mechanics and general pit crew are the unsung heroes, their jobs never done. The drivers are able to bask in any glory. And while the pressure of competing is always intense for them, they are show ponies compared to those in the garage, who are forever racing against time to have the cars ready for each round. Sometimes the turnaround time between rounds is ridiculously short, and it is even worse for teams whose cars have suffered severe damage. When that happens it invariably means many days that turn into long nights, working against the clock to have the repairs finished in time.

The first year started slowly but Jones finished second at a couple of rounds to end the championship in eighth place. He was also third in the non-championship round at Surfers Paradise. At Bathurst, Jones passed Craig

Lowndes's Holden on lap 16 to take the lead, giving the new team its best exposure yet, only for disaster to strike 10 laps later, going up Mountain Straight, when the Falcon burst into flames.

Jones produced some solid results in 1997 but his best was saved for the last round at Oran Park in August when he was third overall after a couple of seconds. It turned out to be his last race. Shortly after, the Stones bought out Jones's share in the team. They mortgaged their Gold Coast homes to finance the new venture, now called Stone Brothers Racing.

The Stones kicked off in 1998 with one car. It was driven by newcomer Jason Bright, who had captured Ross's attention with his performances in Formula Holden single-seaters. But it wasn't a signing that pleased the previous team's principal sponsor. At a team sponsor's meeting it was adamant that the Stones get an established driver, rather than a little-known rookie, or it would be out. Things reached a stalemate when Ross Stone refused to budge. Ross left the meeting and was followed out by Glenn Duncan, who had been newly appointed

Craig Baird's Ford Falcon suffered considerable damage from flying stones in his one season driving for the Stone brothers in 2000.

Gietty Images

Craig Baird acknowledges the cheers after one of his few crowning moments in Supercars. It came after winning race two and finishing third overall first time out for the Stones in 2000 at Phillip Island.

as the general manager of Pirtek Fluid Systems. At that time Pirtek was a subsidiary sponsor, but out on the street Duncan had a quick conversation with Ross and within 24 hours the company had signed a contract to be the naming rights sponsor at SBR. 'It was one of Glenn's first decisions in his new job, and he did not have universal support for it,' Ross said. 'It turned out to be great for both of us, starting a happy association that lasted eight years. The Pirtek people became part of our racing family.'

It was a topsy-turvy first year for Bright. He demonstrated his raw potential, and learned a few lessons the hard way. In the first round at Sandown he set a lap record, but ruined it all when he finished with a badly damaged car. By round seven, at Melbourne's Calder Park, Bright showed he was becoming more comfortable in the Falcon EL when he achieved his first podium finish. He then claimed the team's first pole position at the Hidden Valley circuit in Darwin. The season was made memorable when Bright and co-driver Steven Richards scored a stunning win in the 1000 km race at Bathurst, after starting from 15th place on the grid. And this after a nearly disastrous accident in qualifying on the Friday morning. Bright crashed on top of Mount Panorama, causing extensive damage to the car's right-hand side, and it was a battle to have the car fixed in time for a late appearance in the official qualifying rounds that weekend. The Holden Racing Team's Craig Lowndes and Mark Skaife were overwhelming favourites, Lowndes having collected a second touring car title in 1998, and Skaife arguably the best driver in the field. Their car was leading till a puncture on lap 114, which left the car bogged in sand at The Chase, costing the Holden pair two laps and any chance of victory.

The result enhanced the Stones's reputation for engineering excellence and team efficiency. It was the second time they had provided the expertise for a Ford to win at Bathurst in the new V8 era (the other being with Dick Johnson in 1994), and it was an early vindication of the Stones's decision to form their own team. Victory was achieved by a superior fuel strategy and the driving skills of the emerging pair of Bright and Richards. In those days Richards was racing two-litre super tourers in England, and Ross approached Richards' father, Jim Richards, about Jim partnering Bright. Jim suggested Ross contact Steven, and the decision to hire him worked perfectly. Bright ended an encouraging ninth in the championship in the last season before Bathurst was included as a round in the competition.

In 1999 Bright benefited from a new AU Falcon, giving the team its first championship round victory in No. 5 at Hidden Valley. He was on the podium at three other rounds, and started from pole position at three others. Despite failing to finish at the big-scoring last two rounds, Sandown and Bathurst, he still finished eighth in the chase for the touring car title. That year SBR also prepared a car for Mark Larkham, who finished 21st in the championship, in a separate entry run under Mitre 10 sponsorship.

With Bright leaving to try his hand at Indy Lights single-seaters in the United States, the Stones gave New Zealander Craig Baird an opportunity in 2000, though he was still inexperienced in Supercars and

was unfamiliar with most of the circuits. He became a team-mate of more-accomplished Australian Tony Longhurst in the team's first year of running two cars.

Baird created an immediate impact in the opening round at Phillip Island when he won the second heat, SBR's first sprint race victory, and came third overall. It proved to be a one-off performance. He struggled to come to grips with the car and the succession of new tracks, though finishing seventh overall at Hidden Valley and Bathurst, the latter alongside Simon Wills, and ninth at Winton, helped lift Baird to 15th in the championship. Longhurst and new recruit Dave Besnard came within a few laps of winning there, but their race was ended by Longhurst's brush with a back marker. Longhurst was 10th for the year, but Baird's disappointment at his performance was shared by the Stones, who cut him halfway through a two-year deal. 'We never got the best out of Craig that year, which was probably more our fault than anything,' Ross said. 'He was much, much better than the results showed.'

... the Stones gave New Zealander Craig Baird an opportunity in 2000, though he was still inexperienced in Supercars ...

Australian Tony Longhurst walks away dejectedly after a brush with a back marker ruined the leader and the Stones's bright prospects of victory at Bathurst in 2000.

Marcos Ambrose's arrival in 2001 to join Besnard provided the spark that would propel the Stones from being among the better teams into becoming the most professional and successful in the championship. Ross was so sure about the ambitious Ambrose that he signed him before he had even driven a Supercar. He knew all about Ambrose's single-seater exploits in Europe, and liked what he saw when Ambrose contested the Honda Young Guns Challenge at the Gold Coast V8 round in late 2000. Ambrose was just back from Europe, and was keen to make an impact against a number of top young drivers all racing in identical cars, including soon-to-be SBR team-mate Besnard, and three other Supercar regulars in recent years, Steven Johnson, Paul Weel, and New Zealander Simon Wills.

While some of the others regarded the Challenge races as a bit of fun, Ambrose saw it quite differently. He looked at it as an ideal opportunity to impress a Supercar team, and approached it in a professional

'No. 1' on his car's front doors for 2006.

Going to Bathurst for round 10 of 13 in 2005, Ambrose was on course to emulate Holden's Mark Skaife by winning the title three years in succession till he and New Zealand's No. 1 V8 driver Greg Murphy collided on the entry to The Cutting near the end of the race. A 'dnf' (did not finish) cost Ambrose his series lead. He fell two points behind new leader Ingall, and he was never able to gather sufficient momentum in the last three rounds to finish any higher than third. The intensely competitive Murphy and Ambrose have had a testy relationship with neither prepared to concede any ground to the other. The bad blood spilled over at Bathurst when they leapt out of their cars at the chaotic crash scene — which blocked the track and claimed several other cars — and confronted each other. There was a heated exchange of words, and they looked one step away from coming to blows.

The bad blood spilled over at Bathurst when they leapt out of their cars at the chaotic crash scene . . .

manner. He duly won the second race to claim overall victory in the Challenge. Ambrose's attitude and performance were not lost on Ross. He put Ambrose in a special category when he contracted him, but conceded that it was hard to see anyone else ever being signed without having had a few laps behind the wheel of a Supercar.

Ambrose proved to be an inspired choice. SBR had the car, the technical know-how, and a finely-tuned support crew, and Ambrose had the driving skill, and soon the confidence and poise, to make the most of the superb package he was presented with. Together they created a tsunami and swept all before them in 2003 and 2004. Ambrose and Besnard's replacement from 2003, Russell Ingall, were first and second in the championship in 2004, the first time that two drivers from the same team had ever taken out the two top places. The wave was still powerful enough in 2005 for Ingall to finally secure an elusive championship, after four times having to accept being runner-up, and earn the much-prized

However, the Confederation of Australian Motor-sport's investigation determined that neither driver was at fault, and no further action was taken.

The incident left Ambrose without a win in five attempts at Bathurst, the one glaring omission on his otherwise glittering Supercar CV. His chances of victory had earlier been reduced when he twice had to return to the pits to complete a drive-through penalty after first his co-driver Warren Luff and then he himself were found not to be wearing the obligatory balaclava under their racing helmets.

Ross Stone declined to comment on the Ambrose-Murphy debacle apart from saying he had spoken to Murphy about it, and they remained friends. But he offered a little more on the balaclava issue, which created quite a stir in pit lane, and even led to a suggestion that SBR had been victimised. Ross understood from talking to Ambrose that there was a gentlemen's agreement they not wear them as they were too hot, and were not considered essential to a driver's safety. A 'blind eye' had been turned to drivers not wearing them in the heat at the Clipsal 500 km at Adelaide earlier in the year, Ross said. However, he said that the marshal scrutinising the SBR pit stops was 'only doing his job' when he reported that the drivers were not wearing balaclavas.

New Zealand driver Craig Baird had a different view. He felt sorry for the Stones, his former employers, believing they were set-up. He was among a number of drivers not wearing balaclavas at Bathurst, he said, and if the Stones were being penalised so should all the others who transgressed. Baird said he did not wear the required full-length underwear under his layered racing suit either, as he found it too hot in the often stifling temperatures in the cars, and believed it was unnecessary. One of a driver's biggest fears was fire, he said, and he was well protected without either the balaclava or the underwear.

Fellow New Zealand drivers Jason Richards and Greg Murphy also commented. Richards said he did not wear the long johns underwear until Bathurst, because it was too hot. Murphy said that Ambrose and Luff being penalised for not wearing balaclavas had resulted in a tightening of procedures to ensure that the drivers observed the rules at all times.

Even with the drive-through penalties, Ross Stone said Ambrose, on fresh tyres, was still in a position to win Bathurst, till that emotion-charged tangle with Murphy on lap 145 of 161. 'It was good that Russell [Ingall] gained a good points haul for finishing fifth, but in Marcos's case things weren't working for us.'

There are some likenesses between Ambrose and his Australian replacement for 2006, the 25-year-old James Courtney. Courtney headed off a number of potential contenders in what became a protracted selection process. There was much conjecture in the motoring press with the SBR seat among the most sought after in Supercars, and emerging talent Jason Richards was mentioned as a possible candidate. Like Ambrose, Courtney had spent a lot of time racing single-seaters overseas — in Courtney's case as a test driver for the Jaguar Formula One team — and he was signed with little Supercar experience. The two-time world karting champion did have more touring car experience than Ambrose though, having driven a Toyota Supra with success in the Japanese GT championship. But he had never raced on any Australian tracks other than Sandown and Bathurst. Courtney's signing tasted even sweeter for the Stones as he was lured away from Holden, having appeared for HRT at Sandown and Bathurst in 2005. In fact it was at Bathurst that his early lap times caught the Stones's attention. 'Jimmy and I turned to each other

Marcos Ambrose's battered Ford is carted away on the back of a truck after his car and that of Greg Murphy crashed into each other at Bathurst in 2005, creating a heated standoff that was shown live on television across the world.

Getty Images

Marcos Ambrose's background in the cut-throat single-seater scene in England and France was ideal preparation for Supercar racing. He won the Eurocup Formula Ford championship in 1999 before a stumbling Formula Three campaign in 2000 in France convinced him that, despite his undoubted ability, there were too many obstacles in his way for Formula One to ever become a reality.

He returned to Australia without a job or a drive, and was essentially broke. He set his sights on a seat in V8 Supercars, and having achieved that he was hell-bent on proving that he deserved the opportunity. He did not waste any time, snatching pole position from a disbelieving defending series champion Mark Skaife in his first racing weekend at the non-championship round attached to the Australian Grand Prix weekend in Melbourne. Ambrose was on the way when he secured his first round victory in round four at Darwin's Hidden Valley, and three days later Ford signed him to a five-year deal. Nicknamed 'The Devil Racer', after his native Tasmania's ferocious little marsupial, the Tasmanian Devil, he finished 2001 eighth in the championship, and was named rookie of the year. Ambrose did even better in 2002, climbing to third in the series, and being the leading Ford driver.

SBR had two of the most abrasive competitors and complete drivers for 2003 when the wily Russell Ingall, commonly known as 'The Enforcer', ended seven years of racing Holdens for Larry Perkins and replaced Besnard in the SBR team. The team was now one of the few with two genuine title contenders and they were driving cars superior to any other. SBR had the total package, as was made clear when Ambrose and Ingall won an incredible eight of 13 rounds between them, with Ambrose claiming four in succession.

Ambrose's 2003 victory gave the long-suffering Ford fans and the manufacturer something to savour after the Holden Racing Team's Craig Lowndes and Mark Skaife had outpaced all comers, at times with almost ridiculous ease, in the previous five seasons.

and without saying a word we knew that James had to be a priority signing for us,' Ross said.

Craig Baird, is a huge admirer of the thoroughly grounded Stones. He says Ford should be rewarding them for their success. 'Ford would be pretty sick in this competition with-out the Stones,' he said. 'It took the Stones to stop the Holden Racing Team winning everything. Ford piggybacked on a couple of blokes from Pukekohe.' He describes Ross as 'a very average bloke you'd run in to on the street'. 'He's got no ego, he doesn't care what other people think of him,' Baird says. 'He sticks to his own bundle of knitting [he sticks to what he knows]. He's a general all-round good bloke.'

Baird likened Jimmy to 'a wind-up toy', so busy was he building anything and everything in the garage. 'Jimmy's a hard worker, the ultimate head-down arse-up type. He's an innovator. He's not afraid to try things. The Stones design and develop things themselves within the rules, and do it better than anyone else.' He said Ross and Jimmy's strength is that they have a partnership that works, they know each other's strengths. 'Ross runs the business, Jimmy runs the cars,' Baird said. 'They know each other better than they know themselves. All they want is to have a good race team.' They have enjoyed huge success because they have had everything working at 100 per cent, Baird said. 'For instance you can have the best engines in pit lane, but it's no use if all the other things aren't up to scratch.'

As Ross Stone puts it, success has come because 'we have fewer weaknesses than anyone else'. 'It gets harder and harder,' he said. 'Everyone wants to beat us. We have become a target. We keep refining and reinventing what we do. If we're doing the same thing as we did last year we're not going forward. Essentially though we're not doing anything different to the other teams. Our methods are based on good, sound preparation and engineering, and hard work.'

Those methods have created a remarkably stable and loyal workforce. At the end of 2004 only one person left, and that was to go to Europe. Twelve months later, again just one person was lost. Marcos Ambrose emphasised that when he said the crew on his car had been basically the same for five years. This is quite different from a number of other teams, where as many as 10 to 15 people will depart annually. Among the more able of SBR's staff have been crew chief and pit crew manager Les Laidlaw, former team manager at Dick Johnson Racing, and electronics and computing expert Ken Douglas.

Ross says life has become a little easier. It can take as many as 1700 hours to simply build a car's chassis, and that's before it's painted and assembled. When the eagerly awaited Falcon BA replaced the often uncompetitive AU in 2003, Jimmy and Ross took just two days off between January 1 and June 30. Since then increased staff numbers have reduced the burden, but it has meant other people doing jobs the Stones did previously, and perhaps with not quite the same quest for perfection. It has been speculated that running costs for the SBR team were around $A5 million in 2005, which indicates just how high the stakes have become. Even that might be a conservative figure.

But despite the numbers in the SBR team, it has remained very much a family concern. Ross's wife Dianne runs the merchandise department; their daughter Emily has worked part-time in that area; son Nick does the team's IT; and his other daughter, Anna, is in charge of the team's travel and administration. Jimmy's son Matthew works in the engine room, and Kevin's son Jody, named after a past Formula One world champion Jody Scheckter, is a mechanic on Russell Ingall's car.

The Stones had to broaden their skills to keep up with the various developments that have been made in Supercars over the years. There is much more now to staying on top of things than simply hiring the right drivers, building the best cars, and having a huge appetite for work. It has been a large adjustment for a couple of modest, increasingly grey-haired mechanics, who are generally more at home on the workshop floor than mixing it with corporate sponsors; and, in Ross's case, developing business opportunities and being in constant negotiations. Supercars is now more than just motor racing.

As Ross concedes, it is increasingly just as much about entertainment as sport. A good example of

Dirk Klynsmith/Graphics Dak Photography

Russell Ingall, the 2005 Australian touring car champion, is flanked by Ross (left) and Jimmy Stone after he signed to drive for them from 2003.

this is the revival in 2006 of the reverse grid in the second heat at all rounds with three races. This is not a decision Ross supports, as it gives the weaker teams a leg up they have not earned, and threatens to penalise the leading teams and drivers by putting unnecessary extra pressure on them.

The Stones's philosophy about what keeps them going is thoroughly down-to-earth. As Ross says: 'It's the next race'. It reflects a philosophy that belies the amount of sophistication and planning required for them to stay ahead of the pack. Jimmy was once quoted as saying: 'I enjoy the competitive part of racing. I think if I stopped doing it I would just keel over and die. I just love the next challenge. It's always around the corner.' Ross said new driver James Courtney had given the Stones a new lease of life. 'It might take James a couple of years to get fully up to speed in this formula,' he said. 'We were not looking for someone as good as Marcos Ambrose. We were looking for someone better.' Leading New Zealand driver Greg Murphy also expects big things from Courtney. 'He'll do a good job. He's very talented,' Murphy said. 'There'll be no let-up from the car that Marcos [Ambrose] would have driven. He'll be just as tough.'

Ross gained a lot of satisfaction from Ingall's championship victory, believing that after Ambrose's successive title wins it was important for the team to produce another champion, rather than having the departing Ambrose securing the hat-trick that looked so likely most of the year. 'It would have looked "all Marcos" otherwise,' Ross said. 'We'll see the best of Russell Ingall in the next two years. Now that he's won the championship he can be his usual aggressive self without the pressure of before. With Russell in a position to win the title he raced to a more conservative plan in the later rounds than would normally have been the case.'

Though Ambrose was still contracted to SBR for 2006, and the Stones stood to lose plenty with their most successful driver going to the United States, they did not stand in his way, knowing Ford was very much behind Ambrose's desire to take his career to another level. Ross described Ambrose as 'single-minded with the talent to match. He was special, of that there is no doubt. The first time he drove for us I knew it was the right decision to sign him,' Ross said. 'The timing was perfect for him, and perfect for us. He was less enthusiastic about the public relations side of the business. He could be very difficult at times.'

on the raceway running out, 2005 would be the Stones's last opportunity to win at Pukekohe. And with continuing problems there, it seemed that the contract was unlikely to be renewed. However, with no other suitable New Zealand circuit available, Pukekohe was granted rounds for two more years — hopefully enough time for another New Zealand venue to be found. Not surprisingly the Stones were delighted, the decision allowing them to have their dream rekindled. 'There are some racetracks you go to that have no atmosphere at all, but that's not Pukekohe,' Ross said. 'The place always has a great buzz, and the fans are so knowledgeable.'

When the skills that Jimmy and Ross bring to motor racing are discussed it inevitably invites comparisons with fellow New Zealanders. One, Bruce McLaren, stands out above all others. Back in the late 1960s and into 1970, the year of his death, he was doing extraordinary things that put him at the forefront of world automotive

'There are some race tracks you go to that have no atmosphere at all, but that's not Pukekohe,' Ross said.

To illustrate just how special Ambrose's feats are to the Stones they are keeping the Falcon he has driven for the last three years. It's the first time they have held on to a car. Previously when it's been time for them to retire a car, it has been sold off as just another business transaction. 'We need to have something to show for what's happened in the last three years, and we couldn't do any better than keep the car that's won two championships,' Ross said.

Though Ross is softly spoken, approachable and seemingly mild-mannered one soon senses a steely resolve within, an attitude the brothers have needed in their quest for success. The Stones have achieved much, but still have some unfinished business. One ambition that's still to be realised is a Supercar round win on their 'home' track of Pukekohe. Over the five years that Supercars have raced there, Greg Murphy has enjoyed an incredible four round victories, and Jason Bright stopped Murphy's run with a win in 2004. The word was that, with the five-year contract

engineering. Dick Bennetts is another who has made special contributions to motor racing. He has based himself in England for many years, and his West Surrey Racing team has continued to be at the cutting edge of single-seater racing below Formula One, including running the New Zealand team in the new A1 championship.

The Stones have established similar credentials in Supercars, becoming progressively better over a long period, and steadily moving up the grid as they have had the drivers to capitalise on their engineering and team management talents. The test for them is whether they can continue to set the pace without their star driver, Marcos Ambrose. To maintain such high standards is asking a lot. However, given the Stones's constant striving for excellence there is unlikely to be any lessening of intensity on their part.

Russell Ingall, on the limit at practice at Surfers Paradise in 2005, before winning the Australian touring car title for the first time.

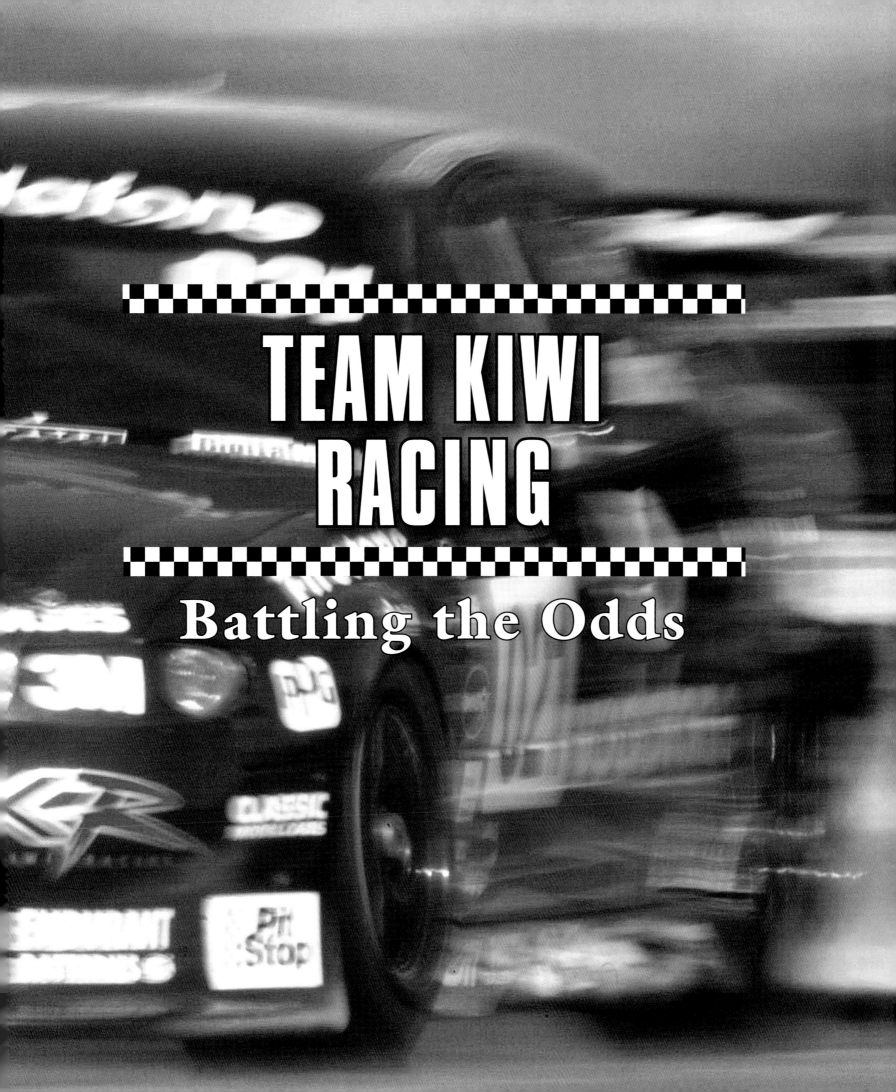

TEAM KIWI RACING

Battling the Odds

Team Kiwi Racing (TKR) owner David John has a reputation for never taking 'no' for an answer. It is a trait that has served him remarkably well. TKR would almost certainly have gone under without it, such was the battle to keep going before 2005. But the burly Australian's bulldog attitude ensured that for the first time that season, the team started with a package good enough to consistently run in the top 10. It resulted in the team's best year in V8 Supercars since first testing the water in the series' blue-ribbon event, the Bathurst 1000 km at Mount Panorama, in 2000.

For the first time TKR had a new car, a Holden Commodore VZ, prepared by the team's new partner Paul Morris Motorsports, and a new driver in expatriate Kiwi Paul Radisich. After being dropped by Triple Eight Race Engineering in favour of the much higher-profile Craig Lowndes, Radisich relished the package John was able to put together. There were any number of people telling Radisich he was mad to join the perennial strugglers. He had similar thoughts initially, but after TKR met his demands he

was happy with the partnership with Morris, and the results started to come almost immediately.

By season's end Radisich had finished 14th in the Australian touring car championship, five places higher than he had been at Triple Eight's Betta Electrical Ford team the year before, and 13 spots better than TKR managed in 2004. It provided John with further impetus to keep pushing towards his dream of having a New Zealand driver, from a New Zealand-owned and based team, winning the title.

TKR finally achieved its first podium finish in 2005. It was in round five, in the Supercars' debut race in Shanghai, when Radisich was third overall after placings of sixth, fifth and third in the three heats. It was a special moment for John, who was present at the race, and one that brought the team instant credibility and welcome congratulations from their competitors. 'Seven or eight drivers came up to offer their congratulations,' John said. 'It was a turning point for us.'

The knockers, and there have been a number of them, will still say John is a dreamer, that any

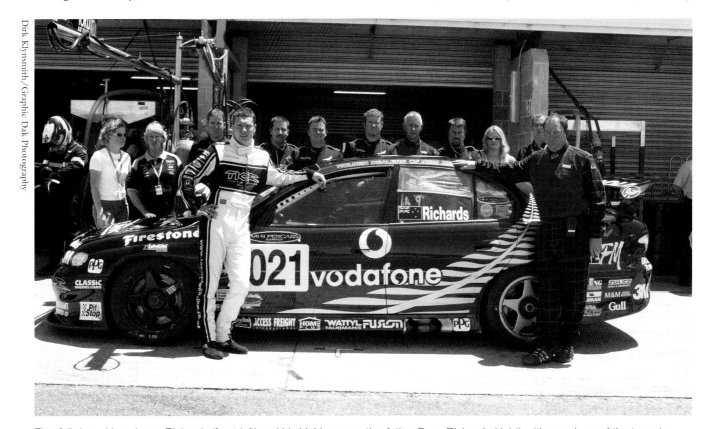

First full-time driver Jason Richards (front left) and his highly supportive father Dave Richards (right) with members of the team in the early days.

notion of TKR having the champion driver is preposterous when they are pitted against teams such as Stone Brothers Racing, the Holden Racing Team, and the Betta Electrical team of 2005. Yet John is essentially a realist; an unpretentious man and a problem-solver. Against the odds he put a New Zealand-based team on the Supercars grid, and after surviving for four years he was able to bask in a little well-deserved glory in 2005.

What made the 36-year-old John more than a little different though is that he is an Australian. After leaving his Adelaide home at the age of 16 and driving across the massive, desert-like Nullarbor Plain with a couple of mates, John made a swift impact in the Australian automotive industry; first as a cadet salesman for Holden in Perth, and next when he suggested to his car dealership-owning father, Dale John, that they sell the Hyundai cars that were then being introduced to Australia. On the back of exceptional performances in his early

raised Steven Richards, for the Australian Kmart Racing Team — and it got him thinking. The prospect of tackling the Aussies in one of their iconic V8s with a team out of Auckland excited him, and he immediately started investigating the prospect of entering a car in 2000.

He talked to Ross Stone from Stone Brothers Racing about buying a Ford from them, and actually did. He then approached Ford New Zealand about support, but they didn't take him seriously. John was fortunate to be able to sell the Ford within a week, and he started again. An option came up with one of the great V8 drivers, the feisty Larry Perkins, whose engineering business had a reputation for excellence. The deal was for Perkins to sell him a used car, and service the engine, but it also came with the warning 'don't even think you're going to pass me on a straight'. Otherwise TKR was on its own, with gear inferior to that being used by Perkins's Castrol team. However, there were still a few major hurdles

The prospect of tackling the Aussies in one of their iconic V8s with a team out of Auckland excited him . . .

twenties working for the Astre Group, his Malaysian boss, CK Lieu, transferred him to New Zealand in 1994 to launch the Jeep Cherokee. It was a very successful move, and even resulted in him being invited to the United States to work in the centre of its car industry, Detroit. Instead, John returned to Australia to successfully rescue the struggling Audi franchise for the Astre Group, before his methods clashed with those of the car's German manufacturer. He had worked extremely hard since leaving school at the age of 15 with no real qualifications, and he decided it was time to take a rest from the business.

He returned to Auckland in 1998, and entered the corporate hospitality business by buying two launches. Before long, with all the work he was getting as a consequence of New Zealand hosting the America's Cup, he bought a third launch. The next year he was watching the Bathurst 1000 km race on television — won by New Zealander Greg Murphy and the Auckland-born and Melbourne-

to negotiate before the indomitable John could have the opportunity of qualifying for the Bathurst grid — things that would easily have frightened off anyone with less determination.

The biggest obstacle initially was that V8 Supercars Australia was unconvinced of the validity of his proposal. 'I was 20-something with no background in motor racing, and someone they'd never heard of,' John said. Eventually AVESCO, as it was then, agreed to give him a wild card or one-off entry before suddenly changing its mind. 'Then they said to us "you can't just turn up any more",' John said. 'In a few months they came back and said as proof of your intentions you have to make a commitment to race in the full championship for the next two years as well. . . . But hang on they weren't finished. They made it bloody difficult for us. They kept on thinking we were full of shit. They demanded we had to buy a franchise to take part, something never required before.'

John was taken aback. There were no previous grounds for determining the value of a franchise. The playing field had become even more uneven. It was another test of how serious he was. He eventually agreed to the request, even though he felt it was unfair. John will not say how much the franchise cost other than to say it was in the 'lower triple figures', when at the time they had no value at all. 'We were being used as a guinea pig,' he said. 'In hindsight it helped the championship. Now a franchise is worth $A1.4 million, and we wouldn't be here without it. I guess what we were being asked to do was probably only a sign of good faith on our part. We came on the scene at a time when Supercars had stepped up to be just about the top touring car championship in the world.'

John says he could not afford to become involved today, and he believes no one else based in New Zealand would be able to do so either. Besides the Supercars company, John has constantly had to battle the exchange rate, and the problems that go with being in Auckland, and for most of the time being totally funded from New Zealand. He allows himself a satisfied smile now when he talks about the Gold Coast-based V8 company of which he has a financial share as a team owner. 'The company is very impressed with what we are doing,' John said. 'It acknowledges our tenacity as a one-car team. It's good for the formula. When we started, AVESCO didn't have much time for us. It probably thought we'd be gone in two years. It acknowledges that it is important to have a New Zealand-based team with a round at Pukekohe, and it rates Paul Radisich.'

Supercars chairman Tony Cochrane said he had wondered how long TKR would last, and he was delighted at what it had achieved. 'That first podium in Shanghai was a very proud moment for the New Zealand set-up,' he said. John had excelled in doing a deal with Morris and securing the services of Radisich, and his loyal sponsors continued to believe in the project despite the escalating costs, but he was still facing the usual financial hardships

Getty Images

Paul Radisich is all smiles but it took a series of protracted negotiations before he finally agreed to sign for Team Kiwi.

Dirk Klynsmith/Graphic Dak Photography

Paul Radisich racing in the shadow of the spectacular architecture at Shanghai in 2005, where he secured Team Kiwi Racing's first round podium finish in its fifth full-time year of trying.

Jason Richards was part of a group that tried to buy Team Kiwi before his ill-fated move to Team Dynamik for the second half of 2005. He continued to be handicapped by not having a naming rights sponsor. Holding him back was his insistence that the TKR car remain painted black with a silver fern emblem proudly emblazoned on both sides. He kept looking for more sponsorship, and it was suggested by his team manager, Martin Collins, that he meet Tauranga building tycoon Bernie Gillon. Collins, who had managed the team since day one, had naturally become frustrated at the team's often pauper-like existence, especially when he could see teams performing worse but attracting superior income through their willingness to accept whatever paint jobs the sponsors wanted.

There are limited opportunities for corporates to be involved in Supercars, with 19 teams starting in 2005, and a maximum of 34 cars. However, given the worldwide exposure of the series on television, potential sponsors in Australia were lining up. The live-wire Gillon appeared a promising and welcome proposition. He already had a strong reputation in motor racing, having twice been runner-up in the

New Zealand touring car championship in a BMW behind TKR's first driver, Jason Richards. He had raced in the single-seater Formula Vee championship, successfully raced a Mustang in TransAm events on both sides of the Tasman, and competed in the since-discontinued two-litre race at Bathurst.

He and John talked over the possibility of building a house and selling it for a profit without reaching any decision, but the more often they talked the better became their rapport, and it encouraged John to think that maybe the best solution was to sell Gillon a share of the company. As John said, it was like giving up a fraction of 'your baby'. He had already sold his launches and his house to keep the dream alive, and here he was on the brink of conceding some of his stake in TKR.

'Bernie and I were on the same wavelength,' John said. 'He had a passion for TKR, he loved what we'd been able to achieve, and he knew both sides of the business. I asked myself, "do I start to make it easier?", and when the answer was "yes" I knew I wanted Bernie aboard. I was open with him.

Getty Images

Paul Radisich opens up during qualifying at Pukekohe in 2005. His first weekend racing with Team Kiwi at the track was an encouraging one when he was sixth in all three heats for a fifth placing overall.

I told him I was struggling to maximise the team's full potential. I put a value on the business, and he said "yes" within 24 hours.'

Gillon, 47, initially bought 25 per cent of TKR, and John called it a 'very good decision'. Overnight some of his pressures evaporated. Instead of buying a second-hand car from Morris they were able to purchase a new one, and Gillon's involvement guaranteed the team's future. He was delighted. He recognised TKR's hand-to-mouth existence, and was happy to be a positive influence. 'David's done an exceptional job of running a multi-million-dollar team on a shoestring budget,' Gillon said. 'He reinvested the money I paid him straight away. The team has a good solid base now. It's sound for the first time. We don't have a bottomless pit in terms of money the way some teams do. Some of their spending excesses border on the obscene. Our financial position keeps us focused on what we have to spend money on. We have to make ours go a bit further.'

He also likes John's style. Gillon has heard John referred to as a 'brash Aussie' but he refuses to buy into it, preferring to call him 'single-minded'. 'We gel well. He tells you what he's thinking. I'm in it for the long haul.' As proof of that, last year Gillon increased his state in TKR to 49 per cent. He sold his company, Jennian Homes, in March 2005 after having built it up spectacularly. He had been appointed general manager of the building company in 1987, and he bought the Tauranga branch in 1991 to become the first franchise owner. He then bought the 'whole show' in 1997 when it had six franchises and an annual turnover of just under $NZ40 million. When he sold out he had 25 franchises and an annual turnover of $220 million. Gillon was a master of understatement when he said: 'It's set me up. I worked really hard. I don't have to work again.'

John started the ball rolling for 2005 when he made a second approach to Morris Motorsports

'David's done an exceptional job of running a multi-million-dollar team on a shoestring budget . . .'

in mid-2004. He had first spoken to them about sharing resources the previous year. With TKR and Morris both being one-car teams, and the way costs were spiralling, he saw advantages in them sharing the costs of transport, car and engine building, development, data, and catering facilities. But it didn't work out. Morris was not in a position to help. By 2004, however, there was more common ground. It was agreed they would both have new cars, and engine builder Alan Draper would be invited to come aboard. Draper made his name with Dick Johnson Racing and the Adelaide-based Team Dynamik — in John's words, giving the latter team's cars a 'shitload of firepower'.

Craig Baird, the TKR driver in 2003 and 2004, created a stir when he joined the better-resourced but non-performing Wright Patton Shakespeare (WPS) Racing for 2005. Suddenly TKR was without a driver, and there was an immediate scurrying on both sides of the Tasman to find a replacement. A couple of talented New Zealand-based drivers were possibilities, only to be rejected. Though John was hanging out for a Kiwi driver, there were none

in New Zealand of the standard required to progress the car up the grid.

Always the thinker, and not afraid to look outside the square, John wondered about Radisich. The previously England-based two-times World Cup touring car champion had arrived in Australia for his first full-time drive in V8s in 1999 with a glowing reputation. However, despite some stunning performances for Dick Johnson Racing, Radisich's involvement in V8s was largely one of underachievement. He was said to be unhappy in his second season at the Betta Electrical-sponsored Ford team, now owned by British company Triple Eight. 'Everyone said, "you're wasting your time with Paul", he's of a calibre way out of your league,' said John. 'My philosophy was it would do no harm approaching him. Paul could only say "no". It's been said I've not been one to take "no" for an answer. At the end of the day though it's not about having a silver tongue, it's a matter of arriving at a deal that suits both parties.'

John's first approach to Radisich was unpromising. It was at the 10th round of 13 in 2004, at Bathurst,

Getty Images

Craig Baird racing at Adelaide with the Hyundai Construction Equipment signwriting that upset Holden New Zealand.

where Radisich's best had been two second placings. His mechanical misfortunes in 2004 continued when a brake hub broke on lap 119 of 161. 'We met for 20 minutes, and Paul made it clear he wasn't interested. But he said if we wanted to pursue it we needed to put to paper the details of our plans for 2005,' John said. 'He said he was more than likely going back to England with his wife, Patricia, being English and their only child at the time around school age.'

John and Radisich continued to liaise. Radisich remained sceptical, saying that teams had given him similar assurances of grandiose plans before, only for them to turn to custard. Undaunted, John continued to strengthen his case. But Radisich remained unsure. At the time other teams were also seeking his services, as Triple Eight had declared that it had dropped Radisich and signed Australian golden boy Craig Lowndes. John finally flew to the Gold Coast

Craig Baird, like Radisich, having first established himself in single-seaters, replaced TKR's original pilot Jason Richards from the 2003 season after Richards went to Adelaide to join Team Dynamik, a move that was to go sour. Baird's single-seater accomplishments included winning the New Zealand Grand Prix three years running, before the costs became prohibitive, and he was offered a lifeline in touring cars by Lyall Williamson in the 1990s. He was out of a drive at the end of 2002 when his team, Team Brock, collapsed, and TKR presented him with a chance to stay full-time in V8s.

He came with a lot of touring car experience, and there was hope that he could build on the promise displayed by Richards. John said that at the time there was an expectation that Baird would achieve more than he eventually did — his best effort being to grab pole position for round seven at Winton

Triple Eight had declared that it had dropped Radisich and signed Australian golden boy Craig Lowndes.

— where Radisich was then living — for two days to see if he could stitch together a deal. His stay stretched to four days while he worked through a list of demands made by Radisich, which included that he have a new car, that engine builder Alan Draper was secured, and that Morris would be providing a car development programme. Two weeks after the Gold Coast visit, Radisich signed for two years. After initial disappointment, John described Baird's resignation as 'a blessing'. The team had stagnated for two years, John said, and Baird's going opened the way for Radisich's arrival. Right from the non-championship round at the Australian Grand Prix in Melbourne in March 2005, which signalled the start of the new season, it was evident that Radisich was an excellent signing. It was a huge boost to TKR's confidence and a welcome relief after two tough years using second-hand equipment and failing to make any significant impact, while on much bigger budgets, the frontrunners left TKR in their dust.

in 2004 by winning the top 10 shootout. That, however, was an outstanding, if thoroughly unlikely, feat, coming in the rain and against clearly superior cars. A review of Baird's drive said: 'He mastered the consistent rain of Saturday to scoop the first-ever series pole for himself and the tiny Team Kiwi. The soft chassis of his Commodore proved itself a gem in the wet, and Baird drove the shootout like a master to dominate some of the biggest names in the sport.' With the track dry the following day, Baird was no longer the same force, drifting back in the field in the 300 km race to finish 22nd. After a series high of sixth place in the championship after round three at Pukekohe, Baird lost ground to end 2004 in a disappointing 27th place.

John said that Baird should probably have been more competitive more often, given his experience and previous record, and this was particularly so in 2004 when he had a better car than the previous year, after TKR had acquired a more potent package from Morris Motorsports. 'I'm still not convinced we got the best out of Bairdo,' John said. 'He

was talented. When switched on, one of the best drivers in V8s, and he stood out at Bathurst. It's all about results, and he didn't have the new stuff like Paul, but I still don't think he was special. You hope the driver shares your vision, and hope they do everything to try and achieve it. A true champion driver will outshine many with top equipment. He'll over-drive the car, and get good results.'

Team manager Martin Collins was a fan of Baird's, saying he always did a professional job for TKR given the limitations of his equipment. Baird's last weekend for them was less than memorable when he had to start from pit lane at Eastern Creek Raceway, in New South Wales, after a misfiring problem prevented the team posting a lap time in the last 20-minute session. He did not finish the first heat, and despite solid 16th and 17th placings in heats two and three his overall result of 24th for the round completed an anonymous ending. Baird summed up TKR's limited resources well when, after the Eastern Creek practice, he said: 'There's no use pulling the engine out, we don't have another one.'

Collins and Baird have a strong friendship which stems from the seven years Collins spent managing

BMW Motorsport in the New Zealand touring car championship — a competition that Baird won four years in a row, prior to Collins joining TKR. The pair was together for the Bathurst 1000 km for two-litre cars in 1997, a race that ended in heartache and despair for Baird. He and Paul Morris were first in a BMW M3, only to be disqualified because Baird had driven for longer than permitted. The remarkably loyal Collins created a stir toward the end of 2005 when he resigned, taking up an opportunity to manage BMW's new series in New Zealand in 2006 for Mini Coopers. Bernie Gillon was to take over Collins's duties.

There had been some sadness when Jason Richards departed TKR, having been the team's initial full-time driver. In company with Angus Fogg, he had created a favourable impression when he placed 16th in TKR's first outing, the 2000 Bathurst. The car had suffered considerable damage in practice when another car spun in front of Richards, and, with nowhere to go, he ended in a fence. With the help of local panel beaters the car was patched up sufficiently to race, but it missed the final qualifying session. They made the grid with

Fairfax Sunday Newspapers

Craig Baird in a BMW 320i leads his successor at Team Kiwi, Paul Radisich, in a Ford Telstar in the days when they were rivals in the New Zealand touring car championship.

little time to spare, hardly the ideal scenario for a raw team whose drivers were making their V8 racing debuts on one of the most demanding circuits in the world. Richards, who started, had made his debut there three years previously with countryman Brett Riley, but the two-litre BMW super tourer they had driven then was a completely different machine. Just to make things more harrowing, it rained.

'It hosed down. I couldn't see with all the spray,' said Richards. 'On the first lap I was following Steven Richards and in the white mist I almost ran off the road. It was nerve-wracking but I wasn't intimidated. At times you just had to pray no one was having trouble just in front of you. There was water running across the track, and when we arrived our pit was so flooded we couldn't unpack.'

With repeated mishaps the safety car became an all-too-regular intrusion. Richards was delighted his only race indiscretion was an excursion into a sand trap, and with Fogg keeping out of trouble in the closing stint, TKR headed off numerous more accomplished teams to finish 16th. 'It was a pretty special start. We were happy. Making it even better I got engaged that weekend to an English girl, Charlotte Bridge, who I'd met when I was racing Formula Ford there,' Richards said. 'We had a big party afterwards. It was just Kiwi spirit that got us there, and our almost 400 supporters. We were the new boys on the block, fighting out of our depth. Martin [team manager Martin Collins] had a lot of BMW experience, I had raced in England, and Angus had done his own thing, but most of the guys had bugger all knowledge of what they were doing. We turned up with hardly anything.'

Originally TKR had four drivers it wanted to test prior to Bathurst: Richards, Fogg, the successful Ashley Stichbury (who tragically died of a brain haemorrhage in 2002), and Shane Drake. Richards recalled that Stichbury dropped out when he could not make a full commitment to the TKR project, and Drake looked elsewhere, having a V8 test in Australia in a Gibson Motorsport Commodore (which ended when he crashed at the Winton circuit). The first full season in 2001 was daunting, and on occasions heartbreaking. Richards remembers crying after

they missed pre-qualifying at Sydney's Eastern Creek by a few hundredths of a second. They were battling blind. Unlike the other teams, TKR was learning from scratch, with the totally New Zealand personnel having no experience of the tracks they were racing at or the set-ups required to make the car competitive. They had no data, and no one was falling over themselves to help them. Team members even had to ask for directions to the circuits. Not surprisingly, there were two occasions when the team packed up without getting to race — at Phillip Island first up, and Eastern Creek two rounds later — having failed to post a time good enough to enter qualifying.

Restrictions on testing made it even harder for them to catch up. Practice only lasted 20 minutes in those days, and pre-qualifying five minutes less, which made everything pretty instantaneous.

Richards was delighted his only race indiscretion was an excursion into a sand trap . . .

David John's decision to agree to Bernie Gillon buying a portion of Team Kiwi ended the financial hardship.

Teams had no time to muck about, and hardly any to change the way the car was set-up.

In the circumstances, Richards performed well above expectations by finishing an encouraging 24th in the series in that torrid first full year of 2001. The season started diabolically badly at Phillip Island when the Holden VT did not even complete a single lap of the cut-throat pre-qualifying after the spark plug leads came adrift. The top 25 cars were exempt from pre-qualifying, leaving the others to battle for the last seven places on the grid. For round three at Eastern Creek, 14 cars were chasing seven spots, and it looked as though TKR would qualify until the last few seconds. Richards was handicapped in that he was trying to qualify on used tyres, and he was mortified when someone with the advantage of new rubber pipped him at the last possible moment. 'I have to say I shed a tear with the sheer frustration of having to battle against rules which were so unfair for us,' Richards

said. 'No one seemed to care. We were nothing to the big boys. Most of our crew were virtually volunteers. Pre-qualifying was for the battlers.'

The almost 4000 km journey to Darwin from Melbourne for round four at Hidden Valley was worth it when Richards won the pre-qualifying, and from then on pre-qualifying was no longer a problem. However, it was not a case of Richards suddenly being more competitive; it was just that he became better accustomed to the V8's capabilities in the sprint races. The Perkins-built car was reliable but Richards lamented its poor handling and lack of grunt. 'It had miles too much understeer. It was like taking a knife to a gunfight,' Richards recalled. 'Larry [Perkins] held our hand to a degree. We had a little bit of info but not enough. The car was not set up properly.'

TKR again held its head high at Bathurst when it finished 16th, the same placing as the previous year. As in 2000 there was a practice drama, this time involving Richards' co-driver Angus Fogg, who was

'I have to say I shed a tear with the sheer frustration of having to battle against rules which were so unfair for us . . .'

Getty Images

Jason Richards spinning off in a cloud of dust at the Queensland 500 km in 2001, the same circuit at which he feared for his life after a frightening crash there four years later.

shunted at The Cutting going up the 'mountain', late in qualifying. The car was a wreck, and it was something of a miracle that it made the start. Again, the local smash repairers excelled when the car had originally looked a hopeless case. Even after an all-night session, the TKR crew were still finishing repairs as the car was required on the grid. 'The car was still understeering in practice,' Richards said. 'With some outside help we made some major shock [absorber] changes, and it did the trick. I equalled my qualifying time with a full tank and used tyres.'

In the circumstances, 16th represented a re-markable effort, and there were other useful results for Richards in the season. The penultimate round at Pukekohe started with easily his best heat perform-ance of 2001 when he finished an excellent fourth in the wet in Saturday's race — his knowledge of the track coming to the fore.

There was improvement in 2002. TKR bought a second Perkins Holden toward the end of 2001, and Richards' greater familiarity with the circuits, and the team's better grasp of what was required, resulted in him climbing five places to a commendable 19th in the series — the top position for a single-car team. He and another New Zealander, Simon Wills — who would become his fellow driver at Team Dynamik the following year — combined to graft their way to 11th at Bathurst. At Oran Park, one of Australia's older tracks, Richards achieved his first top 10 placing in qualifying; and in the controversial reverse grid for heat two of the last round on the streets of Canberra, Richards shone with a second, which helped earn him ninth place for the round — his best finishing position in his time at TKR. 'It was a good year. It showed the value of teamwork, that it was just as important as technology,' Richards said. 'We had a lot more info, we got more out of the car, and our pit stops improved. The guys were dedicated, and our results were a lot better. We still didn't have the equipment though to win races.'

Simon Wills only became available to join Richards at Bathurst after he suddenly parted company with John Briggs Motorsport (and almost immediately responded by winning the Queensland 500 km, driving for Stone Brothers Racing).

Dirk Klynsmith/Graphic Dak Photography

Jason Richards battling at Barbagallo — not one of his most productive circuits. In his two rounds there for Team Kiwi he was 23rd twice, and in the three years since, his best overall placing has been 15th.

The modest staff numbers at TKR mirrors the team's frugal attitude. Those in New Zealand are heavily involved in the supporters' club and the lucrative merchandise market, which brings in around $1 million annually. When there's been a cash-flow problem David John has been known to go out and sell gear in order for the team to pay for essentials. John has been grateful for the loyalty and patience displayed by his sponsors; in particular, More FM, Pit Stop, BNT, Dunlop, Makita, Wattyl and Avanti. He is conscious of the huge obligation he owes to them, and is consistent in his desire to honour the commitment he made to them that the team would be wholly New Zealand owned and operated, and would continually strive for improvement.

For the first four years TKR only stayed afloat because John used his personal wealth to underwrite the shortfall. For the first time, he expected to break even in 2005.

Among John's more testing moments occurred in 2003 when he secured Supercar sponsorship from Korean earthmoving company, Hyundai Construction Equipment. At the time Holden New Zealand was a TKR sponsor in the New Zealand V8 series, and it objected to the Hyundai signwriting on the car as there was also a popular make of car by the same name. Holden New Zealand saw the sponsorship as a conflict of interest, and a representative, and another from Holden Australia, made their feelings known to John in the pits at the Australian Grand Prix meeting in Melbourne. John disagreed with them, saying that the advertising was clearly for construction equipment, and he was committed to the signage remaining. He tried to broker a compromise, without success. Holden New Zealand withdrew its sponsorship, and an unhappy Hyundai dropped out at the end of the season.

Though lawyers were involved, the matter never reached the courts. Holden Australia recognised TKR's growing profile when it became a sponsor in 2005, but to John's disappointment Holden New Zealand has continued to stay away — even though it provides backup to two other Supercar teams, Tasman Motorsport and Super Cheap Auto Racing.

John argues that those teams cannot promote New Zealand the way he can, despite having a strong New Zealand component with Greg Murphy driving for Super Cheap; his father, Kevin Murphy, managing the Tasman team; and Nelson-born Jason Richards being one of the Tasman team drivers.

Despite the strength of the combination it mattered little when, in the Friday afternoon final qualifying, Richards caught the Commodore VX's right wheel on the exit wall at McPhillamy Park at the top of the hill. The impact smashed the rim, but Richards managed to park the car safely instead of leaving it in a dangerous place on the track. However, this worked against TKR. The officials left it there and Richards and Wills were denied the chance to post a final practice time. This meant they were forced to start from 37th, almost last, on the grid. 'I felt it was unfair to leave the car up there,' Richards said. 'I did the sensible thing, and got penalised for parking the car out of harm's way.'

His opening stint was among the best drives of the day. By lap 23 he was 17th, and he had wiped out the disadvantage of starting so far back. However, as the race progressed the car developed a steering problem, which Richards attributed to something being missed when the car was repaired following the damaged rim. 'The car wouldn't turn properly,' he said. 'It became a wrestling match. We might have finished as high as seventh, which would have been a pretty fair result.'

Richards was satisfied, though, that the TKR car finished on all three occasions he drove it at Bathurst, and he praised the enthusiasm of the team's supporters, who he said had cheered every lap in 2002. By the end of the year Richards was heartened too by the knowledge that his star was on the rise, that people were starting to take notice of him and the team. 'People knew we were not a big operation, but they appreciated some of our results were remarkable,' Richards said proudly.

He still had concerns for TKR, believing that the team's owner, David John, was trying to be too ambitious with his racing programmes on both sides of the Tasman — which included contesting the New Zealand two-litre and V8 championships. Richards considered the Supercar project was suffering. TKR subsequently dropped out of the New Zealand series, returning to the V8s in the 2005–06 season. 'I had some difference of opinion with David. I was focused on achieving results in Australia, but it did not seem to be David's No.

1 priority,' Richards said. 'In my opinion we were spreading ourselves too thin. The Supercar was too often starved of resources.'

Richards, who has a business management diploma from Nelson Polytechnic, even gathered a group of people, including his half-brother Anthony Boyd, in an attempt to buy TKR. Richards said consultants were paid $40,000 in the process, and he even approached Morris Motorsports with the suggestion that they run a second car, with him at the wheel. The idea collapsed, Richards said, when John would not sell. That decision contributed to Richards' decision to sign for Team Dynamik in 2003.

John acknowledged Richards' interest in buying TKR, but feared that the philosophy the team was built on would be lost. He said the team would no longer be based in New Zealand, and would not be interested in contesting New Zealand championships or fostering local talent. 'Jason did some good things for us after we'd given him the opportunity to carve out a career in Supercars,' John said. 'He's very talented. The grass was greener when he went to Team Dynamik, and what happened there slowed down his progress. It was a backward step, and in the end a disaster.'

John said Richards' leaving, and later Craig Baird's departure, set the team back — and Baird's year at WPS in 2005 hardly justified his move. John says the deal with Morris Motorsports, very much a 50-50 joint venture, has worked well. There are three elements to it, John said, TKR, Morris Motorsports, and in the middle, the combined project. The cars for the two Pauls, Radisich and Morris, are both prepared for each round in the same workshop in Norwell, Queensland, and Alan Draper splits his time between the two cars, which are otherwise worked on separately by TKR's New Zealand pit crew, and Morris's people. The venture allows them to have many of the advantages of a two-car team. Data is shared, and more can be achieved, faster, with the teams limited to just six testing days annually — a restriction designed to keep costs down and to maintain the appearance of a reasonably level playing field (though clearly it is not). 'It can look like we're just a customer of Morris's, the way we were with Larry Perkins, but that's not what's going on here,' John emphasised. 'The teams are billed the same for services provided.'

'It was a backward step, and in the end a disaster.'

A Team Kiwi car waits for the pit crew to finish their work.

TKR has been very ambitious. Not only has it raced in Supercars but it has also tackled the New Zealand two-litre and V8 competitions. On top of that, it has established a development academy aimed at trying to promote motor racing in New Zealand and helping provide a pathway for Kiwi drivers toward Supercars. All of this also helps add value for the sponsors.

In the team's opening domestic season John McIntyre and Andy Booth were third and fourth, respectively, in the V8s; and Richards and Angus Fogg were first and second in the two-litres. The following year Booth won the V8s, and achieved a third in the smaller cars the year after that. But Supercar costs, which leapt out of control, snookered a continuation of racing in New Zealand. Over the five years that TKR has vied for the Supercar title, the costs of running one car in a season climbed from $A1 million to $A2.5 million.

The drivers also share the same engineer, Paul Ceprnich, a South African, who designed the TKR chassis and has the tasks of producing greater speed from the cars and improving their handling. Radisich was keen for Ceprnich to be his engineer, having known of his background, which included working for BMW (Europe). 'Paul Ceprnich could work for any team around the world,' John said. 'He's very highly regarded in pit lane. He thinks outside the square. He's always looking for a winning edge, and that's no surprise given South Africa's reputation for being very competitive.'

Interestingly, with the cars being pretty well identical, it was Radisich who was the faster out of the blocks at the start of 2005. That advantage was maintained throughout the campaign without appearing to impede the relationship between the still-competing teams. Morris was 19th in the championship, five places behind Radisich.

Getty Images

Paul Radisich pushes his Holden Commodore through a corner at Pukekohe in 2005.

John derived much satisfaction from Radisich's performances, and the obvious enjoyment they created for other members of the team. 'I can take or leave the motor sport environment,' he said. 'I don't understand it in New Zealand. It can be so negative with people bagging the shit out of us. I'm happy to provide the opportunity for people to be successful, and what happened in Shanghai was special. Budgets have doubled in our time, and the competition has become even more intense, with most of the cars on the grid often separated by mere fractions of a second. At times you can't see the light at the end of the tunnel. Pit lane is hardly an even playing field, with Ford pouring big money into its high-profile teams, and Holden devoting a lot of its attention to HRT.'

John said Shanghai was the first occasion in his time when the playing field was reasonably even, with everyone having to start from scratch on a new and unfamiliar track. Radisich had shown his class, John said, in being able to get to grips with the circuit a lot more quickly than most other drivers, despite his car lacking the speed on the straights of a number of his opponents. John had had no intention of making the long journey to China, but when the opportunity came he was able to secure the necessary visa at the eleventh hour, and catch a flight just in time to witness what became a memorable, ground-breaking occasion.

It was the V8s' first appearance outside of Australasia, and it put the formula on a truly international stage for the first time. Radisich was 'blown away' by the support he received once driving for TKR, John said. 'Paul didn't understand the support for the black car or how pleased people were to see him driving it,' John said. He says the soft-spoken Radisich's professionalism and modesty have shone through to the benefit of everyone, in particular Radisich's pit crew, who reacted well to him. Radisich is not one to blow his own trumpet, preferring his results to do the talking for him — very much the New Zealand way. TKR gave him the opportunity to regularly run in the top 10, something that Radisich did not have a lot of in the previous two years, and it fired his enthusiasm when his career appeared to be on the wane. 'We get on extremely well,' John said. 'There's no bullshit with Paul, and a lot of mutual respect. I gave him what he asked for and he gave us the results. That freed me up to concentrate on building the business, which gave us a stronger base for bargaining with sponsors.'

After having previously largely existed on a number of smaller sponsorship deals, John managed something of a breakthrough when he secured two lucrative sponsorships for 2006 — Makita NZ and 3M New Zealand. It put the seal on what John regarded as a hugely satisfying season, with Radisich's 14th placing in the 2005 championship making TKR the highest-placed one-car team, and superior to a number of two-car operations. Despite the disappointment of Bathurst, when Radisich did not even get behind the wheel after Paul Morris crashed the Morris team car they shared, the TKR Commodore, which Radisich had driven all season, finished 10th.

The scratch team of 53-year-old Palmerston North veteran John Faulkner, who came out of retirement at Sandown the round before, and Sydneysider Alan Gurr, earned TKR its best finish at Bathurst. It would have been even better had the car not been required to pit twice late in the race, when the brake lights were not working.

Faulkner, who still regards himself as a New Zealander and travels on a New Zealand passport, is an interesting guy. He went to Australia when he was 16, and, after a late start, raced solidly in V8s between 1996 and 2002, often running his own team, John Faulkner Racing. His best year was 1997. He was fourth in the Sandown 500 km, fifth in the Bathurst 1000 km, and 10th in the championship overall. After recently running the Holden Young Lions team in the development series, he will help manage the Paul Morris Supercar team, which has secured another licence to run a second car to be shared by Gurr and New Zealander Fabian Coulthard in 2006.

David John had good reason to be excited looking toward 2006. After scrimping and scraping for so long, and spending just about every waking moment in the last five years striving to make TKR better, the team finally has the financial stability and structure to compete more vigorously with the big boys.

THE RICHARDS DYNASTY

Getty Images

Getty Images

Jim Richards

Born: Auckland, 2 September 1947

Championship debut: Oran Park, 1976

Starts: 129 (a record)

Pole positions: 16

Round wins: 22 (4th equal overall; first win: round 1, Winton, 1985; last win: round 10, Bathurst 1000, 2002)

Wins in succession: 6 (a record, rounds 4 to 9, 1985)

Podium finishes: 48

Best championship finish: 1st (1985, 1987, 1990, 1991)

Bathurst record: debut 1974; 34 starts (a record), 24 finishes; best results: 1st (1978, 1979, 1980, 1991, 1992, 1998 (two-litre), 2002)

There's just no holding back New Zealand touring car great Jim Richards. Even at the age of 58 his enthusiasm for racing and love of motor sport are undiminished. One only has to sit down and talk with him at his Ringwood workshop in suburban Melbourne to know how blessed he feels to have been able to convert a teenage obsession into a highly successful career and immensely pleasurable lifestyle.

Gentleman Jim, as he is universally known in Australasian motor sport, is an appropriate nickname. It was bestowed on him many years ago by Australian Channel Seven commentator, Mike Raymond, and, not surprisingly, 'just stuck'. The still-lithe Richards is likeable, laidback, modest, and mild-mannered, not one to court the media or air his grievances in public, and on the track he has long been regarded as a hard but fair competitor.

When he gets behind the wheel the competitive instincts that have been honed over more than 40 years of no-quarter racing are quickly to the fore. It is a tribute to him that it is hard for anyone to recall an occasion when Richards was unnecessarily foolhardy or reckless on the track, or could be accused of poor sportsmanship. The elder of his two sons, Steven Richards, a similarly accomplished

racer, might just as easily have earned the nickname 'Gentleman Steve'. He is among the top tier of V8 Supercar drivers, and has inherited his father's attitudes and approach to racing. Like Jim he has tended to let his driving do the talking for him, and he is good enough to one day fashion a record as impressive as Dad's.

Though Jim dropped out of full-time V8 racing a decade ago, he feeds his competitive urges by being in the thick of the Carrera Cup series for Porsches — one of the supporting events at V8 rounds — and the Targa Tasmania and AGP Rallies, also driving Porsches. The competition keeps him in racing trim and ensures his continued appearance at the long-distance Supercar rounds at Sandown and Bathurst when each car has two drivers. He readily accepts the annual invitations, not just to make up the numbers for old time's sake, or to play the part of a legend for a battling privateer, but to be involved in high-calibre teams with genuine race-winning chances.

Driving for HRT he created history in 2002 by becoming the oldest driver to win the Bathurst 1000 km showpiece, alongside Mark Skaife. It was their third victory together and their first since 1992. The win was Richards' seventh at Mount Panorama, just two behind the record set by Peter

Brock, at the age of 55 years, one month and 11 days. He became the oldest driver to win Bathurst, and also the oldest to win a round of the Australian touring car championship — eclipsing the mark set by Brock, who was almost three years younger when he finished top of the podium for the Perth round at Barbagallo in 1997.

The feat made it a proud day for the remarkably durable and motivated Richards. 'It was my most prized win,' he said. 'Ten years earlier Mark and I had done it together at Bathurst, and here we were doing it again. At my age it was good to know I was still driving as well as ever. I love the circuit. It will be my last win there. I was flattered when Mark, at the top of his game, invited me to drive with him. I was sure I could do a good job. He hadn't approached me before because I was with other teams.'

Richards said there had been some drama too when a plastic bag blew into the radiator inlet, and with 20 laps to go the car began overheating. Skaife was driving, and it was decided not to stop to remove the bag. 'It got tight toward the end.

Steven [Jim's elder son] was second and cutting in to our lead,' Richards said. 'Mark drove as fast as he could, within reason.' They won by less than three seconds. That victory took him to 22 round victories in the touring car championship, and placed him fourth equal on the all-time list with Dick Johnson and Craig Lowndes, behind Peter Brock (37), Mark Skaife (36) and Allan Moffat (32).

Richards derived almost as much satisfaction the following year when he qualified HRT car he shared with Tony Longhurst third on the grid at Bathurst. It was a staggering achievement, particularly as he was very much a V8 part-timer. Typically, the self-effacing Richards made nothing of it at the time, but he later said he regarded it as 'a great personal achievement'. 'I drive one of these cars twice a year

. . . he created history in 2002 by becoming the oldest driver to win the Bathurst 1000 km . . .

Jim Richards enjoys one of his greatest triumphs as driving partner Mark Skaife takes the chequered flag at Bathurst in 2002. The result made Richards, at the age of 55, the oldest championship round winner.

and it showed my skill level had not slipped after all this time,' he said.

In 2005 Richards was still competing at Bathurst, being good enough to qualify ninth on the grid. However, his 34th appearance, two more than Brock, who last raced there in 2004, was a non-event when his partner, James Courtney, eliminated their Holden Commodore VZ before Richards had the chance to race it. After promising so much, it was a huge disappointment for Richards. Skaife, now the owner of HRT, had engaged his old friend to partner Courtney, a former Formula One test driver for Jaguar, who was making his Bathurst debut and was a Supercar novice. Though Richards was the most experienced driver in the race, had excelled in qualifying for the top 10 shootout, and there was some uncertainty about the weather, it was decided that the raw Courtney should start. The wisdom of that decision was called into question on lap eight when Courtney clipped a wall, damaging the car seriously enough for it to be withdrawn.

Concern about the incident was, however, dwarfed by Skaife and Todd Kelly's victory in the team's other car. It was a win that ended a lengthy victory drought for Skaife, who had lost some of his driving edge, perhaps weighed down in recent times by the responsibility of team ownership. Had both cars dropped out the team would have been bathed in embarrassment. Ever the diplomat, Richards made light of the decision to start Courtney. The new pair were an encouraging 11th in their first time together in the Sandown 500 km, and would have finished considerably higher with a better-timed pit stop late in the race.

Richards' passion for his sport knows no bounds. At a time when most other drivers his age would long since have called it quits, having got tired of it, lost their edge or perhaps scaled down their activities, Richards is as busy as ever. 'Motor sport is my passion, my work and my life,' he says. 'I'm more passionate about racing than ever. I'm at the workshop every day unless I'm away racing.'

He even drives his own 13 metre (40 foot) 14-wheel, four-door, dual-cab, Scania transporter

Getty Images

Jim Richards giving it heaps during practice at Bathurst in 2005 — still good enough to qualify for the top 10 shootout at the age of 58.

vast distances all over Australia to compete — something none of the other drivers would contemplate. There are usually three Porsches in it, two for racing in the Carrera Cup, one for himself, one for a wealthy Melbourne hotelier, Dean Grant, and the other, a registered road car, for Richards' hot lap days with corporate clients, who don crash helmets to sit in the passenger seat while Richards drives them around the track.

Richards started his own team, Jim Richards Racing, in 1995, and since 2001 he has been travelling in the transporter. It takes three or four 12-hour days to make the 3750 km trek from Melbourne to Perth. The distance from Perth to Darwin is even further at around 4000 km, and it's 3700 km from Melbourne to Darwin, 3000 km from Darwin to Brisbane, and a mere 1700 km from Brisbane to Melbourne, to complete the round trip.

Richards has never had a blowout in the middle of nowhere, but he is prepared if the need arises. The closest he has come occurred on one occasion when he was travelling from Darwin to Melbourne and had stopped at a roadhouse. A check revealed one of his trailer tyres had a flat spot, and was down to the canvas, so he averted what might have been a far more difficult scenario.

Richards and his mechanic, Luke Gelding, prepare two of the Porsches, but his 3.6-litre twin turbo-charged, factory-made cup race car is worked on by Karl Batson, a Porsche master technician with 18 years' experience. It has been a deadly combination, with Richards continuing to be desperately hard to head off in his 911 GT3 in the Carrera Cup. On race days he also has Gelding's father, Brian, alongside. They have been friends since the former Aucklanders raced in New Zealand, and Richards

The wisdom of that decision was called into question on lap eight when Courtney clipped a wall, damaging the car ...

Then there's the so-called shorter trips of 900 km between Sydney and Melbourne, and 800 km from Melbourne to Adelaide — huge by New Zealand standards, but not by Australian.

His philosophy is a simple one. If he flew to all the meetings, as he used to, he would need to employ a driver, and when the cars are on the road they are not able to be worked on. 'That no one else does it [the driving] probably shows how keen I am,' Richards said. 'My wife, Fay, sometimes comes with me. It's not a hardship. I enjoy the travelling. The transporter is really comfortable. You can sleep in it. The rigs are actually more comfortable than a car.'

The law requires that they travel no faster than 100 kmh, which, Richards says, given the variance in speed cameras, allows him to push up to 104 kmh. On occasions it is not worth returning to Melbourne between races, and he has a chance to do a bit of touring, which he thoroughly enjoys. He has to complete a logbook to discourage himself from sitting behind the wheel for too long. He cannot drive for longer than 12 hours in 24. Fortunately

estimates the elder Gelding has been to just about every race meeting with him in the last 30 years. Richards won the Carrera Cup in 2003, its inaugural season, but in 2005 he had to accept second behind another New Zealander, Fabian Coulthard, after he uncharacteristically ran into a barrier in the penultimate round at Surfers Paradise.

Richards is equally comfortable racing his beloved Porsches on the open roads, having won the Targa Tasmania seven times since it began in 1992, and been the victor on five occasions in the AGP Rally. He also crosses the Tasman to contest the week-long North Island Targa Rally, which he won handsomely in 2005.

In all he runs five fabulous Porsches, and is a master of understatement when he says he is 'one of Porsche's better clients'. No one has done more to promote the precision German marque in Australia, and this has been acknowledged by his status as Porsche's official ambassador there. Richards is similarly grateful to Porsche, with whom he has had a 'fantastic relationship' for 10 years. It all started in

Getty Images

Jim Richards' Porsche 996 twin turbo has its lights blazing as it hammers along the open road in the Targa Tasmania Rally, an event Richards has dominated over the years.

1993 when he was invited to drive in the Bathurst 12-hour race by accomplished Porsche driver Peter Fitzgerald. Fitzgerald had been loaned two factory cars for the event, and it was Richards' first experience of a racing Porsche. He was impressed with the car when he finished second. 'I liked the Porsche so much I bought one, and Peter purchased the other,' Richards said. 'It was smaller than the V8s I was used to but I didn't know how good Porsches were till then.'

He drove Porsches with success in the Australian production series against the factory Mazdas, starting with a 968 Clubsport. The series attracted a number of other V8 drivers who also warmed to the Porsches. Before long, as a result of this increasing popularity, they started racing on their own in the Carrera Cup, a competition that is contested in several countries.

Though Richards has had plenty of offers to race Porsches in Europe he has always declined, but he was delighted to compete against the top German Porsche drivers when they and their cars were brought to Melbourne in 1999 to be part of the Australian Grand Prix meeting. He excelled in finishing fourth. The cars, which had shone in races all over Europe, were superior to those in Australia at the time, but after 1999 they started appearing Down Under.

Richards counts himself fortunate to have raced in a wide variety of touring cars, and invariably it has been with excellent results — in particular in the 1000 km classic at Bathurst. His first appearance there was in 1974 when he was third in a Holden Torana L34 belonging to good friend and fellow Kiwi, Rod Coppins. He collected his first two Bathursts in 1978 and 1979, sharing a Torana A9X with Brock, and they made it a hat-trick the following year in a Holden Commodore VC. He drove BMWs there for seven consecutive years in the 1980s from 1982, twice achieving a best placing of fourth when driving with Longhurst — in a 635 CSi in 1985, and an M3 in 1987. Four years later Richards was again top of the podium in company with Skaife; this time in a twin-turbo, four-wheel drive Nissan GTR, and they repeated the victory the following year, again in a Nissan GTR.

From 1993 Richards has raced various Holden Commodore and Ford V8s at Bathurst, winning again with Skaife in 2002 in a Commodore VX. He also won the 1000 km event for two-litre super tourers at Bathurst in 1998, in partnership with slick Swede Rickard Rydell, this time in a Tim Walkinshaw Racing Volvo S40. Though the separate two-litre race lasted just two years — losing out to the superior excitement and crowd-pulling power of the Holdens and Fords — both the super touring and V8 winners in 1997 and 1998 are recognised in the Bathurst records, allowing Richards to claim a seventh victory there.

The 1998 victory is easily forgotten, but for Jim it was the toughest to achieve. At the time it was still the official Bathurst event. The reason Richards found winning so difficult was none other than his son, Steven Richards, who shared a Nissan Primera with top-flight Englishman, Matt Neal. 'Steve and I battled against each other for a big part of the day,' Jim said. 'We were

Jim Richards in the super-fast Nissan GTR, derogatorily dubbed 'Godzilla' after it controversially dominated touring car racing in the early 1990s.

Richards was again top of the podium in company with Skaife; this time in a twin-turbo, four-wheel drive Nissan GTR . . .

going at it from the start. He led and then I led. We were absolutely flat out. It was the hardest race I had there, to finish just ahead of Steve.'

Steven remembers it well. He had been racing V8s for Garry Rogers Motorsport, till he was released to test-drive for the Nissan team in the British touring car championship. Steven was supposed to receive a number of racing opportunities as well, and when it did not work out as well as anticipated, the team felt some obligation to enter him at Bathurst. 'Dad and I ended up having a great scrap,' Steven said. 'There was never more than five seconds between us.' Jim has had three other podium finishes at Bathurst, all in Commodores, being second with Skaife, and son Steven, and third with Jason Bargwanna.

Richards has competed in numerous other car categories in New Zealand and Australia, including loose metal and tarmac rallying, speedway in saloon cars on a one-mile track, single-seater Formula 5000, and NASCAR and Oscar racing — the latter being the Australian version of NASCARs — winning

Australian titles in both. He has also raced trucks, and motorcycles in enduro events. As Australian NASCAR titleholder, Richards was invited to Japan's Suzuka Raceway in the mid-1990s to test his skills against the top-notch Americans, who included Rusty Wallace, Mark Martin, Jeff Burton and the late Dale Earnhardt Snr. Driving a 700 hp six-litre Pontiac GP for a Canadian team, Richards qualified second and finished fourth. It was a remarkable result and helped reinforce the belief among some Kiwis that he deserves to be regarded as among New Zealand's very best motor racers — perhaps only surpassed by former Formula One drivers Denny Hulme, Bruce McLaren and Chris Amon.

When he moved to Australia in 1975 it was to race the Sidchrome Mustang with which he had set a new benchmark for big-banger tin-top racing in New Zealand. He was similarly successful across the Tasman, and won twice at his first outing, at Sandown in Melbourne. Yet despite driving some of the very best touring cars Richards says his all-time favourite is a Ford Falcon six-litre V8 two-door built in Sydney by an Auckland friend Murray Bunn. It tied for the Australian GT/sports sedan title in 1978, losing on a countback to a Chevrolet Corvair run by Australian great Frank Gardner, and driven by Allan Grice. 'Your favourite tends to move with the improved equipment, year by year,' Richards said. 'But if I had to nominate one standout for all time, this was it. It was a car ahead of its time, and one I'd still like to have. I was equal with Allan on points but he had one more win than me.' Richards said what made the Ford special was that the engine was next to him, in the middle of the car, rather than in front of him, and that gave the car superior balance and weight distribution.

He happily says he 'wouldn't change anything' when he reflects on a glittering and deeply satisfying career, and looking at his record it is easy to agree with him. However, if he could change one thing it would surely be to have won Bathurst with son Steven. They have raced there three times, and their best effort was coming second in 1997 in a

Garry Rogers Motorsport Commodore VS behind Larry Perkins and Russell Ingall in another Holden, winners for the second time in three years.

'When I ended probably the best period of my career in leaving Fred Gibson Motorsport in 1995 I wanted to drive with Steve,' Richards said. 'I joined Garry Rogers for no other reason.' Their first time together, 1996, ended after an accident on lap 33 of 161 when Steven hit a wall. 'Steve was driving brilliantly, he was in second or third place,' Richards recalled. 'Then he spun out of Castrol Chase, and unfortunately the back wheels caught the white paint, and the back of the car hit the wall.'

The following year the Richards performed with considerable consistency. There were no mishaps, but the pair were never able to put Perkins and Ingall under sufficient pressure for them to make a mistake. By 2004, and their third attempt together, Dad had joined his son at Perkins's Castrol Holden team, and despite a sticking throttle, a podium place was still possible after Steve had put them on pole position on the grid. Jim was on the second part

A Valiant Charger, which Jim Richards and Rod Coppins raced with success in the 1970s.

of his double stint when an extraordinary thing happened on lap 110. A kangaroo jumped out in front of him going up Mountain Straight toward The Cutting, and the car and animal connected at around 170 kmh. The car was 'roo-ted' after the front left was badly damaged. Somehow Jim managed to coax the car back to the pits but the damage was so severe it seemed unlikely it could be repaired. 'The car looked pretty sick,' Jim said. 'The radiator was leaking, the air intake was broken, the bodywork was shot, the bonnet was knackered.'

The team was determined to get the car race-worthy as Steven's touring car championship bid stood in the balance. It eventually returned to complete 148 laps, and be classified 21st, which, though earning Steven 112 points, was too few to keep him in the championship race. 'It was all a bit hard to take in — to be taken out by a kangaroo,' Jim said. 'It was the most bizarre accident I've been involved in. There are plenty of roos in the outback, they leap across the road all the time when I'm driving the transporter, but you wouldn't expect them to be in the middle of a racetrack. I was lucky. If the kangaroo had jumped out a second later it could have gone through the windscreen, and killed me. You tend to be a bit philosophical about the dangers of motor racing. What occurred was just one of those things and you move on.'

Jim was more concerned that Steven was a partner in the fastest car in the race, and the accident had ruined their prospects of ever being the first winning father-and-son combination at Bathurst. 'Some fairytales don't come true. I won't drive with Steve again,' Jim said. 'Another two Bathursts [2005 and 2006] will probably be enough for me. Realistically, it's harder for me to get a drive when I'm not a regular V8 driver. Teams need two regular drivers to be a winning combination.'

Steven lamented the lost opportunity. 'We were going strongly. It was on for a podium finish, if

The car was 'roo-ted' after the front left was badly damaged.

Father and son, Jim and Steven Richards, were among the leaders in this Castrol Commodore at Bathurst in 2004, until Jim had the misfortune to collide with a kangaroo.

not a win, when it happened,' he said. 'There wasn't anything we could have done to avoid what happened. Over the years there's been a few kangaroos and horses on the course, but ours was the first car to be put out by one.'

He agreed that the chances of them again being a driving partnership at Bathurst were slim. Steven said that the race became more professional every year, and those drivers who graduated to the podium were largely full-time Supercar drivers. 'I wouldn't say never, but looking at where my career and Dad's are at, the reality is it's unlikely we'll be together again at Bathurst,' Steven said. 'Co-drivers who do not race V8s full-time tend to be a bit tentative and cautious, and if you're going to win you can't afford to drop any time. Our weakness in 2004 was that Dad was a bit slow to start with on cold tyres, time you won't make up.'

a Holden ute to carry their karts to meetings. Richards helped his father maintain and modify the karts, and he had a good slice of success. However, once he left school the teenager was eager to try his hand at more serious motor racing. One of his earliest experiences was to contest the standing and flying quarter-mile on the Tamahere Straight, near Hamilton, where he finished well back. He did contemplate open-wheeler racing but the costs, and the need to have his road car as his race car, dictated his path. As a struggling apprentice he had no money, so his parents, Albert and Joyce, bought him a Ford Anglia 105E.

They were not flush for cash either but they recognised their son's developing passion. He soon fitted the Anglia with twin carburettors, a mild cam, and an extractor exhaust system. It was still no match for other better-quality modified cars,

Steven has won two Bathursts himself . . . being the first driver to win in a Ford and a Holden in consecutive years . . .

Steven has won two Bathursts himself, in 1998 and 1999, in the process being the first driver to win in a Ford and a Holden in consecutive years — firstly with Jason Bright in a Ford Falcon EL, and then with Kiwi, Greg Murphy, in a Kmart Commodore VT.

Jim Richards' interest in cars started in Manurewa, south Auckland, when he visited the premises of a local garage on his way home from school. The owner, Brian Yates, built, prepared and raced speedway midget cars, and young Richards was fascinated. It wasn't long before the youngster was performing menial tasks for Mr Yates, and when he narrowly missed out on passing the old School Certificate examination, it was no surprise that when he left school at 16 he started an apprenticeship to become a motor mechanic, a decision that has hugely benefited him over his racing career.

Four years earlier Richards, like so many others, started motor racing in karts. It wasn't long before his father, Albert, joined him, and they used

and in about a year he had traded it for a faster, more competitive Anglia. His first outing in the original Anglia occurred at Pukekohe, and it was thoroughly unremarkable, at least until he received the chequered flag near the rear of the field. He was so relieved to see the flag that he missed the turn at the end of the front straight and collected the strawbales safety barrier, denting a front mudguard.

He took the second Anglia on a South Island tour, following the Tasman single-seater series to the runway track at the Royal New Zealand Air Force base at Wigram in Christchurch, and then to Invercargill's Teretonga circuit, which in the 1960s featured some of the big names in Formula One in the off-season. Among them were the great Scot Jimmy Clark; John Surtees, a world motorcycling champion who later became the world champion on four wheels; Australian ace Jack Brabham; British world champion Graham Hill, whose son Damon Hill

The Wynn's Commodore that unexpectedly powered Steven Richards and Greg Murphy to victory at Bathurst in 1999.

Fairfax Sunday Newspapers: *Auckland Star* Collection

One of Jim Richards' tougher opponents over the years — expat Canadian Allan Moffat.

eventually emulated him; New Zealand's 1967 world champion Denny Hulme; the brilliant car builder and racer Bruce McLaren; Ferrari driver Chris Amon; and Australian Frank Gardner, who was later to help Richards further his career across the Tasman.

Richards had an Anglia van to tow his car, and he tells the story of how two of his crew had to travel in the car on the A-frame trailer because there was insufficient room in the van.

In 1968 Richards graduated to a Ford Escort. Though the car didn't make him significantly more competitive it brought him in contact with well-heeled fellow Escort driver Jim Carney, who managed the oil refinery at Marsden Point, near Whangarei. After a year filling each other's mirrors they became good friends, and at the start of the 1969 season Carney floored Richards when he offered him his more powerful 1600cc Escort at all the major meetings, saying, in addition, that he would pay for the maintenance and repair bills. Richards was immediately able to beat the best drivers in the open class, and he rapidly earned their respect, finishing the season as something of a star. That summer he had done all the preparation on the car, save for the engine, which was in the hands of another young Aucklander Murray Bunn (who would later build Richards' favourite of all time, the Ford Falcon V8 he would race in Australia).

The pair, who did their motor apprenticeships at the same time, started to forge a partnership that would lead to the championship-winning Sidchrome Mustang, and its superior successor, the Falcon. Carney was even more generous when he imported a more potent Escort twin-cam from England, which competed more than favourably against the growing band of grunty V8-powered Mustangs, Camaros and Pontiac Firebirds. Richards was the New Zealand saloon car champion, and furthered his motoring education competing in speedway and rallying events. After also successfully campaigning a 1000 cc Hillman Imp and a Falcon GTHO, the now well-established, polished and immensely popular 'JR' first raced the Sidchrome Mustang at Mount Maunganui's Baypark track at Easter, 1973.

The late 1960s was a memorable time in New Zealand saloon car racing. The crowds loved the throaty chargers, and they flocked to Pukekohe, the now defunct Levin circuit, Manfeild, Baypark, Wigram and Teretonga to watch their heroes led by Richards and 1986 Australian touring car champion Robbie Francevic, who became a legend in his highly modified Ford Customline. Also there were proven performers Paul Fahey, Red Dawson, Rod Coppins, Jack Nazer, Neville Crichton (later to become a big player in ocean yachting classics like the Sydney to Hobart), David Oxton, Graham Baker and Dennis Marwood.

Richards was pretty well invincible in a Team McMillan Falcon GTHO and later a Falcon GT, and he drove a Valiant Charger when he won the Benson and Hedges six-hour race two years in a row with Coppins. But the 1969 second-hand Boss Mustang,

which Richards helped Bunn transform into the Sidchrome version in a secret location in a rundown shed on a farm south of Auckland, was something else. The objective was to win the 1973–74 New Zealand saloon car title by crushing the opposition, and crucial to that was keeping the project under wraps till the last possible moment. Within a year Richards had secured the 0–6000 cc national title but was pipped by Fahey's nimble little Capri in his farewell full New Zealand season in 1974–75.

Richards had the satisfaction, though, of beating a crop of visiting Australian sports sedans that summer, driven by, among others, Allan Moffat (Mustang), John McCormack (Repco Charger), and Ian 'Pete' Geoghegan (Porsche) over a six-race series. That effort sparked the idea of racing the car in Australia, and it became an even more appealing prospect when Sidchrome New Zealand decided to

Richards was pretty well invincible . . . when he won the Benson and Hedges six-hour race two years in a row . . .

Fairfax Sunday Newspapers: *Auckland Star* Collection

Allan Moffat in his potent Ford Mustang in New Zealand. It had numerous jousts with Jim Richards' outstandingly successful Sidchrome Mustang.

end its support. The tool-making manufacturer's parent company in Australia was approached, and agreed to take over the car's sponsorship, also inviting Richards to drive it. Originally the move was seen as temporary, with Richards only agreeing to compete at 15 main events over 12 months.

There were suggestions he would commute between New Zealand and Australia. But such was his success in the first few weeks that it became apparent that shuttling back and forth between the two countries was impractical. Richards accepted that the move needed to be permanent. Suddenly he was faced with having to pack up, sell the house and move a young family to Melbourne, and he described it as 'a huge jump'.

Richards was excited at the prospect of testing himself against the best Aussies on their own doorstep, and it made all the difference that wife Fay was happy to make the change. With Richards pouring any spare cash into motor racing he had little, and it was only the help of Auckland car dealers Jerry Clayton, who owned the Mustang, and Colin

Giltrap — two very passionate and influential motor racing followers — that made it possible for Richards to race in Australia. Richards' mechanic, Don Harper, came with him and lived with the family, and the pair were more than happy to ready themselves for the car's debut at Melbourne's Sandown track in July 1975 without any great fanfare.

The car was shipped to Melbourne and cleared by customs just in time, and they worked on it in a borrowed workshop near the track. Here he was competing against some of the biggest names in Australian motor sport in Moffat, McCormack, and Colin Bond in sports sedans. Richards won both races that weekend, one of them in the wet, where he is an acknowledged master. It was an impressive start, creating anxiety among the normally cocky Aussies, and signalling that the distinctive red-and-yellow Mustang was a genuine threat.

Richards argued, though, that at the time the standard of New Zealand sports sedan racing was superior to that in Australia. Though there was greater depth in the fields of Camaros and Mustangs

Fairfax Sunday Newspapers: *Auckland Star* Collection

Jim Richards piloting the thundering Sidchrome Mustang, which was such a hit on both sides of the Tasman in the 1970s.

at home, Richards said there was a much better chance of being a full-time driver in Australia, and that was what he was after. 'I'm proud of what I've done,' he said. 'It was a struggle for a long time, but you didn't know any different. I spent everything on the cars. There was just enough money to keep the family alive. In the Sidchrome Mustang days I'd pay myself $A100 a week for the basics. I've been spending my own money on motor racing for more than 40 friggin' years. I guess I won't know what I'm worth after all that till I finally sell up.'

When the Richards moved to Australia they had two little boys, Steven and Jason. Daughter Danielle was born in Australia.

In the five months to the end of 1975 Richards' efforts had yielded 28 major placings from 30 starts, including 13 wins, 12 seconds, two thirds and a few lap records. But the outstandingly durable Mustang

meticulous Sheppard had a fine reputation as an engineer, and was in the process of replacing the old 'seat-of-the-pants' approach with a slick professional factory team. The partnership proved a winner, Richards and Brock completing an unprecedented hat-trick of victories, a feat Brock was later to repeat with Larry Perkins.

Richards does not look back on the three-peat with great fondness. As the co-driver he raced in Brock's shadow, and by 1980 Brock was the team boss as well as lead driver. It left Richards yearning for the opportunity to be a lead driver in a team with genuine winning prospects. When all the glitter was stripped away and the applause had died, Richards said he was just doing his job, albeit a very desirable one, in contributing to the victories. However, Richards did have the satisfaction of knowing the partnership with Brock had changed the dynamics

It was an impressive start, creating anxiety among the normally cocky Aussies, and signalling that the distinctive red and yellow Mustang was a genuine threat.

never managed to win Richards an Australian sports sedan title. The best Richards managed was to lose to New South Welshman Allan Grice on a countback in 1978, driving the replacement for the Mustang, the Ford Falcon V8. However, Richards was still able to win the prestigious Marlboro $A100,000 series, and the Tasmanian Ten Thousand, the biggest single sports sedan event of the year, before the Mustang ended its racing days in August 1977.

Richards' deeds had made him a star in Australia, and with the experience of four appearances at Bathurst and having run his own Falcon XB GT in the Australian touring championship till he ran out of sponsorship, Richards was offered a lifeline from an unexpected quarter for the Bathurst 1000 km in 1978. Knowing Richards was out of a drive, John Sheppard, the Holden Dealer Team manager, offered him an invitation to be Peter Brock's backup driver. By then Brock was a huge name, having won twice on the 'mountain', in 1972 and 1975. The

of the 161-lap event. They turned it into a six-hour sprint race in which only the best prepared had any chance of surviving at the hot pace set by the front-runners from lap one. To maintain that pace, the role of the co-driver suddenly became more vital. He was no longer there just to complete the lunchtime shift at a pace smart enough to keep the main man in contact with the leaders.

Richards regarded the 1978 win in a Holden Torana A9X as entirely scripted. Brock and Richards drove just six laps each in qualifying, with Brock on pole almost a second clear of his first challenger, and Richards eager to have driven more laps. In the race Brock handed the car over to Richards when it was comfortably ahead, and it was still in front when Richards ended his spell, almost as if Brock had never left the car. The next year, when the combination won by an unprecedented six laps, Richards' value to the team was fully recognised. The ease of the win was no great surprise to Richards, since the

Torana was more powerful and easier to drive. Victory might not have been so easy though had not Richards eased the car through a treacherous period brought on by rain. Just as Richards started his stint, the rain started at the top of the circuit. It was among the most slippery conditions he had experienced. With the track virtually dry elsewhere it was a potentially lethal mixture, and it took all Richards' skill to negotiate the varied conditions.

His value to the team was underlined in 1980. It was the first year of the Holden Commodore (in this case a VC), a car that was in most areas better than the Torana, apart from its initial lack of power. The Commodore was being pressed by the Falcon XD of Dick Johnson and Chevrolet Camaro of Kevin Bartlett, and Brock tangled with a slower car as the big boys started lapping the back markers. It meant a visit to the pits to check the car's left-front corner. For the first time in three years the Holden Dealer Team

time. My wins with Mark Skaife in 1991 and '92 and 2002 mean a lot more to me.'

After 1980, Brock had extended the number of his wins at Bathurst to an impressive five. Richards freely acknowledged Brock's brilliance and imposing record as a driver and enjoyed his friendship, but Richards said Brock's reputation for being almost without peer in Australian motor racing and a great Australian was not the full picture. 'In his own way Peter is a major drama,' Richards said. 'He's a very complicated guy. He fell out with Holden and his friends over his [controversial] polariser concept, but time healed all that. Peter's quite an individual. He has his own ideas, he lives in his own world.'

Brock's army of fans still call him 'Peter Perfect', and, as Richards said, Brock has 'the gift of the gab', which helped in making him a legend, and in opening doors that might have been closed to others. 'He's still bigger than anyone in Aussie motor racing,

'I don't have really good memories of that time. My wins with Mark Skaife in 1991 and '92 and 2002 mean a lot more to me.'

was feeling some pressure, and Brock stayed in the car, slicing through a big chunk of Richards' middle shift, and getting dangerously close to using up all his allowed time at the wheel. Brock did not have the benefit of a significant lead when he finally pitted, and that meant that Richards could not afford to slacken the pace. For the first time, the team instructed him to 'go for it', and he loved it, setting the fastest lap till Brock pipped him by a 10th of a second. With Brock now too close to his driving-time limit the team decided not to risk being penalised for racing him too long, and Richards was at the wheel when the one-lap victory came — a new experience for him. It allowed the Kiwi to savour the exhilaration of the emotion-charged final lap when the wildly excited, banner-carrying Holden fans showed their appreciation of a job well done. 'Looking back over my career those three wins with Peter don't stand out,' Richards said. 'I was the co-driver in the best team. Any number of guys could have done the same job I did. I don't have really good memories of that

bigger even than [former Formula One champion and constructor] Jack Brabham.'

Brock and fellow V8 Supercar great Dick Johnson's courting of the media and sponsors, and their preparedness to be controversial has made them celebrities. Richards, however, has never sought publicity, often rejecting the opportunity to be interviewed or front a promotion, something he now admits might have cost him and his family financially. 'Some guys, like Peter, love to be in the public eye, but it's not me,' Richards said. 'I've not always felt comfortable. I preferred to let my driving do the talking for me. I'm happy when no one knows me. I like being able to go to the movies in a tee-shirt and tracksuit pants. I could have made more money had I been more publicity-conscious. At the end of the day I'm happy with, and proud of, what I've achieved.'

Richards is seen as a trailblazer in being the first New Zealander to make it big in Australian saloon and touring car racing. Typically, he does not see himself in that light. 'I've never felt I was paving the way for other Kiwis to make it in Australia,' Richards says simply. 'I like to think people have admired me for what I've done. I've just tried to do as well as I can. I always tried to be polite. Some worry about what others think of them. That's not me. All I've worried about since day one was driving a car as well as I could.'

Like son Steven, Richards still has a New Zealand passport, and has never felt the necessity to become a naturalised Australian. 'I've lived here [Australia] for over 30 years but I'm still on New Zealand's side when they play Australia,' Richards says proudly. 'People still talk of me as a Kiwi, and I've lived longer in Melbourne than I have in Auckland. I don't think it's held me back, if anything it's helped being seen as an international driver. I've always felt Australians have treated me as an equal but I still get a few sheep jokes.'

Richards doubted his profile or relations with people in motor sport would have been any different were he an Australian. 'I'm 58, and I've got sponsors who will stay with me as long as I continue to race,' he said. 'I've got no written contracts. It's all been done on a handshake, and I'm enjoying racing as much as ever. I'm not motivated by chasing records. It's more a love of racing hard. I'm thankful I still make a living out of it. I get a thrill out of coming to the workshop, and driving the truck thousands of kilometres around Australia.'

Richards said he could have made more money had he been a full-time mechanic and owned a service station. He did go in to business with a cousin, Ralph Jones, which proved a godsend financially. They bought a small Bob Jane T Mart franchise in 1978, which he retained till 1985, and he owned another between 1989 and 1991.

He ran with Brock twice more at Bathurst; in 1981, again in a Commodore, and in 1988 in a BMW M3. Their winning prospects in 1981 were ended by a long pit stop to fix a faulty axle and tighten a loose linkage, relegating them to a distant 21st. It was worse seven years later when Brock hit a tyre on Conrod Straight, which eventually led to the car's retirement.

Jim Richards racing a Winfield Holden Commodore for Fred Gibson's team in the early days of the new V8 era, after the Nissans were outlawed.

With touring cars the way of the future, rather than the hybrid sports sedans Richards loves so much, he welcomed the chance to join Frank Gardner's factory-backed BMW team full-time in 1982. It allowed him to tackle Holden and Ford's stranglehold on Australian touring car racing in a sophisticated European car. Richards had huge respect for Gardner, an Australian who raced Formula One in the 1960s and won numerous British and European touring car and single-seater titles. After a split with driver Allan Grice, Gardner made it clear that he saw Richards as the best candidate to replace him. At the age of 35, Richards found himself with his best-paying job since he'd been in motor racing. The partnership with Gardner lasted six years till the end of 1987 when BMW withdrew its support, and during that time Richards won the first two of his four Australian touring car titles — in 1985 and 1987.

The black-and-gold John Player Special BMW 635 took time to become competitive. Fortunately, BMW Australia and Gardner were realistic, understanding that the Australian group C regulations, which many considered unfair, made it

difficult for Richards. They assured him they were in for the long haul, and never put pressure on him to do any better. Their patience was borne out when the group C rules — which had required the 3.5-litre car to carry as much weight as a 5-litre Commodore (something Richards could never fathom) — were scrapped for the 1985 season in favour of the far more favourable international group A regulations.

Richards still managed a creditable fifth in his first full season of the Australian touring car championship in 1984. And the wait proved worth it the following year when the BMW 635 CSi suddenly became the car to beat. Richards took full advantage of the car's superiority, achieving a record six straight round victories in a golden period that has still to be equalled — and he also had a further four wins from five appearances in the later discontinued endurance series. It left him largely in a class of his own. He accumulated 233 points in the championship, beating Dick Johnson, who amassed 192 points for second place, with a decisive win in the penultimate round at Sydney's tight Amaroo Park track. It was the first time a European marque had

BMW drivers (from left) Denny Hulme, Jim Richards and Tony Longhurst 'view' themselves through a new video camera used to telecast the Bathurst 1000 km in 1984.

been the championship-winning car, and Richards was the first New Zealander to claim the title, a year before countryman Robbie Francevic.

One of his few blemishes in 1985 was the Bathurst round, where Richards and co-driver Tony Longhurst were fourth. That year The Great Race was won by a Jaguar XJS V12 run by Tom Walkinshaw. Richards led on Mount Panorama before a third of the distance had been completed when the thirsty Jaguars pitted. With the race capturing more world attention than before now that it was being run under international regulations, the fuel-efficient, ultra-reliable 635 was poised to strike. But it all turned sour when Richards had the misfortune to strike oil on the track, and slid off into a new sand trap at Hell Corner, which precedes the start-finish straight. Unfortunately, another car was already stuck in there, and Richards' attempt to drive through the trap met with no success. He was beached for four laps, and slipped back to 23rd place, before he and Longhurst managed a pretty useful salvage job in clawing their way back to fourth, which included setting the fastest lap. 'It was

one of my best opportunities to win at Bathurst,' Richards recalled. 'The car had been great all year, and we had everything going for us.'

It was Richards' belief that under the international regulations his team had provided him with the fastest 635 in the world at the time. It was difficult to make comparisons with the best group A BMWs from the northern hemisphere, but he gained a strong indication at Bathurst. The Schnitzer BMWs were setting the benchmark, and at Bathurst Richards' car was 'a lot quicker' than the Schnitzer one. Significant too was the fact that the new 635 for 1985 was down to 1185 kg under the new regulations, rather than being burdened with 1420 kg as it had been previously, significantly lighter than the Aussie V8s.

Richards' deeds were recognised by the Bavarian Motor Works in Munich, Germany. He was placed third-best performing BMW driver worldwide in 1985 on a points basis, and was invited to a vast concert hall in Munich to receive an achievement award. His accomplishment eclipsed two particularly worthy efforts, the Schnitzer team's victory at the

Fairfax Sunday Newspapers

A Jaguar XJS V12, similar to this one winning the Spa 24-hour race in Belgium, was victorious at Bathurst in 1985, raced by Scot Tom Walkinshaw's team.

Spa 24-hour in Belgium, and former world Formula One champion Nelson Piquet winning a grand prix in a Brabham BMW turbo.

Richards had a Kiwi team-mate in 1985, Sydney-based businessman Neville Crichton. Although he had been a long-time adversary of Richards in the New Zealand GTX production championship, the two had been partners in a Camaro drive in 1975, just before Richards left New Zealand. Crichton was now a fully-fledged, but paying, member of the John Player Special team, and to the shock of their rivals they started the championship in spectacular fashion at Winton with a one-two finish.

Richards was hugely grateful for the input of astute team boss Frank Gardner, who did all the painstaking testing on the car in pursuit of victory. Gardner's thoroughness and Richards' driving skills and calm in the heat of battle were never more apparent than in the win in the Castrol 500

Gardner had been closely following the exploits of the 635 in Europe, and had noted the occasional electrical fault. The culprit, according to a tip-off from Germany, was a potentially faulty relay in the wiring to the car's black box. The Gardner cars had never had such a failure, and the relays had never been changed since the car was built. Still, Gardner was not one to take any chances. The drivers were given a quick auto-electrical lesson, being told that should the car stop for any reason, they had to grab one of the spare relays in the glovebox, and replace the one being used. So it was that when the car stopped in the middle of the race, Richards did not panic. Although he had no clear idea of the problem, he remembered his boss's words. He dived into the glovebox and changed the relay. The car started, and he was back in the race.

Crichton was an encouraging fourth in the championship, one place above the colourful,

Gardner's thoroughness and Richards' driving skills and calm in the heat of battle were never more apparent ...

km at Sandown. Richards was closing in on the second-placed Peter Brock, just eight laps into the endurance race, when the engine cut out. It was the only time the seemingly bulletproof 635 had stopped all year, and here it had happened in the most important event to that stage of the season. It seemed Richards' race was over prematurely and he was marooned out on the circuit. Yet within a few minutes he was going again, having lost one and a half laps, and fallen back to 28th place. The car was going as if nothing had happened as Richards carved his way through the field in one of the better drives of his career. Within 30 laps he was just about in the top 10, and in another 30 he was back in third spot. Soon after, he was running second to the team's other BMW. Richards' partner, Longhurst, took over at halfway, and he passed the Crichton-George Fury 635 to complete an unlikely victory. What made the win possible was Gardner's attention to every detail, and Richards' poise when his race looked to have been run.

Auckland-based Robbie Francevic, who, in a Volvo, showed glimpses of the skills that were to carry him to the title the following year.

By the 1985 season's end Richards' competitors were starting to close the gap on him, and the arrival of faster Commodores, new Nissan Skyline turbos, and the factory-backed Volvo turbos, meant that Richards was on the back foot again in 1986. After his seven round wins in 1985, Richards managed just one win in the next 12 months — at Winton in the penultimate round, and only after the winning car, a Nissan, was disqualified for having illegal front brakes. He was simply outpaced by the turbos. His 147 points for third were light years behind the 217 points of Francevic in a Volvo 240T, and the 212 points of second-placed Fury, now in a Nissan.

The series was also notable for the appearance of another New Zealander, Graeme Crosby, who made a swift and successful transition to four wheels in a Holden Commodore after having been an outstanding world championship motorcyclist. The

Fairfax Sunday Newspapers: *NZ Truth* Collection

popular 'Croz' was sixth in the championship. Three other New Zealanders raced that year: David Oxton, who finished 17th; Neal Lowe, who came 23rd; and Andrew Bagnall, who placed 36th equal. Richards' season was made more meaningful, however, when he held off Fury to secure the endurance title — though the 635 was blown away by the speed of the frontrunners and only finished sixth at Bathurst (after starting from eighth on the grid).

With the 635 having become increasingly obsolete, Richards gained an edge again with the appearance in 1987 of the new BMW M3 — a smart machine, which achieved a distinguished record in international touring car racing. Though harried by the Nissans of the emerging Glenn Seton and old hand George Fury, Richards held his nerve to win a second Australian touring car title — achieving victories in four of the nine rounds, including three of the last four, when it counted most, at Surfers Paradise, and Sydney's Amaroo and Oran parks.

Richards remembered some drama in the concluding round at Oran Park. Seton held a three-point lead, which meant Richards had to finish ahead of him to grab the title. The Kiwi was being dragged off on the straight by the Nissans, and was trailing the pair. Not for the first time, Richards' ability to keep it together in the wet proved a winner when, with all the cars on slick dry-weather tyres, it started raining. 'The BMW handled the changed conditions more comfortably,' Richards said. 'I came from a fair way back. I was able to get by George [Fury] and finally young Glenn. I made contact with Glenn in passing him, and it was said I'd spoiled his chances of winning. It wasn't quite like that. Glenn dropped out when he blew a turbo.'

Richards' glowing reputation in the rain started from his very first appearance at Bathurst in 1974, when he was unfazed in the latter stages. In a barnstorming run he lifted to third, the Holden Torana he shared with fellow New Zealander Rod Coppins when other drivers struggled. 'People said my ability in the rain was because I came from New Zealand,' Richards said. 'It was a bit of a fallacy. We didn't race in the rain a lot in my time.' But Richards said he did have 'better results than most in the wet'.

Extrovert Aucklander Robbie Francevic, whose performances in a Volvo in 1986 wrested the Australian touring car title away from fellow Kiwi, Jim Richards.

Fairfax Sunday Newspapers: *NZ Truth* Collection

Jim Richards is all smiles in 1989 after making the smart career move to drive a Nissan Skyline.

It was not to do with driving style or technique, he said modestly. It was more about taking advantage of everything you can. His approach when it rained had a lot to do with remaining positive, when some drivers were less confident.

Despite the success, BMW decided to withdraw its factory support at the end of 1987, and there was a parting of the ways. Gardner, who Richards rated 'as good as anyone I drove for', dropped out. The two BMWs were taken over by Peter Brock, under Mobil sponsorship, during a period when Brock and Holden had fallen out. After six years a successful partnership was over, but it was one that Richards would always remember fondly. Gardner ran a slick operation, which included doing all the painstaking testing, something he had had much experience of in Europe, leaving Richards largely to just focus on the racing.

Though Richards still had a team in 1988, it became obvious that he needed to be in a faster car. He was fourth, just ahead of Brock in the touring car championship, which was dominated by the Ford Sierra RS500s of Dick Johnson and his new team-mate John Bowe. That pair were first and second respectively in the championship, winning eight of the nine rounds. Richards and Brock were together one last time at Bathurst, qualifying a modest 16th,

and retiring before halfway after Brock hit a tyre on Conrod Straight. 'The little BMW [M3] carried on a year too long,' Richards said. 'It was only 2.3 litres against the turbos of the Ford Sierras and the Nissans, and the V8s of the Holdens and Fords.'

Richards had been watching the development of the Japanese Nissans with considerable interest, and he grabbed the chance when team owner Fred Gibson, himself a Bathurst winner in 1967, offered him a full-time position from 1989 when Seton left to start his own Ford team. It was to be the start of an association that was to last seven years, and that was probably the best and most pleasing period of Richards' career — even with all the turmoil generated by the runaway success of the Nissans. 'I could have continued with Peter [Brock], who raced Sierras in 1989 and 1990,' Richards said. 'I received an offer but I decided to join Fred's team. It was a better offer, and I thought a better career move, and the Nissan appealed to me. It wasn't as competitive then, and Fred, who looked like he was going places, had the only Nissan team. It was before the arrival of the GTR, but I liked the challenge. I didn't want to be just another Sierra driver. There were now four or five teams running them.'

Richards said he didn't really know how good the Nissan would be. The Nissan HR 31 he drove in 1989 was only a two-rear-wheel drive, and the motor lacked the power of the Sierras. However, there was strong talk of a better car coming. That Nissan, the GTR, which had been built for Japan's group A racing, was a rocketship and Gibson had the good sense to realise that from an early stage. It so upset the fans of other makes, that when it started racing, the twin-turbo, four-wheel drive Skyline was disparagingly dubbed Godzilla (King of the Monsters). Richards and Mark Skaife were just about unbeatable for an extended period, particularly in 1991 and 1992. Richards earned his third Australian touring car title in 1990 and he retained it the following year. Skaife was second to Richards in 1991, and the positions were reversed when Skaife prevailed in 1992. The pair won Bathurst both years, and their reign only ended when the Nissans were thrown out for 1993, following fierce opposition from Holden, Ford and the other teams.

The GTR first appeared in June 1990, at Mallala in South Australia. As it was still on trial, and Richards was in a position to win the touring car title, Skaife drove it. But with the car making an immediate impression, Richards had one himself for the last two rounds. Going to Oran Park for the final round, the title was in the balance, with Peter Brock, Richards, Dick Johnson and Colin Bond still in contention. Richards, who was three points ahead of Johnson and 12 in front of Brock, ended the uncertainty when he qualified on pole and won the race to bury his opposition.

The hostility against the GTR reached its peak at Bathurst in 1992. Heavy rain resulted in the race being called off after a series of incidents, and although Richards and Skaife were among those whose cars had crashed, they were declared the winners. Fuelled by some derogatory comments from the second-placed Ford driver Dick Johnson, the fans turned ugly at the presentation. They greeted the announcement that Skaife and Richards had won with loud booing, prompting the normally mild-mannered Richards to utter the best remembered and most controversial words from the presentation balcony at Bathurst — 'you're a pack of arseholes'.

'I'm just really stunned for words. I can't believe the reception,' Richards was quoted as saying at the time. 'I thought Australian race fans had a lot more going [for them] than this. This is a bloody disgrace. This is going to remain with me for a long time. You're a pack of arseholes.'

Skaife and Richards were without doubt the winners, the rules clearly stating that when a race is red-flagged and cannot be restarted, the finishing positions are taken from before the carnage occurred. The safety car had been used earlier, but in this instance, with the race 75 per cent over, the rain intense, and so many cars having crashed, it was considered impossible to continue. Richards was driving at the time. At the top of the circuit he encountered a torrent of water, and the uncontrollable GTR slid in to a wall, breaking its left suspension. 'It

Jim Richards with his Nissan Skyline at the 1990 Wellington street race.

Fairfax Sunday Newspapers

was spitting rain climbing through The Cutting but when I got out of there it was just torrential,' he said at the time. 'It [the car] understeered straight into the wall. I could do nothing. Other cars had gone off where I did.' The track was in chaos. Three Holden Commodores and a Toyota Corolla had also hit a wall up the hill, and three other Holdens were stuck at nearby Forrest Elbow, and it was this that led to the appearance of the red flags. Richards had no idea that he had won. 'I expected a punch in the mouth [for crashing] when I got back [to the pits],' he said. 'Instead I was told we'd won.'

It was said that his inflammatory comments on the podium may have been further triggered by the death of one of his heroes, Denny Hulme, at Bathurst earlier in the day. Hulme died of a heart attack at the wheel of his BMW, somehow managing to drive his car safely off the track on Mountain Straight before slumping over the wheel. 'Denny was a fantastic guy and a great driver. I got to know him for the last 10 years of his life,' Richards says now. 'When I was in New Zealand he used to take me motorbike riding. During the race people had an inkling Denny might have died, but I didn't think about it till later. I shed a tear and had a drink to him. There were a few signs he had had a problem [with his health]. A few people knew. Had he done something about it, he might still be alive.'

More than 13 years later Richards regarded his outburst as completely out of character, and probably triggered by the extraordinary circumstances of the day. 'A few things came home afterwards. I'd never have talked about arseholes in public,' he said. 'It was more something I might say to some guy who'd just cut me off. We deserved to win. We'd been at the front all day. We were nearly a lap ahead of the second car a lot of the time, but the pace car would

'I expected a punch in the mouth (for crashing) when I got back (to the pits),' he said. 'Instead I was told we'd won.'

Photosport

Jim Richards (left) talking to Winfield team boss Fred Gibson.

come out [when the race was neutralised while the track was cleared following a race incident] allowing the other cars to catch up. At the prize-giving Dick Johnson knew the race rules but he still played up to the crowd asking: "How can a crashed car win?" The crowd was more pro-Ford than Nissan, some people were throwing cans at us, some were yelling and screaming. When it came time for me to speak I could hardly hear what I was saying. "It wasn't fair", I said, and with all the noise, and knowing Denny had died it all suddenly got to me. I laughed about it 10 minutes later. It was all good fun really. I wasn't too wound up.'

Skaife, however, was still upset with the crowd's behaviour, and said at the post-race press conference: 'I just felt that what we got out there wasn't warranted. I felt sorry for Dick [Johnson] and John [Bowe] — their car was running at the end, but rules are rules. Winners are grinners, and the rest can go to hell.'

Understandably, Richards' comments were not well received in some quarters. Nissan even received calls from people who said they would no longer consider buying one of its cars. However, Nissan managing director Leon Daphne remained steadfast in his support of Richards' stance. After all the hard work done by the team Richards was understandably unhappy that CAMS (the Confederation of Australian Motorsport) scrapped the international group A formula, which outlawed the rampant Nissan. 'At the time it was not a good decision, but in hindsight it was,' Richards said. 'Nissan didn't like it, but to be realistic the cars were twin-turbo and four-wheel drive. We were winning everything, most of the time easily, and the cars were expensive to run. The changes allowed Australia's two biggest manufacturers to compete on their own, and for more drivers and cars to be competitive.'

With the Nissans ineligible from 1993, Richards and Skaife raced Holden Commodores for Fred Gibson in the first three years of the new V8 formula, before Richards opted to end his full-time involvement. In that time, Skaife picked up a second touring car crown in 1994, and the pair were second at Bathurst in 1993 in a Commodore VP, similar to that of the winners, Larry Perkins and Gregg Hansford.

That second was yet another case of 'what might have been'. Richards was in the car for the last spell, and after 150 laps was 10 seconds behind Perkins, and closing in. He was within four seconds of Perkins when fate dealt him another heavy hand. A car spun in front of Richards, who was left with two options, one unpalatable, the other probably bad enough to ruin his victory prospects. He could either crash into the car, and end his race, or avoid it, and take the escape road. Not surprisingly he opted for the latter option, pulling up as quickly as possible in a puff of smoke, putting the car into a controlled, spinning U-turn, and haring back onto the track. 'That was our race. I didn't catch Larry. Even if I had it might have been difficult to get past him,' Richards said.

The two Bathurst wins with Gibson were far more special for Richards than the three earlier victories with Brock. 'I was a lead driver, not a co-driver as I was with Peter,' Richards recalled. 'It was the height of my career. We had fantastic times over the seven years. Mark, Fred and I became close friends. There was a lot of mutual respect. Fred was generous to a fault. He had two drivers who were as fast as each other. The team was a unit. Mark did all the testing, but I never felt I was coming in to just be the co-driver.'

Richards says Skaife 'would say' he had learned from him. Richards recalled: 'I was happy to tell him things to improve his performance . . . We talked all the time in those days. Mark was in his early 20s when I joined the team, and I was in my 40s.' The pair completed the 1000 km at Bathurst in 1991 in a record fastest time of 6h 19m 14.80s — a time which is still to be bettered. Richards rates Skaife as the best he's driven with or against, believing him to be more complete than any of the others.

In the early 1990s Skaife also found time to win the Formula Brabham Australian single-seater drivers' championship three years in a row.

Skaife has a huge regard for Richards as a driver and a person. 'In the mid- to late-1980s, Jim was arguably the best touring car driver in the world,' Skaife said. 'I learned a lot from him. I was a young bloke coming through and Jim was a superstar.

Mark Skaife, Jim Richards and Fred Gibson needed to be tight to survive the flak aimed at their nasty Nissan GTRs. The other teams were constantly griping about how unfair it was having to race against the three Nissans (Gibson's team had built another one for privateer Mark Gibbs to race). Teams even stayed away from meetings in protest at what they considered the lopsided competition — something they would not get away with today, when a no-show can cost a two-car team a fine of $A150,000 for each car.

By May 1991 Skaife and Richards were on fire with 1-2 finishes in the first five rounds of the championship, and Tony Longhurst only managed to break that monopoly in round six at Amaroo Park after Richards' engine packed up in practice and he was forced to start from last on the grid. Even then it was a close-run thing. Despite the handicap, Richards finished second, closing to within 1.6 seconds of Longhurst's BMW M3. CAMS became increasingly agitated, making the Nissans carry far more weight than any of the other cars — so much more in fact that cracks appeared on the cars' wheels, and stronger ones were required. The turbos were drastically de-tuned as well, but still the complaints continued. The situation wasn't helped either when Gibbs's car, on occasions faster than the factory pair, was third at Bathurst in 1991 and sixth a year later when he finished sixth in the touring car championship. In June 1992 an increasingly frustrated Gibson threatened legal action against CAMS.

Though the cars were harder to drive they were still invariably the frontrunners and it was decided as early as October 1991 that the Nissans and the Ford Sierra turbos would be ineligible when the V8 formula started in 1993.

He was very honest in telling me things. I've learned more from Richo in motor racing than from almost any other person. Though our ages are 20 years apart we could be brothers. We've never had a bad word in all the time we've been together. Jim's a beautiful guy. He has a soft, lovely nature but he's not like that in a car. He's the most tenacious and competitive guy I've been around once in the car.'

Skaife said that no matter what the state of the track, the day, or the weather, Richards 'knew the best way to get the best result'. Skaife's decision to continue to invite Richards to drive for his Holden Racing Team at Sandown and Bathurst was essentially based on his still superb driving skills, rather than any warm fuzzies surrounding their long friendship. 'We wouldn't have Richo back if he wasn't driving well,' Skaife said. 'You couldn't have a more sound guy to come and drive your car. He's the best driver in this region that's not doing it [Supercars] full-time.' In February 2006 Richards was confirmed to race again at Sandown and Bathurst for Skaife, this time alongside single-seater star Ryan Briscoe.

One of Richards' few racing attempts outside Australasia, in 1981, was a disaster. Australian Porsche detailer Alan Hamilton arranged for Richards, Peter Brock and Colin Bond to race a Porsche 924 turbo at the famous 24-hour endurance race at Le Mans, France. It sounded a hugely attractive opportunity. Unfortunately it was a rushed job, and Porsche's reputation for precision engineering and organisation, and cars of the highest calibre, took a battering on this occasion.

In fact it was so bad the drivers were unable to even qualify the car. 'The concept was brilliant, but the car wasn't ready,' Richards said. 'It was a prototype. It was still being bonneted together on the first day of practice. We couldn't change gear, and it broke a con rod. I only had two laps, and drove down the long, high-speed Mulsanne Straight at 100 kmh with the car jammed in third gear. We had a terrific time watching the race. It was probably better than if we'd had to drive all that time.'

Aside from his bizarre encounter with the kangaroo at Bathurst in 2004, Richards has had only two other serious accidents. While situations can occur that are out of a driver's control, that he has had so few bad experiences is largely testament to his driving ability. The first occasion was in the 1973 Heatway Rally in New Zealand's Southern Alps, when the 1800 cc Ford Escort he and his navigator Richard Halls were in encountered ice and snow on a mountain pass road, and slid off down a bank. Remarkably, they escaped without a scratch, but were left overnight in the pitch black and bitter cold. When they were picked up in daylight the car was still driveable despite the numerous dents. However, on closer inspection the pair realised how lucky they were. The car was perched precariously on a narrow mountain outcrop. Had their fall not been arrested when it was, they would have plummeted to their death down a steep slope that went 'forever'.

His second serious crash was at high speed in a NASCAR race on a banded oval at the Calder Park circuit, near Melbourne, in the mid-1990s. Richards suffered bruised ribs, and may have been momentarily knocked out when his car hit a wall, at a slight angle, at 200 kmh. 'My foot was flat on the accelerator, and I think I blacked out when the car hit the wall,' Richards said. 'The impact ripped the seat off its mountings. I've been pretty lucky. It reflects the preparation of the cars I've driven, and my attitude to racing. There are things that happen, though, that I can't control.'

Richards said he's never deliberately tried to drive opponents off the track — it's just not his style — and this has been borne out by his impeccable reputation as a driver. However, Richards said he was no pushover either. He was prepared to make contact with other cars to protect or enhance his position on the track, although with officials watching your every move these days, Richards said 'you have to make contact look fair to avoid a stop-go penalty' in the pits.

Hardly a Supercar round goes by without serious car damage caused by jousting drivers seeking an advantage, pushing the limits or being decidedly foolhardy. Richards is not surprised at the amount of contact given the level of competition. 'The competition is so tight. There can be not much more than a second between the 32 cars in qualifying,' Richards said. 'Ten years ago there'd have been five seconds between the fastest and the slowest cars. We also got away with more contact then, biff and barge. There are a lot more regulations now. It's harder to get away with anything, with three or four guys deciding whether you deserve a stop-go penalty. Sometimes the drivers are being impatient. The situation gets the better of them. It's tempting to lean on other cars. Most of the altercations take place through competitiveness and frustration, rather than people taking out other drivers.'

Richards does not pay any particular attention to his fitness but, like a number of the Supercar drivers, he enjoys the benefits of off-road motorbike riding. He has the stamina and condition to travel 100 to 150 km at a time on his Swedish purpose-built 550 cc Husaberg. Helping keeping him young at heart are

Jim Richards battling to control his Holden after it has left the track.

his four young grandchildren, Steven's son Clayton and daughter Priya, and Danielle's daughter Alaska and son Jett.

Understandably, Richards holds son Steven in high regard as a motor racer, and even believes him to be on a par with the best he has come across, Mark Skaife. With the Porsches on the same programme as the V8s, Richards has the opportunity to regularly watch his son at close quarters, and cast a critical eye over his performance. 'Steven taught himself to drive. It was nothing to do with me,' Richards said. 'He was a pretty late starter. He didn't start karting till he was 15. Till then he was into his soccer and cricket. He came to the races with me when he was quite small. He wasn't disadvantaged being my son. He's done all the hard work himself, and I'm very proud of what he's achieved.'

Richards has noted the similarities between his driving style and Steven's. 'He's calculated, he's hard, he thinks about it before he does it. He's not like a bull at a gate. His personality is like mine. He keeps out of trouble. He rarely makes a mistake. He's better than I was with the sponsors, he isn't a controversial figure. Maybe some of my attitude has rubbed off.'

Like his father, Steven is disappointed that the two have not been successful in their efforts to become the first father-and-son combination to win either of the classic Sandown and Bathurst endurance races. 'No doubt it would be special to have won with Dad,' Steven said. 'Motor racing is unique in that longevity in the sport allows someone like me the chance to drive with my father. Naturally, if you could share a great sporting moment, like winning Bathurst, it would be awesome.'

The 33-year-old Steven said he had been going to Bathurst since he was very little. 'It was our annual family holiday, and I never thought I'd ever be driving up there with my dad,' he said. 'I've been a part of almost all of Dad's Bathurst career from being dragged up there as a baby in a pram. Later, I wouldn't miss a Bathurst race. I was allowed to wander down to the pits, and watch from a discreet distance.'

'I've been a part of almost all of Dad's Bathurst career from being dragged up there as a baby in a pram.'

Jim (left) and Steven Richards, who were second in the 1000 km V8 race at Bathurst in 1997, their best result from three times driving together there.

Steven finds himself in a bit of a bind when talk of his nationality comes up. Though proud of his New Zealand background, and often being referred to as a Kiwi, the Auckland-born Richards feels more of an Australian. 'It's different for Dad. He has a strong allegiance to New Zealand,' Steven says. 'I was three when we moved to Aussie. I would be a bit embarrassed if I was dropped in the middle of New Zealand. I wouldn't know where I was. I know more about Australia. I still back the All Blacks when they play, and I've got relatives in New Zealand. It's a hard one for me. I try not to make a big thing of it.'

Steven is confident and articulate, and proud that despite his strong motor racing connections he stood on his own two feet much of the time in his formative years. When he started karting, after a friend of his father's offered him the opportunity to try one, he was on his own, racing at weekends while Dad was away earning his living as a professional driver. A number of his competitors would have their fathers to help them, but for young Steven it was often a case of having to work things out for himself. 'Dad helped me when he could. It was just that he wasn't around at weekends,' he said. 'I learned to look after my machine. It was tough, but it was still great fun. It still is. I've Dad's passion and love of the sport.'

Steven is unsure why it took so long for his motor racing involvement to become more than just being an avid supporter of his father's exploits. Perhaps it was because he pursued his own sporting interests, which included showing particular promise at cricket as a wicketkeeper-opening batsman. However, once he tried karting he was, in his own words, 'hooked'. Till then he did not realise the high level of interest he had in motor racing. When he graduated to Formula Fords in his late teens, he secured his own sponsorship, and his parents provided some financial help. During the day he would be studying to be an aircraft mechanic, and work on his car at night.

Despite so much of the family energy and resources being endlessly concentrated on motor racing, Steven can never remember his mother Fay complaining. 'Mum's been through all of it, and she's always been totally supportive of us,' Steven said. 'She once told me she was never nervous when Dad raced, but she felt a few nerves when I started. You forget the pressures you put on parents.' Steven said his parents went through tough times financially in the early days, at a time when money to go motor racing was hard to come by, and he was one of three small children.

Steven ended widespread speculation that he would replace the departing Marcos Ambrose in the SBR Ford team when he confirmed that he would be staying with Larry Perkins's long-standing Holden team for 2006. A possible move to SBR was triggered by some uncertainty about the Perkins team's future, following their loss of loyal sponsor Castrol. He said he was never looking to go anywhere else for 2006, that he was more than happy with the set-up in the Perkins team, though winning the touring car title continued to elude him. 'There's a little unfinished business there,' he said. 'I've won Bathurst twice, and it's one event on the programme. The title is the ultimate for me: 40-odd people in the team, all working for the same goal, over the full 13 rounds. I'm in a pretty good team. We can control our own destiny with 97 per cent of the work on the cars done in-house.'

His standing has been recognised with his chairing of the fledgling V8 drivers' association. He has worked hard for a couple of years to try and establish the organisation which, despite the formula having had fully professional participants since the outset, had been strangely lacking.

Steven ended a barren run in May 2005, when he won the third round at Perth's Barbagallo circuit. It was his first win since joining the Perkins team in 2002, and, despite scoring points consistently, his previous victory had been back in August 2000. However, after being a championship contender for some time he drifted off the pace, not helped by team-mate Paul Dumbrell crashing the car at Bathurst, which left them with no points from that race. A final position of seventh was not a fair reflection of his ability and standing.

With the dream of the father and son winning at Bathurst having faded nothing would give Jim greater pleasure now than for Steven to emulate him in winning the championship.

GREG MURPHY

A Man in a Hurry

Getty Images

Greg Murphy

Born: Hastings, 23 August 1972

Championship debut: Round 1, Calder, 1997

Starts: 102

Pole positions: 12

Round wins: 11 (includes three at Bathurst; four at Pukekohe)

Podium finishes: 35

Best championship finish: 2nd (2002, 2003)

Bathurst record: debut 1993; 13 starts, 8 finishes; best result: 1st
(1996 [not part of Supercar championship], 1999, 2003, 2004)

Greg Murphy's stellar motor racing career is encapsulated in one defining moment. It took just 2 min 6.8594 sec, and it set the Hawke's Bay-raised Kiwi apart from his largely Australian V8 Supercar colleagues. The occasion was the solo top 10 one-lap shootout at the Bob Jane T Marts 1000 km race at Bathurst's demanding Mount Panorama circuit on 11 October 2003. It was the first time a Supercar driver had bettered the 2 min 7 sec barrier for one tour of the celebrated 6.21 km New South Wales country track, and it sparked a reaction on pit lane that Murphy will treasure forever.

The Supercar series is a constant, thorough, and even bitter examination of the best that Australia's two biggest car manufacturers, Holden and Ford, can throw at each other. That rivalry becomes heightened within Bathurst's legendary precincts where ordinary seasons can be rescued by a spectacular result 'on the mountain', as Murphy's example vividly illustrated. He was experiencing a so-so campaign in his Kmart Holden Commodore VY, but on that October afternoon everything was turned around in an instant. His shootout time, one that helped determine the top 10 grid positions for the 1000 km race the following day, was so special it struck a chord with the teams, for a moment breaking down the deep divisions that exist between Ford and Holden.

As Murphy came back to the pits he was greeted with spontaneous applause and cheers, an unusually frank acknowledgement of his achievement from the teams. 'The reaction from the pits made the lap so unbelievably special,' Murphy recalled. 'To have that respect and the congratulations from your peers is what it is all about. They are the ones who know. That one lap is the highlight of my career. We'd been doing 2 min 7 sec times the day before, but next we do a 2 min 6 sec. It was huge. It left me thinking "where the hell did that time come from?" The fans appreciated it, and I even had the president of Ford Australia [Geoff Polites] come out and shake my hand. I felt on top of the world.'

Murphy's time was made even more astonishing by the fact that he missed a gear, selecting third instead of first exiting the corner known as the Dipper, as he worked his way down the hill. 'Missing a gear cost me two-tenths of a second,' he said. 'Without it I'd have been looking at a 2 min 6.6 sec lap. I'm still amazed at that lap, and seeing all of the teams standing out in pit lane applauding on my return is something I will never forget.'

As the top qualifier for the top 10 shootout Murphy had the honour of starting last, and when his turn to race came around he needed to better John Bowe's 2 min 7.9556 sec, set in a Ford Falcon, to be first on the grid the day after. He not only bettered the time, but did so by more than a full second. Bowe was among those to enthusiastically congratulate Murphy afterwards. 'Murph's was just a fantastic effort,' Bowe said at the time. 'To Greg, who's driven beautifully, and to the effort made by the guys in his team — how good is that? We are talking about over a second break on one of the most demanding circuits in the world.'

Bathurst 2003 turned out to be a wonderful weekend for Murphy. As he succinctly put it: 'We literally went from the outhouse to the penthouse'. This was in contrast to the previous year at Bathurst, which had been Murphy's darkest hour when he incurred a five-minute penalty for leaving the pit lane with the fuel hose connected. He regarded the penalty as grossly unfair and it had serious consequences. The extra five minutes meant his prospects of victory were ruined. And his chances of a win had been good as he and Todd Kelly, who had started from the third row of the grid, were holding the lead at the time of the sensational pit stop.

Twelve months on, Murphy and his co-driver Rick Kelly, Todd's younger brother, capitalised on Murphy's domination of the practice sessions and that marvellous shootout time to savour victory the following day. It was Murphy's third victory at Bathurst. 'Following the dramas of the previous year our team went back to the mountain singularly focused on achieving what we had missed out on in 2002, and it could not have gone any better,' Murphy said. 'From the time our team arrived in Bathurst on the Tuesday and the Kmart Commodore rolled out of the transporter for the first practice session, everything felt like it was meant to be. Our season to date had been difficult but in the most important week of the year for the Supercar fraternity

'. . . our team went back to the mountain singularly focused on achieving what we had missed out on in 2002 . . .'

Greg Murphy crosses the line first at Bathurst in 2003 to complete the greatest weekend of his motor racing career. The day before he had set the Supercar lap record — a time which was still standing three years later, in 2006.

Rick Kelly (left) and Greg Murphy celebrate after winning the Bathurst 1000 km for the second consecutive year, in 2004, in their Kmart Commodore.

everything went according to plan. My co-driver Rick Kelly tended to get a little lost in the media hype following that lap. But he drove superbly. His performance was faultless. He was just 20 at the time, the youngest winner of the Great Race.'

Even in the euphoria of victory Rick Kelly was still feeling disappointment that, for the second year in a row, circumstances had prevented his brother Todd from being on the podium. In 2002 Todd was a bystander when Murphy pulled away with the fuel hose still connected, and in 2003 Todd was again out of the car when his new partner Mark Skaife's Commodore was hit on the left-rear door by John Bowe's Falcon. The impact caused the door to flap open, and after seeming to ignore it, the scrutineers decided to black-flag Skaife. The enforced stop for repairs cost them a good opportunity of being on the podium, and perhaps even challenging the flying Murphy.

The Holden chassis he and Rick Kelly used that day, 043, has an extraordinary history. In a five-year period the V8 was driven by Holden greats Craig Lowndes, Mark Skaife and Murphy. Skaife used it to win the touring car championship in 2000 and 2001, and after HRT had sold it to Kmart in mid-2003, it carried Murphy to his special Bathurst victory a few months later. The car did not race in 2002 but was selected in 2003 for new HRT driver Todd Kelly, after the departing Jason Bright had taken his Holden to the re-formed Team Brock. Murphy got to drive 043 for the first time at Oran Park, after it was swiftly rebuilt by legendary fabricator Dencar. This was necessary as Todd Kelly had badly damaged it in a massive smash into the wall exiting turn one at Darwin's Hidden Valley circuit. HRT decided to replace the damaged car with a new Holden VY, and Kmart Racing bought 043 to replace Murphy's aging VX. Driving it, he was 11th at Oran Park, and third at the Sandown 500 km in the build-up to Bathurst. 'I'm not a romantic about race cars: they are a tool to do a job,' he said. 'But that chassis [043] served me very well. The best two minutes and six seconds of my life in a racing car were in that vehicle and I don't know if I will have that feeling again.'

It was intended that the chassis be a Kmart spare

in 2004. But it was dusted off again when Murphy began feeling exasperated with his car's performance after the first four championship rounds. It was a tough time for a disenchanted Murphy, who was soon to announce his plans to move to the Super Cheap Auto-sponsored Paul Weel Racing for 2005.

The mixed results continued for Murphy. After using chassis No. 044 in securing a second consecutive Bathurst win with Rick Kelly, he was back in 043 when he was victorious in the following championship round at Surfers Paradise and second at Tasmania's Symmons Plains.

The 2004 Bathurst triumph put the Kiwi in exalted company. It made Murphy a four-times victor alongside Skaife, and Allan Moffat, and only three drivers had won more often, the legendary Peter Brock (nine), the remarkably durable and popular New Zealander Jim Richards (seven), and Larry Perkins (six). Skaife took his tally to five in

Any mishap or mistake would have been fatal. It needed a cool head, and with Murphy desperate to salvage something from a mediocre series, having already declared his change of team for 2005, he seized the moment. With the car performing for once — something that has a lot to do with the team's understanding of how to set-up the car for Bathurst — Murphy calmly held off the less-fleet Fords. Ambrose was off the podium for once, having to accept fourth place.

The decisive moment occurred on lap 133, and it resulted from slick pit work by Murphy's Kmart Racing crew. Murphy entered the pit lane behind race leader John Bowe and second-placed Russell Ingall, both driving Fords, but emerged in first place. Craig Lowndes, in another Ford, tried unsuccessfully to run down Murphy, being pipped by only 9.57 seconds in the end.

Hugely important as Murphy's Bathurst wins

Craig Lowndes, in another Ford, tried unsuccessfully to run down Murphy, being pipped by only 9.57 seconds in the end.

2005 with victory in partnership with Todd Kelly.

The 2004 victory never scaled the heights of the year before but Murphy and Rick Kelly gave much-needed credibility to Holden's campaign. Though Holden won eight of the 13 rounds, including Murphy's Bathurst-Gold Coast double, it raced largely in the shadow of a Ford team — led by unassuming Kiwi brothers Jimmy and Ross Stone — that had everyone else scrambling in its wake. SBR drivers Marcos Ambrose and Russell Ingall were first and second in the Australian touring car championship, something HRT never achieved when Mark Skaife and Craig Lowndes were similarly superior, and Ambrose was consistently the dominant performer in a season that led to his second consecutive title. Ambrose's only conspicuous failure was at Bathurst when Murphy and Kelly were the lone Holden pairing in contention when it mattered. Although hounded by six pursuing Falcons intent on breaking Ford's drought there, Murphy extended Holden's Bathurst domination to six years.

have been to the success of his career and his standing in the formula, he is disappointed at Holden's attitude towards his achievements. Murphy has been among Holden's best drivers for years, probably second only to Mark Skaife, and he has been loyal to Holden when he could have crossed the great divide to the 'blue oval'. He feels let down and that his endeavours have not been fully appreciated. It leaves him wondering whether he was right to stay with Holden since first becoming a Supercar driver in 1995 for HRT.

'In the last few years I don't believe anyone has given more to Holden Motorsport than I have,' Murphy said. 'It's been quite tough. I don't believe Holden has given me the respect I deserve. I've had the chance to go to Ford for a lot more money. I've had a number of offers and I've always said "no". I've probably shown too much loyalty. I've been a bit foolish. Holden hasn't reciprocated my attitude toward them. I might have won an Australian touring car title by now if I'd gone to Ford.

Ford has invested a horrendous amount of dough in Russell Ingall, Jason Bright, Craig Lowndes and Marcos Ambrose. You do a lot better if you drive with them.'

After trailing Holden for years, Ford has recently smartened up its act. Its first big step was in snaring Holden darling, Lowndes, for the 2001 season. The ramifications were huge. Holden, and its incredulous fans, had lost their No. 1 man.

'Craig must have thought all his Christmases had come at once,' Murphy said. 'Ford looks after all its drivers. It's not Holden's policy to pay its drivers directly. It's left to the teams to top up the salaries. The position is quite difficult. It has created a lot of problems. It's widely known what dough drivers are getting [Bright and Lowndes were said to receive $A1 million each in 2005]. Holden drivers are saying, "Hold on, Ford want me. What are you going to offer?" I've not done a very good job in bargaining.'

Murphy said Holden thought it was a disaster when its flagship team, HRT, did not win Bathurst

in 2003 and 2004. It did not seem to matter, Murphy said, that he and Rick Kelly had won driving a Holden. 'We'd shut out Ford yet I never received a phone call or email from Holden to say "well done",' he said. 'It pisses you off. It makes you question why you don't go across. It was like you beat HRT, and that's not what we wanted. It makes it all a bit of a mockery. We're supposed to be on the same side, and yet Holden put so much more money into HRT.'

What makes Murphy's efforts even more remarkable was that he has mostly driven for significantly under-resourced Holden teams since ending his HRT days in 1998. He had two hard years with Fred Gibson Motorsport in 1999 and 2000, yet he and Steven Richards still delivered Gibson a Bathurst triumph in the first year. The next four years Murphy spent with Kmart, where the team rose above its circumstances to secure two Bathurst crowns, and he had a trying time with new team, Paul Weel Racing, in 2005.

Getty Images

Greg Murphy (left) and Steven Richards look apprehensive at Bathurst in 2000 as they prepare to defend their 1000 km title. They were third.

Mechanical failures cost Murphy a lot in 2005, contributing significantly to the worst full-time season of the eight he has driven in Supercars. Though he enhanced his stunning record at Pukekohe by winning his fourth round there in five years, and was still the first New Zealander in the championship, his final position of 11th was five places lower than his previous worst of sixth, a source of immense frustration for him.

However, he will be best remembered in 2005 for the wrong reason: his ugly confrontation with Ford's Marcos Ambrose on lap 145 of 161 at Bathurst after the pair collided at Griffins Bend on the way up the hill. The shaven-headed pair stripped off their helmets and fireproof balaclavas as they leapt from their cars, and in threatening fashion exchanged some heated words. It looked for a moment like they would come to blows.

Thankfully it was restricted to some finger waving,

but with the track blocked 11 following cars became involved in a pile-up and the repair bill was expected to run in to the millions of dollars. There had been some friction between Murphy and Ambrose, and it spilled over in this instance with neither driver prepared to give any ground as Ambrose attempted to pass Murphy on the outside. Before completing the manoeuvre Ambrose turned across in front of Murphy's Holden, which held its line, and the pair tangled. The momentum speared Ambrose's car into the wall, and for moment it looked as if it might flip over the barrier and down a steep slope. *The Australian* newspaper's front-page headline on 10 October 2005 read: 'Two hotheads crash and burn, leaving damage bill worth millions of dollars'.

Murphy, in search of a third straight Bathurst victory, said at the time he never felt there would be a punch-up, describing any such suggestion as 'pretty silly'. 'Two guys yelling and screaming is stupid

...he will be best remembered in 2005 for the wrong reason...

Getty Images

Greg Murphy's Holden tracking Marcos Ambrose's Ford at Bathurst in 2005. Later that day their aspirations were scuttled when they collided amid considerable acrimony.

enough,' he said. Typically the drivers blamed each other for the incident. Said Murphy: 'Marcos, as always, thinks he's in the right and everyone should give way to him, and move over and that's just not the case. He's got an ego problem that we all know about and that reared its ugly head again and I'm just not going to put up with it. I said he can bugger off and leave [to race in the United States in 2006]. I won't be crying about it.' Said Ambrose: 'Murphy made a mistake coming out of turn two and I had the momentum on him. As usual, nothing is Greg's fault and my reaction has to be pretty conservative. He had the chance to avoid the accident and he did not.'

A day later Murphy said he had 'stuffed up' on the previous corner, and at the next, Ambrose tried to pass him, and 'just carved across aggressively toward the apex [of the corner] as if I wasn't there. Our fate was sealed. I couldn't back out.' Ambrose said he

'We finished the year on a good note,' Murphy said. 'We shook hands and I wished him luck . . .'

had given Murphy racing room, turning across in a wide arc 'not to the apex', and 'you just can't drive in to somebody under those circumstances'.

The Confederation of Australian Motorsport investigation imposed no penalties, determining that it was unlikely to be clearly established whether there was a breach of the rules by either driver. One official observed that it was a difficult part of the circuit to overtake on. The incident again raised the question of racing etiquette, and recalled a time when the onus was on a passing car to complete the pass safely, and people did not run into each other the way they do today.

It was costly for both drivers in terms of the championship. Murphy was fourth and Ambrose fifth when Ambrose attempted the pass. Both were still well in contention for a top three finish and a place on the podium. With neither driver finishing, Ambrose lost his championship lead, which he never recovered, and for Murphy it was a second

successive round with no points, after an engine failure when holding third late in the Sandown 500 km in Melbourne.

Another V8 Supercar driver, Craig Baird, is a good friend of Murphy's. The families are part of a Kiwi motor racing contingent that likes to go on holiday each year. However, Baird wondered at the wisdom of Murphy's decision to maintain his driving line at the expense of colliding with Ambrose. 'The way the rule is written the guy [Murphy] was right but why should you take him [Ambrose] out,' Baird said. 'Why not just lift [the foot off the throttle] and have a crack at the next corner. Sometimes you have to give a guy room.' Baird noted that had Ambrose's car not been stopped by the wall the result would have been disastrous. 'I ran up there one day and looked over the wall,' he said. 'There's a 100 ft [33 metre] drop to a house and a tennis court.'

Naturally enough what occurred upset a number of people. Some blamed Murphy, among them team owner Mark Larkham, who said Murphy should pay for the repair bill on his car involved in the smash derby. Baird said Murphy came across sometimes as an 'angry young man' and even a 'hothead', and this was probably one of those occasions. But even amid all the anger, broken cars and mud-slinging that night at Bathurst — which somewhat overshadowed Mark Skaife and Todd Kelly extending Holden's number of victories there to seven in a row — there was still room for a touch of humour. The elimination of Ambrose allowed his Stone Brothers team-mate Russell Ingall to assume the championship lead, and a mischievous Ingall delighted in ringing Murphy to thank him for taking out Ambrose.

Murphy and Ambrose were later on much better terms. 'We finished the year on a good note,' Murphy said. 'We shook hands and I wished him luck [going to NASCAR in the United States] at the annual awards ceremony. He's taking a bit of a chance but he doesn't have any more to prove in Australia. I've not won a championship yet and he's won two.'

Greg Murphy's Super Cheap Holden running strongly in the early stages at Bathurst in 2005.

The 'Kick-ass Kids' Greg Murphy (left) and Craig Lowndes spraying the obligatory champagne after winning at Bathurst in 1996.

Murphy had always got on well with Ambrose and Ingall's joint boss Ross Stone, and despite what happened at Bathurst they remain friends. 'Everyone was disappointed, everyone was angry about it,' Murphy said. 'Ross and I took our time about making contact. There's no bad feeling between us. There's a lot of respect for each other.' In 1999 they had discussed the prospect of Murphy, who has lived in Melbourne for more than a decade, driving a Ford for Stone Brothers. 'I probably would have moved out there [to the Gold Coast] had Ford shown a bit more interest,' he said. 'Ford's attitude to looking after individual drivers changed soon after.' Murphy was also believed to be a contender to join the Stones in 2003 when they signed Ingall.

Murphy's victory at Pukekohe in 2005 was achieved using a package largely based on that used by Paul Weel Racing the previous year. However, from round six at Darwin's Hidden Valley track, the team had new Holden Motorsport, Perkins Engineering-built, engines, part of a three-year deal, which Murphy said were 'not on par with some of the other Holden engines'. On six occasions Murphy failed to finish races, effectively ending his championship aspirations. Although these included an excursion into the sand at Shanghai, which

Murphy took responsibility for, and the Bathurst debacle, he blamed the engines for a lot of the team's misfortunes. 'Had I finished in the positions I was fighting for at the time I was forced out I'd have been fighting for the championship,' he said.

Murphy first tasted Bathurst success in 1996. Craig Lowndes, then 22, and Murphy, 24, combined in an HRT VR Commodore, becoming the youngest pair to win there. Despite their inexperience, the pair had already won the Sandown 500 km shortly before, and Lowndes was just about untouchable that year in also being the youngest — 19 days before his 22nd birthday — to collect the Australian touring car title.

The New Zealander was amused by the television commentary delivered that day at Bathurst by former great Allan Moffat, a long-time Ford driver. His words suggested he did not have a particularly high regard for young Murphy's driving, and feared the worst for Murphy if he passed wily old Ford driver Dick Johnson, who had passed Murphy illegally under the cautionary yellow flag to take the lead.

The inference was that Johnson would regard it as an indignity, and Murphy, still very much a new boy, had better make a good job of it. Murphy, making his V8 racing debut at Bathurst after mechanical failure had eliminated the car the previous year before he had taken his turn at driving, safely completed the manoeuvre, and left Johnson in his wake. Moffat was left to begrudgingly offer a few compliments. He said it was to Murphy's credit that he handed the car back to Lowndes when it was still leading, and he spoke of the 'prowess' of the Holdens.

Though Murphy refers to his four Bathurst victories as 'all being fantastic', 2003 was clearly the pinnacle. With his fiercely competitive nature he still hates the thought of lost opportunities at Bathurst, and, in particular, the five-minute penalty in 2002 remains an open sore. It rankles with Murphy that the blame was largely aimed at him, and he struggles to accept that the pit foul-up was serious enough to warrant such a severe sentence.

Todd Kelly entered the pits in the lead on lap 71 ready to vacate the driver's seat. Everything seemed to be going smoothly till the Kmart Holden was dropped off its jacks with the car still taking on fuel. As is customary, once the car's wheels touch the ground the driver pulls away, and this is exactly what Murphy did. He left, dragging the hose with him, and it was several metres before he was alerted and stopped. To the pit crew's dismay fuel was spilled everywhere, and the atmosphere was tense till the fire marshals began spraying containment foam. There was no fire, and Murphy left to join the race.

The stop lasted 15 seconds, and allowed Steven Richards to take the lead. Murphy set out in pursuit of Richards, and was about to recover the lead when there was a call over the cars' radios that No. 51 (Murphy) had been given a five-minute penalty.

It was said to be the harshest penalty for a pit lane infringement in Australian motor sport history. Murphy could not believe it. With his team insisting it was true, Murphy reluctantly pitted on lap 81 to serve his sentence. He told crew chief Rob Crawford that he wanted to withdraw the car, that it was pointless to continue with the race effectively over for him and Kelly. While it most certainly was, Murphy was third in the championship at that stage, and there were still valuable points to be competed for. Murphy parked in the pit lane, leapt out of the car and the air turned blue as he stormed to the back of the team garage. He was enraged, and sought the sanctuary of the team's portaloo. He locked the door, and vented his frustration by kicking the plastic walls of the toilet with his driving shoes. When the five minutes were finally up, Murphy was two laps down on the leaders and in 28th place halfway through the race. He and Kelly improved to a final placing of 13th.

Murphy was still seething afterwards. 'It was a

It was said to be the harshest penalty for a pit lane infringement in Australian motor sport history.

Alastair Ritchie

Greg Murphy skating along over the 'mountain' at Bathurst in 1996.

despicable act. It was an attack on our team and me,' Murphy said. 'It was unfair and ridiculous. It ruined our race. There was a lot of misinformation at the time. They [the officials] did not look at the incident properly.' Whether the penalty was appropriate was highly contentious. Murphy believed it would have been more fair to have had a 'stop and go' drive through the pits, and be 'seriously fined'. 'People who looked at it sensibly thought the five-minute penalty was over the top,' he said.

Certainly the Kmart crew was to blame, and Murphy singled out car controller Barry Ryan. 'Our procedure was just like the other teams, it wasn't flawed,' Murphy said. 'Our car controller didn't do his job. I take no blame for it. Our car was dropped by mistake by the air jack man when Barry was in the team bunker looking at the race on TV. It was his job to determine that everything was done properly.'

Murphy likened the penalty to another he received in 2003 at Winton. He incurred a drive-through-the-pits penalty for nudging Craig Lowndes off the circuit. The decision was widely criticised because Murphy's in-car camera clearly showed Lowndes's Falcon was about to spin off the track before contact was made, and Lowndes confirmed this. 'The officials ruined my race,' he said. 'It was unfair. They were wrong and they wouldn't admit it. It was frustrating because what occurred was out of my control, and it damaged my championship chances.'

Murphy is generally satisfied he has made a 'good career in motor racing'. 'I've put a lot in to get where

On occasions he has been unbeatable, driving with breath-taking brilliance, inspired by a wildly cheering crowd.

Greg Murphy's Holden belches flame as it successfully fends off the attentions of Mark Skaife's Commodore at Pukekohe in 2001. Murphy won all three heats on his way to outright victory in the first Supercar round in New Zealand.

I have,' he said. 'Plenty would give a lot for what I've got. I'm never happy, but four Bathurst wins is pretty good. Sitting back and watching the race in the mid-1980s I never thought it would be like that.'

Murphy is married to a New Zealander, Monique, who has been studying for a degree in child psychology. They have two young sons: Ronan, now at school and already fascinated by cars, and Cormac. He is one of the most widely recognised drivers in Supercars as a result of his racing deeds and his willingness to interact with fans. He is also generally respected for his forthright comments, and certainly for his exceptional results.

Many Australians hardly think of Murphy as a New Zealander — he is one of the most experienced drivers in the formula, has a tough, Australian-like attitude in always wanting to be the best, and has also lived there for 12 years. But his reputation for standing up for himself and his team-mates has not always endeared him to officialdom, nor to some of the other drivers.

On the other side of the Tasman Murphy is very much the face of Holden and Supercars, whether it be racing, appearing in television advertisements and programmes such as TVNZ's 'Game of Two Halves', or making articulate and often provocative comments in the media, writing newspaper and magazine columns, and furthering causes, such as road safety, about which he is passionate. With his strong personality and direct approach it is no wonder that he has a sizeable and adoring fan base.

Last year Holden acknowledged his impact and outstanding contribution to New Zealand motor sport with a limited-edition phantom black Commodore dedicated to Murphy. It was badged the 2005 Murph Special Edition, priced at $NZ96,900, and limited to 22 cars exclusively in New Zealand. It was powered by a six-litre Chevrolet V8 engine, and based on the high-performance Holden Special Vehicle Clubsport R8.

His 'home' profile has been hugely enhanced by his wonderful record in the New Zealand round. He has been almost bulletproof, maximising his knowledge of the circuit and the patriotic support to win four of the five Supercar rounds at Pukekohe

Getty Images

An excited Greg Murphy dances on the bonnet of his Kmart Commodore after his clean sweep at Pukekohe in 2001.

since the first in 2001. On occasions he has been unbeatable, driving with breathtaking brilliance, inspired by a wildly cheering crowd.

He has a reputation for wearing his heart on his sleeve, and for speaking with passion, clarity, and even bluntness. One is never left in any doubt about what 'Murph' is thinking. He does not employ a manager, preferring to rely on himself, and invariably his hugely supportive father, Kevin Murphy, to put his deals together.

Kevin managed Greg's career through its formative years, and remains a steadying influence. He is the managing director of Greg Murphy Racing, which has run a number of Porsches in the Carrera Cup, and is the managing director of ambitious V8 Supercar team Tasman Motorsport.

Though Murphy is set to become one of the Supercar greats he still wonders whether he might have realised his dream of racing in Formula One had things been done a little differently. From his earliest days Murphy had his heart set on a career in single-seaters, with F1 the ultimate challenge. He came to realise that for him the cost of getting there was too high.

Murphy had his first taste of racing at the age of eight, when his father Kevin took him karting. It was the start of bigger things and after leaving Havelock North High School Murphy won a NZ$65,000 Shell scholarship that enabled him to compete in the 1990–1991 Formula Ford championship. Aiming to be no lower on the points table than fifth, he demonstrated the value of the scholarship by finishing third. He continued racing with some success in the following years, but his biggest early success came when he won the New Zealand Grand Prix at Manfeild in 1994.

Murphy used the momentum created by that summer's success to contest the 1994 Formula Brabham Australian drivers' championship in a Ralt, with help from long-time Auckland driver, team manager and motoring magazine editor Mark Petch. Heartbreakingly, a gearbox failure in the final round at Sydney's Oran Park cost Murphy the championship, which he had been leading till then. He continued to attract the attention of influential motor sport people. His performances in the Ralt paved the way for participation in the emerging Australian two-litre super touring car championship

Greg Murphy in a Reynard Brabham, which he drove to victory in the New Zealand Grand Prix at Manfeild in 1994.

in a new Toyota Carina, and a first appearance at Australia's most famous circuit, Bathurst.

Englishman James Kaye had raced a similar car in the British touring car championship, and he partnered Murphy in the 1994 1000 km race, the last occasion the two-litre tourers competed alongside the flaming V8s. Murphy was initially blown away by how steep 'the mountain looked in the flesh' after having only seen it on television. Once he started racing though, it didn't feel as steep. He was becoming more familiar with touring cars too, having made a pleasing transition in his debut in Petch's spiteful Ford Sierra Cosworth turbo in the 1992 Nissan-Mobil series with fourths at Wellington and Pukekohe. Murphy had found the ill-handling Sierra a real wrestling match, likening it to 'a bus with a rocket engine strapped to it'.

Capitalising on the downpour at the start at Bathurst, Murphy had the little Toyota just about in the top 10 after the first lap, and he continued to hassle the V8s till the circuit dried out, and the bigger cars' superior horsepower allowed them to pull away. Then complications occurred when the Toyota suffered a broken fuel line. After losing time to fix it, Murphy and Kaye had to be satisfied with a final position of 23rd, completing 136 of the 161 laps.

Murphy's attempt to retain his New Zealand Grand Prix crown in January 1995 ended in sickening fashion at Manfeild. A crash at 200 kmh had those first on the scene fearing he was dead. It happened after six laps, when the brakes on his Formula Brabham Reynard suddenly failed. Murphy found nothing when he applied the pedal and the car went through a fence and was launched three to five metres off the ground after hitting a tyre wall. He flew over a bank, and was fortunate that a few pine trees helped cushion the impact of the fall. Looking at the scattered debris there was huge relief for the crowd of 12,000 when Murphy was found to be largely uninjured. Remarkably all the impact did was leave him winded, suffering from a sore back, although he had badly bitten his tongue.

At the time Murphy was completely in control of the race, having already established a 15 second lead. It was later discovered that a vibration had resulted

Greg Murphy sufficiently enhanced his reputation in Australia driving this Audi super tourer to be invited to test for the Holden Racing Team in 1995.

in a loose brake nipple popping free, and with the loss of the necessary brake fluid Murphy became a helpless passenger. The Manfeild crash was the first major one he had, and happily it remains the worst. Like Murphy, the car came through comparatively unscathed, allowing an increasingly bored Murphy to win the national series against opposition who lacked the skill or machinery to extend him. Murphy was ready for something better in single-seaters, but most of 1995 was spent racing an Audi in the Australian super touring car series where his final position of fourth would have been better had he not been hampered by having to follow team orders.

Murphy was totally unprepared when HRT team manager Jeff Grech rang him at his Sydney flat in 1995 to invite him to a test at Melbourne's Calder track. He thought one of his mates was playing a joke on him. His scepticism suddenly turned to delight when he realised the call was for real. Murphy had been making his presence felt racing the Audi and had approached some V8 teams about the prospect of being a backup driver for the endurance races at Sandown and Bathurst. He didn't have the nerve to approach HRT, regarding the team as a bit out of his league.

HRT showed plenty of confidence in Murphy. After rain made the Calder test inconclusive he was invited to another at Victoria's Phillip Island circuit, which went rather better. He was signed to partner Craig Lowndes, a combination that was to bear fruit in 1996 when they excelled in securing the Sandown-Bathurst double. Not surprisingly Murphy found being a member of such an illustrious team 'an eye-opener'. Lowndes's huge potential was already evident, and the team's other full-time driver was none other than the most famous V8 driver in Australia, Peter Brock.

'I felt confident because the team had confidence in me,' Murphy remembered. 'My first time at Bathurst in a V8 in 1995 was pretty daunting. I was trying a lot harder, and still not getting out of it what I wanted. I wasn't happy with myself. I didn't think it was good enough. I'd mostly raced single-seaters so there were a number of adjustments to make. It was hard to get used to V8s. I didn't feel

were high. Though only 12 Aussie V8s crossed the Tasman, it was a high-quality field with Ford, Holden and series organiser Mobil New Zealand only too aware of the marketing and sales opportunities the races represented. HRT had cars for Murphy and Peter Brock (the latter just about as big a name in New Zealand as his homeland), there were Coke-sponsored Commodores for former world motorcycle champion Wayne Gardner and Neil Crompton, Castrol Commodores for Larry Perkins and Russell Ingall; and the Kiwi Stone brothers had Ford Falcons for a past Formula One champion Alan Jones, and the only other New Zealand driver involved, Paul Radisich. The formidable Dick Johnson, John Bowe, Glenn Seton and Tony Longhurst were also all in Fords.

More than 30,000 fans were at Pukekohe on race day, and the Wellington streets reputedly attracted well over 50,000 for the two days' racing — evoking memories of the numbers who attended the single-

The elation of Greg Murphy's first outings for HRT . . . quickly disappeared when their pacy Commodore failed them.

comfortable in one till Bathurst and the Mobil series in New Zealand the following year, by which time I was fully attuned to them.'

The elation of Greg Murphy's first outings for HRT, partnering Lowndes, quickly disappeared when their pacy Commodore failed them. Lowndes's polished efforts to put the car on pole at Sandown and Bathurst came to nothing when there was a differential problem at the former race, and the motor blew up at the latter race after half an hour, and before Murphy had had any time behind the wheel.

Though it would be 2001 before New Zealand had a Supercar round, the two Mobil events in 1996, at Pukekohe and on the Wellington city streets, were huge for Murphy. His standing in New Zealand was suddenly enhanced by his first victory at Bathurst, and he was in a position to capitalise on that. People who knew little or nothing about Murphy wanted to know more, and expectations

seater Tasman series in the 1960s, when some of the biggest names in Formula One were attracted Down Under to race against New Zealand's world championship participants Denny Hulme, Bruce McLaren and Chris Amon. Murphy more than lived up to his new-found status in winning all three 20-lap sprints at Pukekohe. And then in Wellington he was first in heat three, and became the series victor. He drove the VR Commodore, affectionately known as 'Gabriel', which had been supreme in 1996, carrying Craig Lowndes to championship victory, and he and Murphy had driven the same car in winning the endurance races at Sandown and Bathurst. Lowndes was originally to drive it in New Zealand till there were complications over his Formula 3000 testing for 1997. Murphy proved a more than able substitute. In fact, Lowndes would have been hard pushed to better Murphy's stunning performances.

Sadly it was the last year of the series, and the end of street racing in Wellington. However, the heightened awareness of motor racing created by Murphy, and the success of the series, made the various parties in New Zealand even more determined to host a full round of the Supercar championship. Wellington was not just where Murphy clinched the series win. That weekend he also signed a one-year contract with HRT for his debut full-time season in Supercars in 1997, the year which was to be Brock's last.

Murphy described Brock's announcement of his retirement following the Eastern Creek round in Sydney as 'very emotional'. 'It was a privilege to race in the same team as Brock,' Murphy said. Brock was still attracting huge numbers of fans, and the team would invariably be running late with Brock keen to acknowledge the heartfelt best wishes of the hero worshippers. The Kiwi learned a lot from Brock about how to treat the media and the public, which has served him well.

Murphy's 1996 also featured a second in the GT2 class in a Porsche at the historic Le Mans 24-hour race (where he was racing for Aucklander Bill Farmer's team to celebrate the overall victory of New Zealanders Bruce McLaren and Chris Amon

30 years previously), and continued good super touring car drives across the Tasman in a more potent Audi A4 Quattro.

After safely completing the middle stint in the Sandown triumph that year, Murphy had his first V8 race experience at Bathurst on lap 45, with the track still drying after a downpour shortly before the start. Despite Dick Johnson illegally taking the lead off Murphy when the yellow flags were out, commentator Allan Moffat's questioning of Murphy's ability, and the pressure not to do anything to ruin HRT's prospects of winning, he excelled. The car was still leading when he handed it back to Lowndes, and it was the same when Murphy again vacated the driving seat to allow Lowndes, already the Australian touring car champion, the honour of receiving the chequered flag.

Murphy found it an ordeal sitting in the team pit for the closing laps. The previous year Glenn Seton was leading when his Ford broke down less than 10 laps from home. Murphy was so wound up as Lowndes completed the race that he could hardly watch the television monitor. He felt such

Photosport

Greg Murphy's encouraging first full season for the Holden Racing Team in 1997 counted for little when he was dropped.

elation when Lowndes completed the task that he was moved to tears as the team celebrated. It was Holden's 17th victory there, and the youngest driving combination in the race's history ended the run of the older generation of drivers, led by Peter Brock, who had dominated at Bathurst for many years. The Sandown-Bathurst double rightly reinforced Lowndes and Murphy's label as the 'Kick-Ass Kids'.

Once the assembled horde was dampened by the victory champagne, and the Holden fans had wildly cheered their young guns, Murphy sought out his father Kevin, the biggest influence in his career. As they hugged it was clear the financial sacrifices Kevin had made, and the begging and borrowing he'd had to do to further Greg's motor racing aspirations, were more than worth it. When Murphy and Lowndes returned to the team's headquarters in Melbourne, there was a letter of congratulations from Australian Prime Minister John Howard, a rare honour for a New Zealander.

Murphy was buoyed by his results and his growing stature in Australia, but it did not cloud his vision of the future. He remained firmly focused on single-seaters, and the dream was to drive in Formula One. Though he had the option of a long-term deal with HRT, Murphy chose a one-year contract, with the aim of competing in the US in 1998. After Lowndes failed to crack it in European Formula 3000 in 1997, Murphy became more convinced the best pathway was via the United States. That year he went there for an Indycar test. The venue was Putnam Park, a fast road circuit near the legendary motor racing city of Indianapolis, scene of the Indianapolis 500, the biggest event on the US single-seater calendar. The test went well, so well in fact that he was offered a few laps in a full-blown Indycar in the CART world series, a Reynard-Cosworth. Murphy's time in an Indy Lights Lola was almost two seconds faster than the lap record, and this stunned the people assessing his performance. It took just six laps in the 750 bhp car, massively faster

Getty Images

Eventual victor Simon Wills leads the black car of Greg Murphy (two cars back) at the 1998 New Zealand Grand Prix at Ruapuna. Murphy's winning prospects were ended when rain contributed to him running off the track.

and more powerful than the Formula Brabham he'd been driving, to convince Murphy that this was what he wanted once his 1997 contract with the Holden Racing Team was completed.

A few months later he received a written offer from the Project Indy team. In principle it was generous. It would meet two-thirds of the massive $A9.24 million budget, leaving Murphy to find the rest, $A3.08 million. More than a third of this amount was due in three weeks, and the balance was to follow in another 10 weeks. Not surprisingly, Murphy's frantic efforts to put something together proved fruitless. It was not the end of the matter though. In December 1998 he had another Indy Lights test in Phoenix, Arizona.

It came amid a packed schedule in various parts of the world, and to Murphy's disappointment he did not perform as hoped. He'd just rushed from

through with. I've not played some political games the way some have, the lies and deceit. It could still be a lot worse though.'

HRT knew of Murphy's aspirations in single-seaters but it still came as a withering blow to Murphy when HRT boss John Crennan rang a couple of weeks before Christmas in 1997 to say his services were not required for the following year. He went from being the team's lead driver in 1997, ahead of the legendary Peter Brock, who was in his farewell season, and Lowndes, who was racing Formula 3000 in Europe, to one largely relegated to the sidelines. At the age of 25 Murphy's career was in limbo.

HRT was then owned by Tom Walkinshaw Racing and Lowndes had a 10-year contract with him. When Lowndes's single-seater campaign failed to gain traction he suddenly became available to return

Had Murphy signed the extended deal with HRT in 1996, Skaife would not have been an option for 1998.

driving a Formula Holden Reynard at Invercargill's Teretonga track against rising star Scott Dixon, and instead of going on to France from Arizona to test a Renault Laguna for a possible stint driving in the British touring car championship for Formula One team owner Frank Williams, Murphy had to hare back to New Zealand for the Grand Prix at the Ruapuna circuit in Christchurch. On a wet track Murphy's victory chances ended at the second corner, and immediately afterwards he was back at the Christchurch airport bound for France. Though Murphy tried hard, on a demanding track and in icy conditions, nothing eventuated there either. 'I did everything I could [to get set-up in the US], and it was not enough,' Murphy said. 'We were always a long way away [financially]. It came down to money rather than ability. I had shown I was good enough to be competitive there. I don't believe I've made all the right decisions. I don't dwell on it. Some annoy me a bit. Sometimes I've been too loyal and trusting. People tell you what they want you to hear, they tell you stuff they have no intention of following

to V8s, and with the contract in force a place had to be found for him. The second position in the team would go to either Mark Skaife or Murphy. Skaife was more experienced but Murphy's first season of full-time V8 racing was a promising one. He qualified on pole four times, and won three rounds of the championship, plus the Sandown 500 km (with Lowndes) before it was included in the series. Skaife won out, and went on to achieve great things, including securing a hat-trick of Australian touring car championships and taking over ownership of the team. Lowndes was similarly dynamic in winning the touring car title in 1998 and 1999.

Had Murphy signed the extended deal with HRT in 1996, Skaife would not have been an option for 1998. Given that HRT set the standards on pit lane for years, it is hard to believe that Murphy's results would not have been greatly superior to those he gained. He might well have gained an elusive touring car championship.

Though he was no longer fully employed by HRT he was not dumped altogether. He was offered work testing the new VT Commodore, and he was signed to drive in the long-distance Sandown and Bathurst races. It was still hard going. One of the fastest and most talented drivers in Australasia was being under-utilised. After the kudos that went with driving full-time for HRT his career had lost its considerable momentum.

Despite Murphy's numerous glory days since leaving HRT, one is still left with a feeling he has been trying to play catch-up ever since. That phone call from Crennan has had huge significance.

With his cherished ambition of a Formula One drive now in tatters, his only option for 1999 was to sign for Fred Gibson's Wynn's Holden team alongside Steven Richards. But he was shocked to observe an operation he found totally inferior to the immaculate Holden Racing Team. Murphy regarded most of the season as a dead loss. His win in the first race at Symmons Plains, Tasmania, was the first for

Murphy made one last bid to break in to US single-seater racing at the end of 1999 . . .

Gibson in five years. The season had a silver lining at Bathurst, which for the first time counted for the Australian touring car title.

Gibson had a superior pairing in Murphy and Richards, and over the 1000 km it helped negate the better car preparation of HRT. On the day, the biggest obstacle to a Gibson victory was the Ford Falcon of Kiwi Paul Radisich and Australian battler Steve Ellery. Radisich led with 20 laps remaining, only to clip a slower car in a passing manoeuvre. The resultant damage forced Radisich to bring his car in for repairs, and it was eventually retired. That cleared the way for Richards to safely negotiate the closing laps. He completed the job in the Commodore VT, 25.32 seconds ahead of HRT's Craig Lowndes. 'I don't believe it. This is a fairytale after what we've been through this year. It's hard to fathom,' Murphy said at the time. 'It makes up for the All Blacks not winning the World Cup, and winning at Bathurst is better than a bloody rugby game.'

Murphy qualified 12th on the starting grid and the car led briefly mid-race but did not go to the front again till Ellery pulled in to the pits 30 laps from home. Radisich, now back in the car, recovered the lead from Richards four laps before his accident. The elation of victory against the odds had Murphy screaming in delight as Richards flashed across the line, and he derived a huge feeling of satisfaction after the repeated frustrations and knock-backs of the last two years.

Murphy made one last bid to break into US single-seater racing at the end of 1999, being among half a dozen drivers invited to test for leading Indy Lights outfit Team Doricott in California. This time Murphy did his racing talents justice, but, as previously, the financial demands appeared to be out of reach. He needed to find $US800,000 to be on the team. By now there were other factors to consider. Whereas he was being paid to race in Australia, in America he would be heavily in debt. Neither did he want to risk damaging his relationship with the woman who would eventually become his wife, Monique Van Resseghem. He was now 27, probably a bit late to still be striving to break in to top-line single-seaters. Though it meant the Formula One dreams were finally put to bed, once he had made up his mind Murphy was happy racing Supercars, particularly having won twice in four years at Bathurst.

Murphy had greater V8 options for 2000. Brothers Jimmy and Ross Stone were enthusiastic in wanting Murphy to race for their Ford team (before it became the raging success it did from 2003 onwards), and Garry Dumbrell, who now owned the Gibson Holden outfit, wanted to sign him as well. A change to Ford would have been a radical move for Murphy, but in retrospect it is a step he might well have wished he'd taken. Had he moved, it would have been to replace Jason Bright, who tried Indy Lights in 2000 (a decision that only lasted the year), to fill the spot later taken by Craig Baird. But Murphy remained unsure of how keen Ford's director of motor sport operations, Howard Marsden, was on him switching, and Dumbrell convinced him that the Holden team would have greater resources.

The team's fortunes did not change much, and Murphy's most pleasing effort in 2000 was to coax an overheating Commodore to third at Bathurst, again alongside Steven Richards.

What occurred next angered Murphy, and it required the assistance of sponsor Kmart, and the Holden Racing Team's leading racing executives Jeff Grech and John Crennan to keep him in Supercars. Without consulting his drivers, Dumbrell sold the team back to Gibson, who was going to race Holden's No. 1 pin-up boy, Craig Lowndes, in a Ford. Murphy and Richards suddenly found themselves cast adrift, and Lowndes's decision to defect to the opposition left the massive Holden fan base incredulous, and enraged the many people at HRT who had nurtured his talent and provided him with every advantage.

Never lacking in initiative, Murphy set about trying to salvage something. After Richards secured a Ford drive at Tickford Racing, Murphy discovered Kmart, who had sponsored the Dumbrell team in 2000, was as upset as he was, and was keen to stay

involved. He approached a crestfallen Grech to find out whether Holden might still be prepared to build a Holden team around him.

What followed in 2001 was much better than Murphy had had before. He was now part of a Kmart Holden team closely aligned to HRT. Though he and new team-mate Todd Kelly had cars already raced by HRT, in Murphy's case Lowndes's former car, they still remained highly competitive. Murphy and Kelly were challenging for the lead at Bathurst till a badly timed pit stop during a pace car period ended their hopes. Instead of being second, they found themselves ninth. Murphy made a mad dash over the last 30 laps. He ran out of time and had to be satisfied with finishing third.

His resounding three wins out of three races at Pukekohe's first Supercar round in November 2001, and fourth place in the championship, left Murphy well satisfied considering his predicament at the start of the year. There was an improvement to a career-best championship second in 2002, which again included a round victory at Pukekohe. Without the controversial

Greg Murphy (left) and Steven Richards can hardly believe it as they shout their delight at winning Bathurst in 1999.

five-minute penalty at Bathurst he might well have managed to score that elusive championship.

Murphy was again a victim of the sometimes volatile nature of Supercar teams in 2003. Tom Walkinshaw Racing, then owners of HRT and Kmart teams, was in receivership following the collapse of Walkinshaw's Formula One operation, and Holden Australia had to buy the teams to save them from being two more victims of the debacle.

Holden's involvement created problems among the formula's ruling bodies, whose rules prevented manufacturers from being team owners without special permission. After much unrest, which severely limited Kmart's preparation for 2003, Mark Skaife bought HRT, and Margaret and John Kelly, the parents of drivers Todd and Rick Kelly, purchased Kmart. However, the Kellys' decision took a long time to be ratified, and in the interim the team was limited to one testing day, which placed it at a distinct disadvantage to its competitors.

option. But it was poor timing, as after committing to his new team, the things he had strived for at his former outfit finally started to happen. He was left looking over his shoulder as his new team stuttered along, and yet again he slid out of championship contention. Meanwhile, the man who replaced him at Kmart, big Garth Tander, started to piece together some encouraging results. He was sixth in the championship, whereas Murphy was 11th.

'My move to PWR was the right one at the time,' Murphy says. 'But then the changes finally come at Kmart and you think "what the hell?", and are left scratching your head wondering why things happen. I left Kmart because good results were few and far between, and the team was badly underfunded. The car was very inconsistent in 2003 and 2004. I still won two rounds [Pukekohe and Bathurst] and I was second at Indy [Gold Coast] in 2003, but it was worse in 2004. We were shocking in qualifying, being well outside the top 10 on occasions. It can be

Without the controversial five-minute penalty at Bathurst he might well have managed to score that elusive championship.

Murphy's dogged competitiveness allowed him to become a title contender in 2003 with victories in the 043 chassis at Bathurst, and for the third year in succession at his beloved Pukekohe, a second at Surfers Paradise, and third with Rick Kelly in the Sandown 500 km.

His hot October, successive victories at Bathurst and Surfers, allowed Murphy to convert a potentially less than memorable 2004 into something more substantial. Fourth place in the championship failed to disguise his growing frustration at being unable to be consistently competitive enough to mount a sustained challenge for the title, again won by Ford's formidable Marcos Ambrose.

When Murphy left Kmart, which became the Holden Special Vehicle (HSV) Dealer Team in 2005, he was searching for something better. After four years of pushing for improvements in the invariably struggling Kmart team, Murphy had had enough. The Paul Weel team looked a better

disillusioning not being at the front of the field. I go to Super Cheap and HSV becomes the old Kmart team, and it all changes, there's more resources, everything goes the way it's supposed to go. It's pretty annoying. We had no new people with new ideas at Kmart. Now the team has the money and new staff. You are left asking why life can't work the way it's supposed to for a little while. HSV and Tander get their act together and I'm writing off another touring car title. You only get so many shots at it.'

Murphy believes he *is* 'perceived as a Kiwi' in Australia 'not that it has worked against me. I've been treated really well by Aussies,' he says. He makes no apology either for his approach, which has often been interpreted as being very Australian.

'If I wanted to be successful I couldn't sit around and wait for someone to come to me,' he said. 'My

Greg Murphy joins the 'greats' at Bathurst in 2004 as he wins his fourth 1000 km event there, and his second in succession.

Greg Murphy has had some distinctly acrimonious run-ins with fellow V8 drivers, among them Russell Ingall and Marcos Ambrose. Ambrose's abrasive approach ran foul of officialdom and a number of his fellow drivers in 2004 and 2005, resulting in penalties, and Murphy has not been afraid to tackle him about it publicly. And earlier, in 1997, he and Ingall had become 'sworn enemies' after a race at Melbourne's Calder track when he felt Ingall's repeated whacks from behind were completely unfair, yet they went unpunished.

Ingall, who later moved from Holden to Ford, and Murphy have patched up their friendship, and any reservations about Ambrose's attitude, even after Bathurst in 2005, do not prejudice the Kiwi's admiration of his driving skills. And this is despite an incident with Murphy's then team-mate, Rick Kelly, in the Gold Coast round in 2004. Kelly was in trouble when he punted Ambrose's team-mate Ingall off the circuit in race one. He was penalised for it, and in the second race he upset Ambrose by sticking right behind him, and declining to pass when offered opportunities.

Ambrose showed his annoyance after the chequered flag by braking hard in front of Kelly, and the Kmart team also protested that Ambrose confronted and threatened Kelly afterwards. Ambrose was subsequently found guilty of careless driving, and the post-race media conference became testy when Ambrose declined to answer questions on why he braked suddenly.

Murphy, who had won the round, wasn't happy with Ambrose's reticence, and used the conference to tell Ambrose what he thought. 'I wasn't upset with Marcos,' Murphy said. 'I was offended by his attitude. Who did he think he was? It was like people had no right to get in his way. He tried to pass it off as nothing what he did to Rick. He thought he should get away with it. It was a red rag to a bull for me. He was not being entirely truthful and he knew it. I was the only one prepared to talk about it.'

Murphy was disappointed that Ambrose departed at the end of 2005 to see whether he could foot it in another form of 'tin-top' racing, the helter-skelter NASCAR on oval banked tracks in the United States, where he would be initially racing trucks.

'He's a great driver, he's done a pretty good job with two championships and a third in three years,' Murphy said. 'His ego at times has got too big. It's a pity he's gone, but good on him. I'd prefer he was still in the championship. If I win in 2006 people will be saying it doesn't mean as much because Marcos wasn't there. He and the Stone brothers have done a great job. He's very much an individual.'

attitude was I had to make sure I did enough to make people notice me. At the end of the day I've not got a rich dad or anything else to fall back on. I don't have a lot of other skills.

'It makes you appreciate what you're able to achieve. *I* don't think I'm like an Australian. Some people don't like my attitude. That's life. I have to respect people's opinion. I don't always agree with it. A lot of people don't want you to have opinions because it conflicts with their own.'

The scenario could hardly be more perfect, a V8 Supercar round in New Zealand and a dominant Kiwi winner in Greg Murphy. He loves racing at Pukekohe, and the hordes of petrol-heads who attend love him unconditionally. It doesn't seem to matter whether they are Holden or Ford fans, as long as Murphy is lording it over the Australians. The steadfastly loyal Holden driver freely acknowledges the lift they give him. He can hardly do any wrong at Pukekohe. It's as close as it gets to watching someone walk on water. It's a marketing dream.

'Nothing fires me up more than racing in front of my home crowd,' Murphy says. 'It's the people that make the difference. Whether the fans are wearing red [for Holden] or blue [for Ford] I feel their support and best wishes. There's not a better feeling than being a Kiwi and all those people at Pukekohe willing me to victory. I can hear their cheers over all the noise in the car. With all that expectation and pressure the hardest thing is to keep your concentration and not make a mistake.'

Murphy has made the picturesque 2.82 km circuit, 40 km south of Auckland city, his own domain since the start of the V8 era in 2001. He has an extraordinary nine individual race wins in 15 heats, highlighted by all three in 2001 and 2005, and four round wins over the last five years in the Australian touring car championship, three of these in succession from 2001 to 2003. It is a record of achievement at one venue that places him among the best performers since the V8 formula started in 1993.

Back in 1996 a televison commentator dubbed

Pukekohe 'Murph's Turf' after he stunned the opposition by winning all three sprint races of a one-off non-championship V8 series in New Zealand. Not surprisingly, the label stuck, and as Murphy has continued to enhance his glowing record at Pukekohe it has become increasingly relevant. In 1996 Murphy was very much a new boy in V8s, and for much of the year was not widely known among New Zealand sports followers. He had yet to earn a full-time contract and was only engaged by the Holden Racing Team to partner Holden's budding superstar, Craig Lowndes, in the Sandown and Bathurst endurance races, which did not have championship status till 1999.

However, all that changed in spectacular fashion. Young guns Lowndes and Murphy upset the older brigade by grabbing the Sandown-Bathurst double, and suddenly Murphy was hot property. He only raced in what was to be the last of the annual Mobil series at Pukekohe, and on the streets of Wellington, when Lowndes became unavailable. Despite the field being limited to 12 cars, the first time the V8s had raced on their own in the series, it contained all the big names. There were Holdens for Murphy's team-mate Peter Brock, Larry Perkins and Russell Ingall,

and Fords for Dick Johnson, Glenn Seton, John Bowe and another New Zealander, Paul Radisich.

Though Murphy had made his debut at Pukekohe in 1990 in a Formula Ford, this was the first time he felt the support that has made him feel so special there. He won the first heat from pole position without another car in sight; then, after a scrap with Seton, he won the second with a blistered tyre about to give up; and when the car's superior speed carried him to a stunning third victory, the crowd erupted. Afterwards Murphy was enveloped by jubilant spectators. It was the start of what has become hero worship. 'That success had a huge bearing on my career,' he said. 'It put it in front of New Zealanders and put the sport back on the main board there.' The crowds were huge, evoking memories of the sport's heyday, when Formula One champions would be attracted to the annual summer single-seater series that included the New Zealand Grand Prix at

He loves racing at Pukekohe, and the hordes of petrol-heads who attend love him unconditionally.

The terraces are packed with many adoring Greg Murphy fans along the start-finish straight at Pukekohe in 2005. He did not let them down when he won all three heats.

With the four round victories at Pukekohe making up more than a third of Greg Murphy's 11 championship round successes it is easy to understand why he has such an abiding love for the place. Three of Murphy's round wins are at the Bathurst 1000 km, the other venue for which Murphy has a special affinity. He has actually won there on four occasions, but his first victory there, in 1996, was prior to the 'Great Race' being included in the championship. His other round victories have come at Surfers Paradise, Tasmania's Symmons Plains, Oran Park in Sydney, and at one venue no longer used, Mallala Raceway, near Adelaide. He also had victories in the Sandown 500 km, in 1996 and 1997, before it too became a championship race.

Getty Images

Auckland promoter Dean Calvert, who has worked hard to ensure the longevity and continued success of the Pukekohe round.

Ardmore, and later Pukekohe, and gave weight to the contention that New Zealand could host a round of the V8 championship. The following weekend in Wellington he signed a full-time contract with HRT. Though Murphy deliberately limited the deal to just one year, in order to keep his single-seater aspirations open, he was to be the team's No. 1 driver for 1997 with Lowndes contesting Formula 3000 in Europe.

By the time AVESCO, now simply V8 Supercars Australia, and the IMG were ready to bring a full round to Pukekohe in 2001, Murphy was firmly established among the series stars. He had won a second Bathurst 1000 km in 1999, had finished fourth in the championship in 1997 and sixth in 1999 and 2000, and in 2001, prior to the penultimate round at Pukekohe in November, he had been placed third in five other rounds.

Auckland promoter Dean Calvert, in those days working for IMG, said that despite the undoubted interest in Supercars among New Zealanders, it was still a 'big punt' to bring the series to Pukekohe. 'No one knew how popular it would be,' he said. 'The budget started off really low, but it kept changing every day once the round was announced in November 2000.'

The crowds were huge that first weekend, more than justifying the decision to take the series off-shore for the first time. Overall around 86,000 people attended, with more than 40,000 of those coming on the Sunday, a number only rugby tests could compete with in New Zealand. The crowds were to continue, with 80,000 in 2002, a record 93,000 in 2003, a drop to 76,000 in 2004 when it rained and the circuit was flooded, and a return to 85,000 in 2005, with again around 40,000 of them coming along on the Sunday.

Undoubtedly many of those fans returned to Pukekohe to see Murphy, who scored his impressive run of three wins in three years from 2001 to 2003. Murphy gave himself the ideal start in 2001 by claiming pole position, just as he had when the V8s were last at Pukekohe five years previously. However, after rain and an accident, the first heat was stopped prematurely, and initially the crashed Mark Larkham was declared the winner. Murphy's Kmart team

---

protested, and it took considerable time before the officials changed their decision and declared Murphy the winner. His victories in the following day's two heats were far more straightforward. The excited round victor leapt onto the bonnet of his Commodore with both arms above his head in a salute to the crowd, which applauded wildly.

His 2002 Pukekohe victory, and the opportunity it created to spray champagne over anyone in the vicinity, was in stark contrast to the anger he'd felt at Bathurst a few weeks earlier when his strong winning prospects were ruined by a five-minute penalty for leaving the pits with the fuel hose still connected to his car. He was experiencing the mind-blowing intense highs and shattering lows of a professional racing driver. Though Murphy won just the second of the three heats this time, the overall victory at Pukekohe allowed him to jump to second in the championship, and he retained that position when he was second overall at the final round at Sandown.

Soon after his clinical Bathurst triumph in 2003, Murphy completed his remarkable Pukekohe hat-trick in his Kmart Holden with victories in heats one and two and a third in race three, which moved him to within six points of Marcos Ambrose's championship lead, with one round remaining. He was brilliant in the wet in winning the first race on the Saturday. On the Sunday Murphy was troubled by tyre wear, and took full advantage of late safety car periods, after separate incidents involving Paul Dumbrell and Garth Tander, to secure the first of the two races. He was still left with a seven-lap sprint to the finish with Mark Skaife and Todd Kelly in hot pursuit, but it was Skaife's tyres which didn't last, allowing Murphy to ease home. Skaife and Jason Bright jumped Murphy at the start of race three but third place was still good enough to make it a memorable weekend for Murphy. 'It's quite unbelievable. I think I talked myself into thinking it was not going to happen before I got here, but it's all sort of surreal,' Murphy said at the time. 'I'm just blown away by the whole thing. We didn't have the best car today, and I really battled with tyre wear, much more than we thought.'

A smiling Greg Murphy holds up three fingers at Pukekohe in 2003 to signify a third successive round victory there.

Murphy's best chance of capturing the championship, in the season finale at Sydney's Eastern Creek track, became a non-event when he hurt his back on the Sunday morning, doing a handbrake slide in the VB Challenge, a fun event where two drivers, one from each of the rival Holden and Ford camps, test their speed, co-ordination and awesome car-handling skills in clouds of blue tyre-smoke. It prevented him racing in the second and third heats, and for the second year in a row he was second.

Pukekohe 2004 marked the first time Murphy had not won the round, his grip there being finally loosened by consistent Holden driver Jason Bright, who started with a second and won the last two races. For a time there was uncertainty whether there would be any racing at all. It rained all Saturday and till late on the Sunday morning, requiring teams to make a hasty return to the track late on Saturday night to save cars and equipment from the rising waters. There was no racing on Saturday, and Sunday's programme had to be hastily rescheduled. Three 36-lap heats, with no compulsory pit stops, were squeezed in, and after qualifying third, Murphy's placings of a fourth and

two seconds were insufficient to better Bright and the second-placed Marcos Ambrose. Amazingly, the crowd still reached 76,000 that often miserable weekend. Thousands had sat in the rain for hours on the Saturday in the hope of seeing some racing, particularly that involving Murphy. 'It was a tough day, the Sunday,' Murphy recalled. 'I drove really hard, and could still only finish third.'

For 2005 Murphy moved from the under-performing Kmart Holden team to Paul Weel Racing, replacing the team-hopping Jason Bright, in the hope it would bring him the car consistency he so desperately sought. When he came to Pukekohe for round two, it was with a degree of sadness, especially among the New Zealanders. After five years, this was to be the last of the V8 Supercar racing at Pukekohe. The contract was not being renewed as the general facilities were the poorest in the championship. They were substantially short of what was expected by the all-important corporates, and the women's toilets were particularly uninviting.

Though there was dismay that the Auckland street race bid had failed for 2006, there still appeared to be a good chance there would be a street race in Wellington.

Dirk Klynsmith/Graphic Dak Photography

Greg Murphy might be contemplating whether he made the right move to Paul Weel Racing in 2005 as he prepares to race.

It provided the New Zealanders with even more incentive to perform, and with his VZ Commodore on song, Murphy hardly missed a beat in winning a fourth round at Pukekohe, even when the conditions became treacherous in the early evening on Sunday.

There had been a race to have the track sealed beforehand. It had to be done a second time when the first effort was not deemed to be of the required standard, and the dodgy drainage was also improved. The track's reputation for being dumpy was reduced, and the grippy new surface improved the lap times. By the end of the weekend Murphy had the lap record, but by his own admission he should have started from pole. A mistake in the top 10 shootout relegated him to fourth on the grid.

It mattered little, as Murphy won Saturday's heat in style, keeping out of a tussle between Marcos Ambrose and Craig Lowndes, and showing welcome car speed. On Sunday, he was similarly convincing in winning race one after getting past Russell Ingall at the hairpin, and he held his nerve in the gloom and drizzle experienced in the second event, which was delayed for more than 30 minutes after a horrifying crash on pit straight. Spectators gasped as Craig Baird's Ford Falcon was slammed backwards into the inside fence at more than 200 kmh after a clash that also involved the cars of Paul Dumbrell and Cameron McConville. While the track was being cleared and barriers repaired, Murphy changed to wet-weather tyres, and he was in a class of his own when the race restarted for the final 16 laps. With headlights blazing he crossed the finish line first for a weekend clean sweep.

'The conditions were interesting. I'd have preferred the last race to be called off,' Murphy said. 'But it was a fantastic feeling to win those races at home again.'

The hold-up upset Television New Zealand's coverage, and a decision had to be made whether to cut off the third race before it had finished or risk upsetting a wider viewing audience by delaying the news. TVNZ stayed with the motor racing, delaying the six o'clock news by seven minutes, and long-time Shell Helix Motorsport producer, David Turner, said it was shown to be justified. 'We got away with it, driven by the success of Greg Murphy,' Turner

Greg Murphy holding his nerve in tricky conditions at Pukekohe in 2005 with Russell Ingall on his tail. It enabled Murphy to complete an unblemished round, when he was first in all three heats.

. . . this was to be the last of the V8 Supercar racing at Pukekohe . . .

said. 'A phenomenal event was unfolding. We had 500,000 viewers at the end. There'd been a big crash, it was dark, it was raining and the track was greasy. We'd have been stupid to have gone off.'

Murphy maintained his support for the track, and said if no other venue was found he could not see why the Supercars could not return to Pukekohe. When the Wellington street race proposal also fell over, Pukekohe was the only option if the V8s were to have a presence in New Zealand. He was delighted when it was agreed that there would be a round there for a further two years while another venue was found. Pukekohe remains the third most successful V8 round in terms of spectator numbers behind the Clipsal 500 km in Adelaide and Bathurst, and excluding the Gold Coast round which is run in conjunction with the Indycars.

'At the Darwin round I told Supercars chairman, Tony Cochrane, how important it was for New Zealand to continue to have a round. And I expressed my concerns about suggestions this might not be the case,' Murphy said. 'I had him on about being anti-Pukekohe, and told him he was wrong to blow up about the facilities.' He described Pukekohe as an 'exciting, full-on' circuit with its high-speed corners, long back straight, hairpin, and two blind bends, the first at turn one, and the other coming over the hill just before the start-finish line, which the visiting V8 drivers enjoyed. The only drawbacks, he said, were that it was too short, at 2.82 km, and the facilities were run down.

Murphy loves to compete, he's very much an in-your-face type, and with the Pukekohe faithful ever eager to inspire their man to greater glory, the normally tranquil south Auckland venue will continue to be the place where he is most likely to perform at his best.

Murphy, who learned to fly a helicopter in 2005, is not big on role models, and he was not mentored, but there have been motor racing people who have fired his imagination. When he was young and racing karts he 'used to think Peter Brock was pretty

Zealand. 'The flag is very easily mistaken for others, especially, and frustratingly, the Australian flag,' he says. 'We are from a small country we should be immensely proud of. Our flag should stand out from the others, one that people recognise on its own merit.' He remains the No. 1 flag-bearer for New Zealand V8 fans. His 11 round victories are far superior to the results of the other full-time Kiwi drivers, but when he looks at his career overall, he doesn't regard it as extraordinary.

Murphy's biggest motivation remains the elusive touring car title; his best efforts in eight full seasons being second places in 2002 and 2003. To better that requires a consistency of team performance that he experienced at HRT in 1997. None of the teams he has been with since then have been of that standard. 'It is extremely tough, a never-ending pursuit for me, which is not getting any easier,' he said. 'The decision to bring in a reverse grid for the second race at each three-race round in 2006 is making it a

'The decision to bring in a reverse grid for the second race at each three-race round in 2006 is making it a lottery . . .'

amazing' and he rated British Formula One racer Jim Clark highly. One person who stands out for Murphy, though, is New Zealander Bruce McLaren.

Murphy has a large painting of McLaren overlooking the staircase at his Greg Murphy Racing garage and offices in Melbourne. Though McLaren died at the wheel, testing one of his cars at England's Goodwood track in June 1970, his racing and engineering legacy remains, with McLaren cars still among the leaders on the Formula One grid.

'Bruce was a great New Zealander,' Murphy said. 'As a driver he won Grand Prix races, and he built his own sports cars and single-seaters. What he achieved is largely forgotten, but it says a lot for him that cars bearing his name are still winning at the highest level 35 years after his death.' Although Murphy is 'still a proud Kiwi' it can be confusing in Australia at times, with the flags of the two countries being so similar. He is very much an advocate of a flag that is more strongly representative of New

lottery, not a true championship.' With 2005 team-mate Paul Weel retiring to concentrate on running the Super Cheap Auto business, Murphy was joined by the experienced Cameron McConville from Garry Rogers Motorsport in 2006. He has sound credentials, having won the Winton round in 2004 and been second at Bathurst in 1999, despite not always being in competitive cars.

Murphy's future beyond 2006 remains a little unclear. He declined to say how long his present contract was for, and was happy for people to speculate on when he might join his father at the increasingly competitive Tasman Motorsport, which was set-up with him very much in mind. 'It is pretty obvious I'll be going there one day,' he said. 'It's just a question of when it will be.'

Greg Murphy snugly buckled into his Super Cheap Holden just before the start of the top 10 shootout at Bathurst in 2005. He was third.

PAUL RADISICH

Unfulfilled Potential

Getty Images

Paul Radisich

Born: Auckland, 10 October 1962

Championship debut: Round 1, Eastern Creek, 1999

Starts: 91

Pole positions: 2

Round wins: 3 (last, round 9, Queensland 500, 2001
(with Steve Johnson))

Podium finishes: 11

Best championship finish: 4th (2000)

Bathurst record: debut 1988; 15 starts, 6 finishes; best result,
second (1990, 2000)

If talent was all that mattered, little Paul Radisich might well have realised his dream of following his great hero, Denny Hulme, into Formula One. Certainly, drivers of inferior ability have secured a seat in motor sport's ultimate competition. Radisich, who had an encouraging 14th placing in the 2005 championship in his first campaign with New Zealand-based TKR, always hoped that his driving skill, and catching the attention of the right people at the right time, would open the door to the opportunity of a Formula One test drive. At one time Ford was heavily involved in Formula One, and there was a hint that Radisich's victory in the FIA world touring car championship, driving a Ford Mondeo, would lead to something. Sadly, it never did. He needed more than results. He needed considerable money and he needed people prepared to back him in the long-term way United States-based New Zealander Scott Dixon has been supported in his quest towards driving in Formula One by a group headed by energetic Aucklander, Peter (PJ) Johnston.

Radisich survived on his talent through 12 years of hand-to-mouth existence in single-seaters in New Zealand, Australia, England and the United States before the Formula One dream petered out. He finally accepted the greater financial security of racing touring cars in England, and though there was some talk of a possible Ford test, it was probably too late anyway, with Radisich being aged around 30 at the time.

Radisich isn't one to labour the point. There's a strong feeling that it is now a long time ago, the mid-1990s, and he has moved on. Touring cars in England and Australia have been his lot since 1993, and till TKR successfully wooed him in late 2004, Radisich was seriously considering going back to England — his wife Patricia's home country — to race sports cars.

His career in touring car racing started spectacularly when he secured the FIA World Cup titles in 1993 and 1994. It was a career high. A New Zealander with a limited profile, he upset the best of Europe's touring car drivers — a number of whom had raced in Formula One, or were to — at the famous ultra-fast Italian track of Monza.

The modest, quietly spoken Radisich came to Australia for the 1999 V8 Supercar season with high hopes after the two-litre British touring car scene had lost some of its impetus, and his Peugeot 106 had become uncompetitive, leading to his team's withdrawal. By the levels of excellence Radisich set himself, it hadn't really worked out despite some pleasing results with Dick Johnson's Shell Helix Racing team, till the move to TKR, and the support of Paul Morris Motorsports, offered Radisich perhaps a last opportunity to recharge his career.

Radisich's father, Frank Radisich, himself a pretty competent racer and car builder, has no doubts about his son's ability to have made a good fist of Formula One. 'On his day, Paul was quite capable of it,' Frank said. 'He was let down through a lack of funds. Heaps of guys have got there because they had the money to buy their way in, and Paul didn't. He was usually quicker than whoever he was racing against. He used to beat his team-mate Damon Hill all the time in Formula Three in England, and Damon went on to be world Formula One champion.'

Frank also loves to recall Paul excelling on a Detroit street circuit competing in the American Super Vee single-seater series in the late 1980s. Paul was on pole for a supporting event at the Formula One United States Grand Prix, and the track announcer made it all too plain that he didn't rate Paul's prospects of victory. 'The announcer said it was a fluke Paul was on pole, and he'd be blown away in the race,' Frank said. 'Paul made a superb start. He disappeared in the dust. The others never saw him. He won easily. It was a tough circuit. There were 25–30 corners.'

The next day Paul shared a full page of motor racing in the *USA Today* newspaper with the grand prix winner, Brazilian great Ayrton Senna, who tragically died at the wheel in the San Marino Grand Prix at Imola, Italy, in 1994.

Over two seasons Radisich had seven victories in Super Vee, similar to Formula Three, and also successfully 'filled in for the rich guys' in Indy Lights, before the money once again ran out. 'By the late 1980s I was getting closer to racing Indy cars,' Radisich said. 'I worked at it, but I needed to somehow raise around $US700,000 for a season. That was out of my league. It was a bit of a closed shop when it came to trying to interest people there to support me. Being a Kiwi I didn't hold much appeal. I still came away with very good memories of those times.'

At the end of 1992 Radisich was feeling a little disillusioned and ripe for a change when an English friend, Andy Rouse, offered him the chance of a well-paid job driving the second car of his Ford Mondeo team in the British super tourers in the coming year. 'By then I'd been in single-seaters for

Paul Radisich putting himself about on behalf of Ford. He drove one of its Mondeos to victory in the FIA World Cup in consecutive years in 1993 and 1994.

12 years since I'd started out in New Zealand in a Ralt RT 4, and it just wasn't happening for various reasons,' Radisich recalled. 'The breaks never came. I'd never had a proper job and I was skint. Then one day, from nothing, I had everything.'

The deal with Rouse had taken four years. A friendship with Rouse had been formed when the pair were members of Peter Brock's Mobil Ford Sierra team at Bathurst in 1989, which Radisich described as 'my real career break'. Rouse and Brock had been forced to retire in one of the team's RS 500s, and Radisich and Brad Jones finished ninth in the other. Radisich stayed with Rouse and his family in a memorable 1993. Despite missing the opening rounds in 1993 he was third in the championship behind two of the greats, German Joachim Winkelhock, who had experience in Formula One, and Briton Steve Soper, and he finished well ahead of team-mate Rouse. There were three wins and two pole positions for Radisich throughout the series, but nothing that prepared the opposition for his cup victory at Monza at the end of the year. Radisich summed it up rather matter-of-factly when

he said: 'I had the best car at the right time and I drove well.'

It was not quite as straightforward as that. Radisich was a newcomer to Monza, one of the world's legendary, and more demanding, circuits, in a country besotted with motor racing. He mastered the track so quickly in the brief practice sessions that he started on pole against a group of expectant drivers with superior credentials. Radisich muffed the start but he had a reprieve when an accident resulted in the race being restarted. He got it right second time around, but there were still potential problems when it started raining. Radisich gambled on dry tyres, which paid off when the rain stopped.

He could hardly have asked for much more. Radisich had shown his class by making a remarkably swift transition from single-seaters to touring cars. The British championship was a powerful one with a number of the top European drivers and cars vying for the title. And it was probably even stronger the following year, when Radisich was again third, this time behind Italian victor Gabriele Tarquini, who had often raced in Formula One, and Switzerland's

Paul Radisch in a Ford Mondeo similar to those he used to secure World Cup super tourer titles at Monza and Donington.

Alain Menu, twice a winner of the title. Britain's celebrated Formula One commentator Murray Walker was prone to make hilarious gaffs when his enthusiasm got the better of him. He was excitedly calling a touring car race when he produced a classic clanger involving Radisich. He said: 'The European drivers have adapted to this circuit particularly well, especially Paul Radisich, who's a New Zealander.'

Radisich's rivals knew what to expect for the 1994 World Cup race at his 'home' track of Donington Park in England's Midlands. They still could not prevent him retaining his crown. Again Radisich was on pole, and, apart from a troublesome gearbox, the race was incident free as he led from start to finish to win the 25-lap sprint by 1.8 seconds from Soper and Winkelhock, both driving BMWs. 'I had a lot of success at Donington Park. It was close to my home at Leamington Spa,' Radisich said. 'The track was very challenging. It was very wide, and very European with a few hills.'

any other driver to help fill the vacuum created by the departure of Kiwi Formula One aces Bruce McLaren, Denny Hulme and Chris Amon. Radisich provided some insight into the difficulties he faced when he said: 'It was a very hard road to break in to the international scene. The path to it was not automatic. You need a lot of people to get to where Scott Dixon has. Perhaps I needed that support too. You need to be able to drive quickly, but you have to also fit into the corporate side to keep pushing your name forward, even pestering people. Some people had the dollars to buy a drive, and I didn't. It's hard for us Antipodean guys if you want to get on that world stage.'

In 2003 Dixon achieved international recognition when he became the Indy Racing League champion, which provided the springboard for a test with the Williams Formula One team.

Hulme, the world Formula One champion in 1967 and still the only New Zealander to achieve

'The European drivers have adapted to this circuit particularly well, especially Paul Radisich, who's a New Zealander.'

Radisich surrendered his title the year after when the cup event was raced over two heats at the Paul Ricard circuit in southern France. The Mondeo was no longer as competitive in a classy field of 38 cars from a dozen countries. In the first heat Radisich suffered a puncture that forced him to retire, and a spin in the second heat cost him a high placing. He finished 17th. His performances in the British championship also declined. He was sixth in 1995 and 13th the next year. A switch to Peugeot didn't help his fortunes either, and after another 13th, and a 14th, he and Patricia packed their bags for Australia at the end of 1998, satisfied that a change was timely, and welcoming the opportunity to be nearer to Paul's family in New Zealand.

Till his move to Australia, Radisich was one of the few New Zealanders able to make much of an imprint on the high-stakes international motor racing scene. For a time he did more than

the feat, recognised Radisich's talent and tried to help him. In the early 1980s they met government minister Mike Moore and made a request for financial assistance. None was forthcoming. The result might have been different today with the government better organised and more able to fund elite competitors. Hulme's assistance only served to enhance his standing with a young Radisich, who first became involved with him when he was a winner of the Bruce McLaren New Zealand driver of the year scholarship to England in 1983.

Hulme had a reputation for not relishing young drivers intruding on his patch. It said a lot for Radisich that Hulme was prepared to team up with him for the Nissan-Mobil series one year to race a little BMW at Pukekohe and on the tight Wellington street circuit. 'It was a great pleasure for me. He was an absolute hero, bearing in mind my aim was to race in Formula One,' Radisich recalled. 'He'd done it all.'

Radisich was delighted when Hulme said he

Photosport

Paul Radisich (left) and Jason Bright acknowledge the cheers of the many Ford fans after finishing second at Bathurst in 2000.

'Before it all finishes it would be nice to put one away.'

could start at Pukekohe, and he has never forgotten the short but very explicit instructions he received. 'In his legendary gruff way Denny said "just bring it home boy", and I made sure there were no slip-ups,' Radisich said. Radisich was not at Bathurst the day Hulme died, but that didn't lessen the impact when he learned of the death of a man who had been very much a mentor to him.

Radisich stayed loyal to Ford when he joined the Dick Johnson team in 1999 as a replacement for departing long-time servant John Bowe. Radisich found himself with big shoes to fill. Bowe, after all, had twice won the Bathurst 1000 km with Johnson, in 1989 and 1994, and had been the Australian touring car champion the year after. Added to that, Radisich was now a member of the longest-established motor racing team in Australia, one with a reputation for high standards, and he was racing for a boss nearing the end of an illustrious driving career, who was expecting plenty from Radisich despite the fact that he knew little about the circuits he would be competing on.

Johnson said that Radisich was chosen only after an 'exhaustive search'. He lasted four years there, from 1999 till the end of 2002, and for two of them, 2000 and 2001, he managed a number of brilliant results at a time when HRT's Mark Skaife and Craig Lowndes (in 2000) were all but unbeatable, and Ford's Falcon AUs were too often left scrambling. The highlight of the period for Radisich was undoubtedly being on pole and winning all three races of the 2001 round at Perth's Barbagallo track. His other round victories occurred at Sandown in 2000 and the Queensland 500 km the year after. He achieved a career best of fourth in the championship in 2000 and was seventh the following year.

Of that special Barbagallo weekend Radisich said: 'There was quite a big difference between the Holden Racing Team and the others when I arrived from England. Ford was in a bit of a mess. There were a whole lot of privateers and HRT. There's greater parity between the Fords and Holdens now.' Radisich said he could be 'right there' but he would always be trailing an HRT car. 'To leave them in my wake that weekend was one of my more memorable occasions in motor sport. The car was on song, and I was able to make the most of it.'

He managed a similar performance the year before, beating the best HRT could throw at him at Sandown when he grabbed victories in the first and third heats. The 2001 victory in the Queensland 500 km at Ipswich was shared with team-mate Steven Johnson after a tropical downpour flooded the track and forced organisers to stop the race. Radisich was a victim of the conditions, and was among those to slide off the track. He was saved when the organisers backdated the positions by a lap, which left him and Johnson victorious.

The Kiwi was joined by Jason Bright in a Shell Falcon for the Bathurst 1000 km in 2000, after the latter had spent most of the year in a failed attempt to establish himself in US Indycar racing. On a day when repeated accidents forced the pace car to appear too often, they were second to the Holden of Garth Tander and Jason Bargwanna by just 2.4 seconds, one of the slimmest margins in the history of the race.

For Radisich it only rubbed in the nagging disappointment of missing out the year before when he was driving with Steve Ellery. They should have won Bathurst in 1999, and would have, had not Radisich clipped a slower car in a passing manoeuvre in the closing stages. That weekend their Falcon AU was the strongest car, and he and Ellery had set the pace throughout. The hard-charging Radisich drove the last leg and with just 20 of the 161 laps to go was in control of the race and poised to end a barren run in the Great Race since his first appearance in 1988. The connection with the other car damaged a tyre valve stem, and with air escaping, Radisich tried to press on. There were complications, and the prospect of an elusive first Bathurst win leaked away. Greg Murphy and Steven Richards, then seized what appeared an unlikely chance to record their second victories. 'I've had no luck at Bathurst. Before it all finishes it would be nice to put one away. There's a bit of unfinished business there,' Radisich said. 'Everybody knows what Bathurst is. The reality is everybody has a shot at it, not everyone has a shot at winning the championship. I've not won either, and Bathurst is now the more realistic option for me.'

Radisich maintained he had not dwelled on his near misses at Bathurst, preferring to take the attitude that as a good professional driver he had given each opportunity his 'best shot'. Dick Johnson was at fault in 1990 when Radisich and British touring car driver Jeff Allam were denied victory at Bathurst. Their Ford Sierra Cosworth was leading by more than 10 seconds late in the race when Radisich, who expected to finish the race, brought the car in for its last pit stop. In those days the team boss, in this case Johnson, was allowed to drive his second car if he wished, particularly if his own car had retired. In the midst of what was to be a fleeting, routine pit stop, without warning Radisich was told to jump out to allow Johnson to finish the race and share in the victory for a second consecutive year. After all, Radisich and Allam were only temporary hired help. They had made their reputations racing in other parts of the world. With Johnson a larger man than Radisich, the seat needed to be adjusted, and it all

Getty Images

Paul Radisich putting the foot down in practice for the Phillip Island round at the start of the 2001 season. It promised much when he qualified fourth, but after placings of 12th and 14th he had to be happy with 11th overall.

went horribly wrong when it jammed. Finally, the only alternative was for Radisich to clamber back in, but the pit stop was considerably longer than it should have been. The lead had evaporated, and Radisich could not catch eventual winners Allan Grice and Win Percy in a Holden Commodore VL. It left Radisich, Allam and a glum support crew with a very empty feeling. There was no joy in accepting second place, with Radisich confident that without the unnecessary delay he would 'probably have won'.

Radisich's class also shone on the testing Surfers Paradise street circuit where he won successive Supercar rounds there in 1999 and 2000 in a Johnson Ford in support races for a round of the United States-based CART single-seaters. It was his misfortune that, at the time, the 'Indy' round did not count toward the championship. Now it does, and the Supercars' huge popularity has resulted in them sharing equal billing with the Indy cars.

By the end of 2002 Radisich wanted out. It was a miserable year. He finished 26th in the championship; and nor could he and Johnson's son, Steven Johnson, salvage anything at Bathurst, where they failed to finish. It was also the last year of four generally disastrous ones for Ford and its aging AU Falcon. Ford was pinning its future on the introduction of the new Falcon BA in 2003, a car that would become a success in the hands of Marcos Ambrose at Stone Brothers Racing when he won the touring car title to break Mark Skaife's three-year Holden stranglehold. 'It was time to move on,' Radisich said of his departure. 'I felt some things needed to be changed. Dick considered it wasn't the case, so my time was up. He had a [new] contract for me but I preferred to leave it.'

Radisich was dissatisfied with his four years with Johnson. The good results were all too infrequent, leaving a strong sense of underachievement for one of

Radisich's class also shone on the testing Surfers Paradise street circuit where he won successive Supercar rounds . . .

Dirk Klynsmith/Graphic Dak Photography

Paul Radisich's biggest moment in Supercars. He is squirted with champagne by fellow Kiwi Greg Murphy after winning all three heats at the Barbagallo round in Perth in 2001.

the most accomplished drivers in the championship. 'I didn't get into the top three, which would have been satisfactory,' he said. 'Steven and I had a good working relationship. We had our ups and downs but we got on well. There's always issues when a son is driving in his father's team. It was Dick's last year [of racing] when I started, and Steven took time to find his feet [as his replacement]. He became a lot more competitive.'

The next two years were similarly frustrating. Radisich found himself replaced by Craig Lowndes before they were over. He signed for John Briggs Motorsport with much optimism. He had a new Briggs-built Betta Electrical Falcon BA in 2003, a car Ford Australia desperately wanted to perform in order to rein in HRT's prolonged supremacy. Though there was little to crow about — apart from a provisional pole (for being the top qualifier) at the Sandown 500 km — Radisich's final placing of 10th in the championship was a big improvement. His sterling effort for seventh at Bathurst with Swede Rickard Rydell was hampered by a car that lacked the grunt of those who finished ahead of them. In the latter part of the season Briggs sold out to British motor racing

team Triple Eight Engineering — a deal Radisich was partially instrumental in bring about through a business association with the newcomer. It mattered little in the harsh world of business as Triple Eight opted to punt Radisich and team-mate Max Wilson, and hire Lowndes and Steve Ellery.

That Radisich slipped to 19th in 2004 had a lot to do with a car that performed erratically. At times the problem was an absence of speed, and too often Radisich was betrayed by mechanical failure. His car failed to finish the top two endurance races, Sandown and Bathurst. He managed to scramble into the top 20 for the year thanks to a rousing second place behind the untouchable Marcos Ambrose, the champion for a second successive year, in the final round at Eastern Creek. However, Radisich's heat placings of sixth, second and fourth were too late to influence the decision to replace him.

Radisich was diplomatic and tended to mask his frustrations in talking of the performance of Briggs and Triple Eight. 'I had to build up with a new team that got taken over for 2004,' Radisich said. 'I had new people again. It took time to be competitive,

Paul Radisich's run of appalling luck at Bathurst continued in 2004 when the Betta Electrical Ford he shared with Brazilian Max Wilson failed to finish.

and for people to learn the pitfalls.' He admitted though that it was a blow to find he was not wanted. 'That's the way it goes. It's a commercial world,' he said. 'I had to pick myself up and dust myself off.'

It was a time for reflection and Radisich examined his options. They included walking away from Supercars and returning to England, where he might perhaps race sports cars. He had expected a lot more from the six years in V8s. 'Overall it was pretty disappointing. I didn't achieve a lot,' he said. 'It didn't help that I didn't have the right equipment to do a better job. Fourth was the closest I'd come to the touring car title when I'd fancy myself being higher. It doesn't eat me away. I can only do my best with what [car] I've been given. I do my best every time. I have a set of rules and parameters I follow.'

His mixed feelings hardly left Radisich all that receptive when TKR boss David John boldly approached him at Bathurst in October 2004. His future was uncertain, and he did not have a high

or the Holden Racing Team. I had some offers in front of me. TKR was the last to come along, and it was the best deal. At the time people thought I'd lost my marbles. I felt it was an exciting package. I didn't have to take anything. David pulled his hair out meeting my demands. I think he could see the value of what I was saying.'

Radisich was confident in his decision to sign for two years given that Morris's people had been working on an engine development programme for some time. 'These things don't happen in five minutes. To be able to tap into that experience was something money couldn't buy,' he said. 'I had an opportunity to examine everything. I drove one of the Morris cars before I signed and it felt good.'

The final decision ended six years of racing cars with the blue oval insignia, which Radisich had stuck with for big chunks of his career. Understandably, forsaking that long-standing connection in favour of jumping over to the opposition, Holden, felt strange

He had expected a lot more from the six years in V8s. 'Overall it was pretty disappointing. I didn't achieve a lot . . .'

opinion of TKR. 'I would never have signed with the old TKR,' he said. 'They had no runs on the board. Craig Baird had done a magnificent job with old cars and old engines, but the team was really run on other people's generosity. David wasn't in the ballpark when I first spoke to him.' But John's persistence and preparedness to meet all of Radisich's demands finally won him over. TKR and Morris Motorsports agreed on a sharing of resources, which included a comprehensive engine-building programme, the hiring of a proven person to implement it in Kiwi Alan Draper, and the buying of a new Holden Commodore VZ.

But it would not have happened without John's agonising, but necessary, decision to sell 25 per cent of his beloved TKR to Tauranga-based Bernie Gillon, who had made a fortune in the building industry. His stake would later become 49 per cent. 'With the merging of resources we now have the ingredients to become something special,' Radisich said. 'There weren't offers from [the big boys] Stone Brothers

for Radisich, and created a mixed reaction. Any swapping between the two fiercely competing makes was the subject of much debate among the fans, and Radisich said comment on his move was split about 50-50. 'At the end of the day you have to put yourself in the right direction, and there was not the right opportunity in a Ford,' he said. 'I would have been near the back of the field. I think most people would see that. Even Peter Brock [the ultimate Holden hero] went to Ford for a time, and Craig Lowndes's move to Ford was a bitter blow for Holden fans.'

Radisich's experiences showed how drivers are living on their wits both on and off the track. As he once said: 'Stability in this game is very rare. It tends to be a two-year by two-year arrangement [provided you keep finding a contract].' Reputations and loyalty can count

Paul Radisich's Team Kiwi Holden showing the way to a number of his opponents on the way to an overall finish of third at Shanghai in 2005.

for little as the teams and the manufacturers constantly jockey for any advantage. With the stakes high it's very much results-driven, and the drivers are often casualties of that. Just ask Radisich.

He comes across as mild and a little philosophical, having survived just about everything a top racer can encounter apart from a serious crash. Equally, one senses that Radisich's mood changes quickly once it's down to the business of racing. Though his career is winding down, he has not lost his hunger for success. That is why his contract with TKR was so important. It offered Radisich the chance of being best remembered for more than winning the world touring car championship a couple of times in the 1990s. 'TKR excites me and suits me at this time because I have got a lot to prove,' Radisich said early in the 2005 season. 'I want to try and finish my career on the right note and on paper this programme has the potential to deliver.'

partner Paul Morris collided with another car and eliminated them before Radisich's turn at the wheel came around. With just a little more luck Radisich would have finished the championship in the top 10, which would have represented huge progress for TKR after its 27th the year before.

The decision to run the two Pauls in the Morris car at Sandown (where they finished a good eighth after an engine blew in qualifying) and Bathurst appeared to be a good one, with two full-timers in the car. However, it meant Radisich had the disadvantage of being the co-driver, and it was confusing for the team sponsors and the fans. With the team having substantial new sponsorship deals with Makita and 3M, Radisich said it would not happen in 2006.

It continued Radisich's wretched luck in the Bathurst 1000 km, which has become more of a graveyard circuit for him. He has started there 15 times, and only finished on six occasions. His nine

It continued Radisich's wretched luck in the Bathurst 1000 km, which has become more of a graveyard circuit for him.

Despite plenty of evidence that Radisich's finely tuned racing edge remained, 2005 did not live up to its initial promise. He was seventh in the championship after a fine fifth placing in round two at Pukekohe, where he finished sixth in all three heats. Following round five in the Chinese city of Shanghai, where he was a satisfying third, despite suffering from serious dehydration in the third heat, to give TKR its first podium finish, he was eighth overall.

Unfortunately, the eagerly anticipated extra racing speed from the new partnership with Morris Motorsports never eventuated. The new engines being developed by Alan Draper had been expected to be ready mid-season but they did not appear. The race was then on to have them ready in time for the late March start in 2006.

There were also annoying oil hose clipping failures in successive rounds, Darwin's Hidden Valley and at the Queensland 500 km, which robbed Radisich of high placings. And he did not get to drive in the Bathurst 1000 km on his 43rd birthday, after his

retirements have come in his last 12 appearances, an unenviable record. However, such disappointments in 2005 did not detract hugely from the overall enjoyment of being with TKR. 'There's not the pressure of big-team politics and dealing with sponsors [such as he experienced at Triple Eight],' he said. 'There's a more relaxed environment at TKR. It all fits very well.'

Radisich's family are Dalmatians; his grandparents came to New Zealand from Yugoslavia in the 1920s, and they worked in the Northland gumfields before moving to Auckland. In Australia he's popularly known as 'The Rat', a thoroughly unlikely nickname that would hardly delight his wife. He was more acceptably called 'Patch' in England, probably because of the association of his name with the radish, a root vegetable. As he says himself, 'I suppose Radisich isn't a name that rolls off the tongue all that easily after a few beers. It's a catchy nickname, but I don't know about being a Rat.'

Radisich did not have the usual apprenticeship in

karting like so many of today's drivers. Motor racing was in his blood, but although his father Frank was very much a part of the national scene on four wheels, Paul opted for motocross. While that ended when he fell off and damaged a vertebra, there was no dampening of his enthusiasm. He was only 17 when he and younger brother Chris raced in their mother Denise's Mazda 323 'shopping basket' in the Benson and Hedges long-distance race at Pukekohe.

Paul had started a motor mechanic apprenticeship by then, and Chris, who was still at school, had to slip out to snatch a few hours of practice. They led in their class till, in the end, a puncture dropped them to third. However, the story doesn't end there. Father Frank and the brothers' stepmother Robyn were also competing, in a Mini GT. Paul took the time to help Robyn, who was in trouble when the dashboard fell out: after putting it back, the gallant young Paul was quickly on his way again.

Soon after racing the Mazda, Radisich took a substantial leap to a Datsun Ralt RT1 which belonged to a former New Zealand Grand Prix victor, Dave McMillan. Though Radisich's talent clearly showed through when he qualified for the New Zealand Grand Prix, a blown motor proved costly. With insufficient spares to rebuild it, Radisich's family nevertheless rallied around to enable him to buy his first race car, a Ralt RT4. He soon created an impression in finishing second

to one of New Zealand's best drivers at that time, David Oxton, at the old Baypark circuit at Mount Maunganui and, in the process, beating a number of proven performers, including McMillan, Kenny Smith and Steve Millen.

Fired with enthusiasm he made his first overseas trip, racing in Australia in the early 1980s. In typical Kiwi style he was prepared to rough it, living for months in a Transit van, which he also used to tow his racer.

Further success, with eye-catching Formula Three results in England, was only curtailed by Radisich's lack of financial resources. But he persisted, and became the Peter Jackson New Zealand single-seater series winner in 1988; the same season he had his only success in the New Zealand Grand Prix driving a Formula Atlantic Ralt.

He was on target to repeat that victory in the 1989 Grand Prix in a Swift, only to be disqualified for jumping the start.

By the end of 2005 one had the strong impression 2006 would be Paul Radisich's V8 swansong unless something extraordinary occurred. 'I'm not looking any further forward than that,' he said. 'Realistically our package isn't a championship-winning one, but a top 10 finish is. I'm keen to be in the top half-dozen drivers each round. . . . I've probably achieved as much as I'm going to in motor sport, and I'm becoming more involved in things outside of it. To win Bathurst would be the icing on the cake.'

Getty Images

Paul Radisich was looking to improve on his 2005 championship position of 14th in what appeared likely to be his Supercar farewell in 2006.

JASON RICHARDS

Getting it Together

Getty Images

Jason Richards

Born: Nelson, 10 April 1976

Championship debut: Round 13, Bathurst 1000, 2000

Starts: 63

Pole positions: nil (best: 4th, round 8, Oran Park, 2004)

Round wins: nil (best: 2nd, Bathurst 1000, 2005)

Podium finishes: 2

Best championship finish: 14th, 2004

Bathurst record: debut 1997 (two-litre); 8 starts, 6 finishes; best
    result: 2nd (2005)

New Zealand's biggest Supercar mover in 2005, Jason Richards, thought he was going to die at Pukekohe in 2003. And he was overwhelmed with the same sickening fear at Queensland's Ipswich track in July two years later. The Pukekohe accident was bad enough. Richards found himself helpless in his airborne Team Dynamik Holden Commodore after a collision with the tyre barrier at turns two and three. It was even worse at the Queensland Raceway. Richards' Tasman Motorsport Dodo Commodore received a push to its back left from Paul Morris's Holden when both were travelling at high speed. It triggered a violent reaction that had spectators gasping in horror. The Richards car was slammed left, off the track, at turn three and hit a dangerously placed 22 cm high ripple strip at an estimated 160 kmh. The impact catapulted Richards' car skywards, and it tumbled wildly, end over end, spinning six times while still off the ground, before coming to rest with a sickening thud, right way up, in a cloud of dust and dirt. It was the worst V8 Supercar accident of 2005, and among the most spectacular and devastating in the formula's history.

A dazed and shaken Richards was struggling to speak and extremely lucky not to have suffered more severe injuries than he did, as he stumbled away with

Getty Images

Getty Images

The day Jason Richards thought he was going to die at Pukekohe in 2003.

a cracked rib, neck and back ligament damage, and considerable bruising. He was in a state of shock when taken to Ipswich hospital for precautionary x-rays, but was unaware his rib was cracked till a day or two after when he nearly passed out with the pain.

The ordeal smashed his 'extremely strong' $A4000 carbon fibre seat. 'I thought I was going to die. I had visions of the Pukekohe crash all over again,' Richards said two days after the accident. 'I was being thrown around like a rag doll. My legs were free to move.' Richards said he was saved from more serious injuries by his head and neck safety (HANS) device, which Holden purchased for all its V8 drivers in 2004, and which became compulsory for everyone the following year. It stopped his brain from spinning, and his neck from overextending. 'I felt the rib pop, and my helmet strap was trying to pull my head from my shoulders and crush my voice box,' Richards said. 'After Pukekohe I knew I needed to hold my head. At my second attempt I grabbed the chin of my helmet, and tried to pull it down, and I curled up into a ball. You go into self-preservation mode. You quickly realise you're just a passenger. With the G forces at that speed, my head can weigh 150 kg. It is so important to keep the head still. I remember the whole thing so vividly. I was seeing stars. I was fighting to stop myself losing consciousness.'

The incident, which occurred on lap 44 of the Queensland 300 km, stopped the racing till Richards' condition was known and his crumpled car was no longer a hazard to other racers. Morris was 'blueing' on his car radio when he was black-flagged and told by his pit crew that he had received a 60-second pit lane stop-go penalty, which ended his prospects of a high placing. Richards was furious with Morris. Though Morris rang him that night to check his condition, he was still quick to suggest the incident was all Richards' fault. 'There's been no apology. I'm very disappointed with Paul, and what happened,' Richards said at the time. 'He just turned hard right in to me. It surprised the living hell out of me.' Morris maintained his innocence. 'Jason didn't have to maintain that line,' he said. 'He should have given me some room. I was going to hit the kerb, so it was either him or me, so I turned right. My instinct said self-preservation.'

Richards had been appalled to witness an almost identical accident the day before, when Cameron McLean's Carrera Cup Porsche hit the same ripple

'I remember the whole thing so vividly. I was seeing stars. I was fighting to stop myself losing consciousness.'

Getty Images

Getty Images

Richards' Holden comes to rest upside down after somersaulting through the air after he cannoned into a tyre barrier.

Tasman Motorsport managing director Kevin Murphy (left) sharing a joke with the team's engineering expert, Ron Harrop.

strip. The car was a wreck, but McLean miraculously escaped serious injury. 'I watched what happened from our pit, and I felt sick,' Richards said. 'I knew what was going to happen when I hit the kerb.' The two chilling accidents could have been easily avoided had the ripple strip not been in the wrong place. Morris's move to the right to hit Richards' car would still probably have spun him off the track, but after an excursion onto the grass he would have been able to resume racing.

The bad blood between Richards and Morris continued at later rounds in 2005. There was an 'altercation' at the Sandown 500 km in Melbourne, and there were further instances of their cars being in contact. 'The problem wasn't going away. We've had a chat, and have been civilised about it,' Richards said. 'We struggled a bit at Bathurst. We have a better understanding now. We've agreed to disagree.'

An initial inspection at Ipswich suggested the Tasman car, new at the start of the year, was too badly damaged to be repaired in time for the next meeting three weeks later at Oran Park Raceway. However, dedicated work, that extended well into the night for several days, managed to have the car pristine at a cost of more than $A180,000. It was all worth it when Richards was third in qualifying.

Early on, Tasman investigated fielding a substitute car for the Oran Park race, but it became evident nothing competitive was available. The team could not afford to be missing from the grid, and for Richards it would have been the loss of valuable championship points. A no-show can incur a fine of $A150,000, but Tasman Motorsport managing director Kevin Murphy said it would never have come to that in this instance.

The Pukekohe accident during practice was the sometimes impetuous Richards' fault. The Dynamik Holden was 'taily' and oversteering, and by his own admission Richards carried too much speed through turn one. Having to avoid some debris on the track meant that he spun in to turns two and three. There was a stack of nine tyres, three lots of three, acting as a barrier to stop drivers cutting the corner. The back of his car hit the tyres, which acted as a spring. The impact jolted the tyres free and the car took off. 'I thought, God I'm going to die here. It was the same feeling as Ipswich,' he said. 'The car dug in on hitting the ground. My helmet hit the ground too. The visor was ripped off, and the helmet was covered in mud. My car was a wreck. That was it for the round.'

With Richards desperate to improve on his heartening final championship placing of 14th in 2004, the Ipswich incident left him without any points for the round, and a drop from 19th to 23rd on the table. 'I was gutted on that score,' he said. 'We didn't have enough pace to be challenging up front, but the car was good for a top 15 finish and a hundred-plus points. I just wanted to stay out of trouble. It was hard to pass anyone.'

Kevin Murphy described what happened to Richards at Ipswich as a 'pretty scary moment'. 'Jason's comparatively minor injuries are testimony to how strongly, as a rule, the cars are built,' he said. 'The design of the current cars is, in most cases, exceptionally good.'

After the ordeal it would have been understandable had the 30-year-old Richards been a little apprehensive approaching Oran Park. It stood out as his most successful V8 track till his best performance, a career-altering second in the Bathurst 1000 km in October 2005. However, there was not a trace of any lingering doubts as he went about his work, even though he was not a 100 per cent fit. Richards was still nursing the cracked rib, which continued to make coughing and sneezing 'annoying'. To make him more comfortable and help spread the load of the G forces and the impact of the high-speed bumps on his body, he wore a karting driver's rib protector. It helped, as Richards and his repaired car turned a few heads in qualifying third behind the two biggest names in the series, Ford's Marcos Ambrose, the championship winner for the previous two years and the points leader for much of 2005, and Holden's No. 1 flag-bearer, Mark Skaife. Richards spent most of the two-hour practice with the fastest time only to be run down by Ambrose and Skaife in the closing stages.

In the top 10 shootout a costly slide at turn two and problems with the way the car was 'set up' left him 10th on the grid for race one. He again excelled in finishing sixth, but was guilty of being overeager in race two. He was in the top 10 when he ran his Commodore VZ off the track at turn two, and it ended up jammed in the sand trap against a tyre wall. The blunder dropped him to a final position of 28th, and 15th for the round. 'I just couldn't pull it up going down in to turn two,' Richards admitted. 'As I came down the straight I was trying to stay ahead of Paul Radisich, who was coming out of the pits, and I was lucky not to take out Cameron McConville. We showed a good turn of speed . . . but not the overall result. I can't say enough about the team. They worked long hours to rebuild the car, and I'm really appreciative of their efforts. To have the car third fastest in qualifying was awesome. The car's characteristics changed in the shootout. It was very taily. I had a bit of discomfort [from the cracked rib] in the two-hour practice. Once the adrenalin is pumping you drive through it.'

Edge Photographics

Jason Richards' Tasman Commodore is horrifyingly airborne after being clipped from behind at the Queensland 500 km at Ipswich in 2005. He was lucky to escape with minor injuries.

Jason Richards made his reputation racing BMWs in the New Zealand touring car championship before venturing into Supercars.

Following that meeting Richards found himself under considerable pressure. While the Tasman team was not for one moment pointing the finger at Richards for what happened at Ipswich, there were concerns that he was prone to compromise his potential brilliance with a tendency to over-cook promising positions with rash driving. His final championship position of 14th in 2004 represented an encouraging debut with Tasman in its opening year. However, into his fifth season of Supercar racing Richards was sometimes making the sorts of mistakes associated with a series beginner.

Richards' contract was running out at the end of the season, and there was no certainty Tasman would seek to retain him, though he continued to show an ability to be among the top 10. He was made aware that the team required a greater level of consistency from him for the remainder of 2005, and it was suggested that he might benefit from visiting a sports psychologist, which he did at his own expense. He started working with one of Australia's better practitioners, Patrick Farrell, who had been involved with the Australian Olympic team and a number of leading golfers, as well as working in the corporate field. Richards credits Farrell with helping him to be more calm when he is behind the wheel, and with easing the pressure Richards felt to be successful.

It appears to have worked spectacularly well. Richards and team-mate Jamie Whincup were third at the Sandown 500 km, Richards' and Tasman's first podium finish, and the pair climbed even higher when placed second at Bathurst. Richards then qualified second in practice to another New Zealander, Greg Murphy, at the Gold Coast sprint round. Those results dramatically elevated his standing. It helped seal a new two-year deal at Tasman, and he became a target for other teams. 'Patrick's philosophy is to let the result take care of itself,' Richards said. 'When you try to do something better is when you come unstuck. When I'm racing now I repeat a saying he gave me, "Today is not the day I will perform better than I ever have done before". He has been extremely helpful. I've learned what to focus on and not focus on. I was desperate to get on the podium, and I was trying to push that along too quickly and it created mistakes. I was making mistakes from driving faster than I or the car was capable of. I've now had some pretty amazing results, the best I've ever had, and I let them happen.'

Richards said Farrell also talked about how trying to push things along had a habit of making them worse. He spoke of how when it was raining people were inclined to make a hash of trying to do simple things, like unlock their cars in their haste to get under cover. If they were less flustered they were more likely to do it quickly.

The Sandown result came in difficult weather after Richards and Whincup started 13th on the grid. Richards' decision to stay on slick tyres, even as other teams were changing to wets, allowed Richards to leapfrog several combinations, and he held off the attentions of the fourth-placed Garth Tander and Rick Kelly. Sandown was highly satisfying but the Bathurst performance, after Richards was seventh in

his first top 10 shootout there, gave him a credibility he had not previously enjoyed, and emphasised the belief that the soundly based Tasman team was very much on the up in its first year running two cars. Richards led briefly nearing the 100-lap mark of 161, and again after 130 laps, when his slick crew allowed him to slip out of the pits ahead of HRT's Mark Skaife when the two VZ Commodores had come into the pits at the same time. Richards' partner Jamie Whincup did well to bring the Tasman car in second behind leader Todd Kelly (HRT), and it was Tasman's smart final pit stop that made the difference. The Kiwi stayed ahead till lap 141, when Skaife came out of his slipstream to zap by Richards at The Chase.

Richards kept in touch without ever challenging Skaife, unlike their race at Sandown two years previously when the two leading cars came together at the end, only for Richards to be left stranded in a sand trap and out of the race, and Skaife still

. . . to stay on slick tyres, even as other teams were changing to wets, allowed Richards to leapfrog several combinations . . .

Dirk Klynsmith/Graphic Dak Photography

Jason Richards' Holden (right) shadowing that of race leader Mark Skaife in the wet at the Sandown 500 km in 2003. Soon afterwards Richards was eliminated when the cars came together as he attempted to pass, just when a first Supercar victory beckoned.

able to claim victory. Making it easier for Skaife at Bathurst, the race was neutralised for a number of the closing laps, which included the period after a crash between the fired-up Greg Murphy and Marcos Ambrose, which unfortunately also claimed a number of closely following cars. Richards said that memories of Sandown, which was shaping as a certain first podium finish and possibly even a victory, came flooding back as he led Skaife at Bathurst. The weather at Sandown in 2003 had been wet and gloomy when Richards caught Skaife, whose Holden was ailing, only for Richards' car to suffer wheel damage when the pair touched as Richards attempted to pass Skaife. 'What happened that day has chased me ever since. I've been haunted by it,' Richards said. 'Some of the things Patrick [Farrell] had said to me came into play at Bathurst. With 30 laps to go I was leading. I was telling myself, "how good is this", but remembering Patrick's words,

the resources — which included its own engine-building programme — to offer him his 'best chance to win races'. Richards was reluctant to say much about his other possible options, except to say that there was a good offer to drive alongside one of the better V8 drivers, the very consistent Jason Bright, at Ford Performance Racing.

Having lost more drivers to Ford than they had gained in recent years — in particular Craig Lowndes and Russell Ingall — Holden Motorsport was anxious to retain Richards, and its marketing manager, Simon McNamara, worked to achieve that. 'Holden was very active in trying to keep me in red,' Richards said. 'I'd been loyal to them for five years, and in turn they showed loyalty to me. I'm rapt with the deal. It allows me and the team the continuity to progress. Tasman has a huge amount of potential. Next year [2006] will be my best chance of winning the championship.'

The twin results of Sandown and Bathurst transformed him into one of the more sought-after drivers in Supercars . . .

I just did what I could do. It was a nice moment when I pulled away from Mark to a three-second lead. Going over Skyline I had to slow down with the debris flags out indicating a crash, and it allowed Mark to catch up. When he passed me I knew I still had 20 laps to get back at him. I went as hard as I could but Mark had a faster car, which he indicated in setting the lap record. Two laps from the end I backed off. I made sure I brought the car home. I showed maturity in my driving in a high-pressure situation, which people saw as a positive in me.'

Richards said it had been 'mayhem' for him in the weeks after Bathurst. The twin results of Sandown and Bathurst transformed him into one of the more sought-after drivers in Supercars, and there was much speculation about his future as his contract was up for renewal. There were huge demands on his time, including high media interest from New Zealand, and other teams showed interest in securing his signature. He was delighted to remain at Tasman, believing it had

With Richards unable to capitalise on his efforts of Sandown and Bathurst in the remaining three rounds, he finished 17th in the championship, one place inferior to his team-mate Jamie Whincup, and three off his best of 14th the previous year. 'It should have been a lot better. The cars were better than where they finished,' Kevin Murphy said. 'Jason disguised the potential of the cars. He let us down a bit with his number of unforced errors, and not being smart cost him too often. There was a lack of fight. He runs conservatively at times. In re-signing Jason we've given him the benefit of the doubt.'

Murphy believed that Tasman moved further forward than any other team in 2005, beating a number with much bigger budgets. He anticipated plenty of improvement in 2006 with the team's engineering expert Ron Harrop having so much more to offer,

Joining Tasman in 2004 came as a welcome relief for Jason Richards after his time at Team Dynamik (right) turned sour, and eventually resulted in him taking Dynamik to court.

and more money to spend. After testing three drivers at Victoria's Winton track in December 2005, Tasman chose Andrew Jones, of Melbourne, to replace Jamie Whincup on a one-year deal. Jones, 25, finished 28th in the 2005 championship, which was distinguished by a fourth placing with Cameron McConville in the Bathurst 1000 km. The team was to be known as the Tasman Motorsport Tigers as it attempted to become a stronger brand, and more attractive to sponsors.

▪▪▪▪▪▪▪▪

The horror of Ipswich was far more fleeting than the problems Richards had in 2003. Disenchanted with Team Kiwi Racing's lack of resources and priorities, Richards formed a group of his own in 2002 to try and buy the franchise from owner David John. When that was no longer an option, Richards' group tried to buy the Romano-owned franchise, which was available. He found himself competing for it with another New Zealander,

Kieran Wills, whose son, Simon Wills, and Richards had combined at TKR in 2002 to finish 11th in the Bathurst 1000 km. Kieran, himself an accomplished driver and successful businessman in New Zealand, secured the franchise, but that was not the end of it. Richards and he got talking, and it was suggested that Richards drive alongside Simon Wills at Wills' Team Dynamik outfit, based in Adelaide. Richards did not need much convincing. After the mostly second-hand equipment he was used to at TKR, he was impressed with the smart new stuff Dynamik had to offer, and was soon enjoying Adelaide too. 'Things looked pretty bright. Kieran had a big budget, and he'd set up an awesome team,' Richards recalled. 'He had a top engine builder Alan Draper on board, some pretty good gear and mechanics, and we had the latest VY Holden Commodores.'

Kieran Wills was in partnership with proven team owner Malcolm Ramsay, and Betta Electrical was going to sponsor them. However, things didn't go as smoothly as they had initially hoped. When

Jason Richards tackling the Pukekohe circuit where his best placing there in two years with Team Kiwi was a fourth in race one in 2001.

Ramsay pulled out after the first round in Adelaide, Richards said it 'changed the whole balance of the team'. With Betta Electrical now not on board, Richards said Kieran gradually 'got sick of spending his own money like water'. Richards' first outing in the Clipsal 500 km street race at Adelaide was a disaster. He crashed his new Commodore into the wall in race two at turn eight at more than 200 kmh, and then there was the airborne drama later in the year at Pukekohe after he struck the tyre barrier.

In both cases the car was badly damaged, and required much rebuilding at considerable expense. Richards' relationship with Kieran Wills and technical director Oscar Fiorinotto was also stretched, and he felt he was unfairly blamed when the team botched up a driver change at the Sandown 500 km, which he and Simon Wills almost won, and he was twice penalised for speeding in pit lane.

Richards was always being paid late, and by November 2003 he was owed five months of his salary. 'We were still going racing but Kieran didn't have the necessary corporate support,' Richards said. 'A lot of others in the team were not being paid either.' Richards lived from hand to mouth in that period. 'I wasn't enjoying my motor racing,' he said. 'I didn't get on with Oscar. I started talking to Kevin Murphy at Tasman.' He received some back pay, but not all he was entitled to, and in 2005 Richards successfully took legal action against Team Dynamik. The South Australian District Court ordered Dynamik to pay Richards $A41,704.44 plus interest, which covered non-payment of wages ($A34,374.99) and a percentage of merchandise and membership revenue ($A7329.45).

Wills tried to counter-sue Richards for more than $NZ700,000 to cover repairs to race cars, future loss of profits and lost sponsorship. The action was dismissed. Richards walked out on his two-year contract at Team Dynamik at the end of 2003 because he had not received payments specified in his contract, and joined the Tasman team. 'This is the end of a long battle and the result vindicates what we have been fighting for: that the contract that I entered into in good faith should be honoured,' Richards said at the time. 'This was an important judgment

because as V8 Supercar drivers we do not have a union or an association to look after our interests. That potentially leaves us exposed to exploitation. This sends a clear message that a driver's employment contract is a legally binding document.'

He was delighted with the outcome. 'It closes the door on something which has been hanging over my head for almost two years,' Richards said. 'Because of it, I was forced to move inter-state, and start afresh with a new team in order to pursue my livelihood.' However, it was not over. Richards was later required to return to court after Kieran Wills defaulted on the agreement to pay the original amount. Towards the end of 2005, Richards was relieved to receive a cheque for $A87,000, a lot of it for legal costs, which belatedly closed a matter that caused him much anguish.

Inevitably Richards' performances suffered in 2003 with a drop from 19th in 2002 to 26th in the championship. There were still occasions when his

Richards walked out on his two-year contract at Team Dynamik . . .

talent came to the fore. He achieved his best round result in Supercars up to that time when he finished fifth at Oran Park after qualifying fifth, and there was the duel with the mighty Mark Skaife for the lead in foul weather at the Sandown 500 km, which ended tragically for Richards.

Richards' partner Simon Wills did brilliantly to qualify their car fifth, and in the race, when Richards pitted as instructed, the car was in fifth place. Richards was to jump out to allow Wills to continue but, Richards said, Fiorinotto changed the call. 'I'd pulled my radio out. I was all disconnected, and Simon wasn't ready. It was raining. It was mayhem,' Richards said. 'We dropped a few spots. I was blamed when it wasn't my fault.' Despite the disruption and the worsening conditions Richards and Wills excelled. When Richards climbed into the car for the last stint they were sixth, and Richards was soon in a position to achieve his first Supercar victory. He passed a couple of cars, and had climbed to second, behind Skaife, when the safety car came out as cars were spearing off in all directions following rain and hail.

Delays meant that the race was running way over time. Instead of the scheduled 161 laps the race was reduced to a final 20-minute sprint to accommodate television. When Richards was finally able to pursue Skaife, there were 11 cars — all placed further down the field — between them. Richards' task was made easier when some drivers let him through, and Skaife's car was ailing. The alternator was failing and the battery draining, so much so, that under instruction from his crew, Skaife began shutting down non-essential accessories, such as the wiper and screen heater. He could barely see through the fogged-up windscreen. The car was slowing a little, and with just a few minutes remaining, Richards closed up. An unlikely Team Dynamik victory in the second-biggest race of the year suddenly seemed possible. Even second would have been like

the 161 laps. With Richards desperate to leave Team Dynamik he was fortunate that Tasman Motorsport was about to enter the arena. It had leased one of the two licences that belonged to the Sydney-based Lansvale Racing team of Steve Reed and Trevor Ashby. Richards approached Kevin Murphy, seeking an opportunity, and the response was favourable. 'It suited us because of the strong Kiwi connection within the Tasman set-up,' said Murphy, father of Super Cheap driver Greg Murphy. 'Jason had been in the category since Bathurst 2000, and had the experience we were looking for. He'd shown he was fast, and not always with the best equipment and in a happy environment. Hiring Jason was a no-brainer. There were not a lot of other drivers available with his experience.'

In 2003 Murphy was approached by a good friend of Greg's, who was interested in buying a licence, and asked whether he would mind doing

But in the squeeze in the braking area at Dandenong Road Corner the two Commodores touched and slid off the circuit.

victory for the newcomers. It was clear though that Richards' car was the faster, and with time almost up, the Kiwi made his move, diving down the inside of Skaife. But in the squeeze in the braking area at Dandenong Road Corner the two Commodores touched and slid off the circuit.

Skaife was lucky to miss going completely into the sand trap, but Richards, his steering damaged, went right in. There was no way out. After a superb effort in trying circumstances Richards and Wills had nothing to show for it. 'It was really exciting, but in the end heartbreaking,' Richards said. 'I made a couple of attempts to pass Mark. We were side by side, and Mark hit my right back wheel, and we slid toward the sand trap. The back wheel wouldn't turn. The tyre rod was bent, and the wheel pulled the car straight ahead. I'd experienced the highs and lows of motor racing all at once. It was pretty disappointing.'

Nor did Bathurst go well. An axle problem after Wills entered the gravel ruined their aspirations and they limped home 22nd, having completed 139 of

some research on the subject. Ideally it needed to be a single-car, level two team. But after investigation and discussions with Holden, it transpired that it would have to be a two-car, level one team if Holden was to support it. The financial return was better, level one teams had more votes around the Supercars board table, and there was less certainty about the future of level two, one-car teams. Near the end of the year Murphy became aware that long-time privateers Reed and Ashby, who used the V8s to promote their big smash repair business, were keen to sell up and were negotiating with a team looking to race Fords the next year. It helped that Murphy and his group — New Zealanders who had sponsored or supported Greg Murphy since his early days — preferred to run a Holden, and Holden Motorsport did not want its opposition to pick up another franchise. 'We spoke to the Lansvale owners at Eastern Creek, and they admitted they were about ready to sign off with people keen to run Fords but they would rather stay loyal to Holden,'

Murphy said. 'That helped clinch it for us. Initially Trevor [Ashby] and Steve [Reed] were part-owners of Tasman.'

New Zealander Tim Miles, a merchant banker who raced Formula Fords at home, and was heavily involved in managing open-wheeler teams in England, helped put the Tasman deal together. He is now the chairman of directors and a part-owner of Tasman with fellow New Zealanders Murphy, Alan Stewart, Jim Boult, Gray Mathias, and Australian Ron Harrop, one of the most respected automotive engineers in Australia. Harrop was a consultant to HRT till 2000, when it decided to keep its engineering base and intellectual property in-house, and he was a key figure in the Team Brock Supercar venture, which did not last. As a condition of Harrop's involvement, Tasman was

required to move from Sydney to the Melbourne suburb of Preston in 2005, and locate its high-tech garage across the road from Harrop's engineering shop. Kevin Murphy makes no secret of his wish that Tasman will eventually have the set-up and credibility to attract Greg's driving skills, perhaps as early as 2007. And even if that doesn't happen, Kevin sees Tasman as becoming so well established that Greg would be proud to own it when his driving days are over.

Richards started racing an older VX Commodore at Tasman compared with the VY he had at Dynamik. It was driven by Cameron McConville at Lansvale, and though it lacked straight-line speed it was reliable. Richards still displayed welcome competitiveness, which was helped mid-season when he was upgraded to a VY Commodore. He was

Jason Richards (orange and black Holden) lies second behind eventual 2005 Bathurst 1000 km winner Mark Skaife, closely attended by a helicopter during a late safety car period following the Greg Murphy-Marcus Ambrose collision. Richards held his position at the chequered flag.

Dirk Klynsmith/Graphic Dak Photography

There appears to be no shortage of personnel in the Tasman garage.

twice involved in top 10 shootouts — Oran Park, where he was fourth, and Barbagallo — and he had four top 10 round finishes, highlighted by sevenths at Oran Park and the Gold Coast, to end the season 14th, 12 places higher than the previous year. With 11 top 10 race finishes it was comfortably his best result since entering the formula, and was the top placing in 2004 among the single-car teams.

Richards and fellow New Zealander Fabian Coulthard were looming as top six prospects at Bathurst till a holed radiator on lap 130, the result of debris dropped by a passing competitor, forced them to make a lengthy pit stop to replace it, and relegated them to a final position of 20th. The 2004 *Supercar Yearbook* was moved to comment: 'Jason revelled at Tasman after taking a back seat at Dynamik the previous year. The arrival of a new VY Holden mid-year heralded a series of top 10 finishes. He is a class act whose fine reputation grows each year.'

It was a satisfying season for Tasman. It continued to employ a number of Lansvale staff, and Murphy said it required a change of mind-set. 'They'd no experience of winning, and limited experience of success,' Murphy said. 'They needed someone to come along who had a passion for achieving results.

We had to change the mentality of a team where being in the top 10 was as good as winning. It upset some people to leave Sydney. But being in Melbourne we're near the car manufacturer [Holden], across the road from Ron Harrop, and with immediate access to the technology required to take the team to the front.'

In 2004 the second Lansvale licence was picked up by the Wright Patton Shakespeare (WPS) team, which raced Mark Noske. The licence became Tasman's in 2005, which added Melbourne youngster Jamie Whincup as its second driver.

🏁

Kevin Murphy's story is an interesting one. It is a glowing example of how a capable, determined, no-nonsense Kiwi, who revels in what he is doing, can successfully reinvent himself in his 50s. When he moved to Australia in 1996 to become involved in motor racing, there was nothing long-term. He had limited resources but a strong desire to make a success of a career in motor sport. His attitude was that 'something will happen', and through the business acumen he had developed in the Hawke's Bay, mechanical knowledge working on Greg's cars, and his understanding of motor racing, he gradually established a footing and credibility among people with strong connections. Though he has largely beavered away in Greg's shadow, and is not one to be boastful, it is clear his influence on his son has been huge, and Greg has inherited his father's strong work ethic.

Kevin's father, Patrick Murphy, Greg's grand-father, raced speedway motorbikes at Auckland's Western Springs, and as a kid Kevin remembers camping with his father at Ardmore when the New Zealand Grand Prix was there, and attending meetings at Levin, and street races in Napier. Born in Waipukurau in Central Hawke's Bay, Kevin was a stock and station agent for many years before working for an agricultural chemical spraying company. In 1995, with his industry changing, he decided it was time to make a move, and he followed Greg to Australia. Kevin had a Formula Holden Reynard single-seater in Australia, and HRT general manager Jeff Grech rang one day to ask if Craig

Lowndes could drive it at the Australian Grand Prix meeting in early 1997 before he embarked on what turned out to be a failed Formula 3000 campaign in Europe.

A deal was agreed, only for it to be broken by HRT's owner at the time, Tom Walkinshaw. But Kevin was still paid as he had prepared the car for Lowndes. 'We taught ourselves enough, and I surrounded myself with people who knew more,' Kevin observed of that time. He worked with a number of other cars and drivers in Formula Holden, achieving success, and for a couple of years had the benefit of using HRT facilities. All the time, Kevin was building a reputation on pit lane for knowing what he was about, and was establishing strong working relationships. A logical progression was to form his own team in 1998. Greg Murphy Racing (GMR) was born with father and son as equal partners, and Kevin as managing director. They have facilities in Melbourne near Tasman.

Initially the team had Formula Holden single-seater cars of its own contesting the Gold Star Australian drivers' championship, before they were sold in favour of running customers' cars. GMR was in the championship for five years till the end of 2002. However, with the formula losing its appeal, which made it harder for Kevin to earn a living, he changed to enclosed cars. From 2003 the team ran three cars for clients competing in the buoyant Porsche Carrera Cup. It prospered, and in 2006 had the prospect of racing four cars in the series. GMR had the satisfaction in 2004 of assisting Australian prospect Alex Davison to the title, and had the cup winner again in 2005 in talented young Kiwi Fabian Coulthard, who was third and cup rookie of the year in 2004. The latter honour earned him a start in the 'driver to Europe' supporting event at the 2005 British Grand Prix at Silverstone.

In 2003 another New Zealander, old enough to be Davison and Coulthard's father, the amazing Jim Richards, won the inaugural series in his mid-50s — and, until his title aspirations were extinguished when he hit a wall at the penultimate Gold Coast round, he was still providing Coulthard with his biggest headache in 2005.

Jason Richards suited up ready for action.

Dirk Klynsmith/Graphic Dak Photography

Kevin Murphy said that despite Richards being in competition with Coulthard he had 'helped me out with Fabian in 2004'. 'I valued Jim's honesty and opinions,' Kevin said. 'He was good and easy to talk to. Jim's still a pretty tough competitor. He's a very good yardstick for team owners and talent scouts looking at the younger drivers.'

Coulthard again drove for the Tasman team in the long-distance rounds at Sandown and Bathurst in 2005, teaming with teenager Tony D'Alberto, who came from the V8 Supercar development series. They failed to finish on both occasions. Coulthard moved on in 2006 when he joined Morris Motorsports to share a Holden with Alan Gurr in the full Supercar championship.

🏁🏁🏁

Richards' racing start was like so many others. He was eight, like Greg Murphy, when he began karting in

with his company, Speed Freak Industries, which he is looking to develop.

After being second in the New Zealand Formula Ford championship he was offered an opportunity in the British equivalent. It sounded great, but there were problems with the team, and Richards dropped out, spending much of his time in England as a parts delivery boy. His potential was recognised in 1995 when he was signed as the third driver to Craig Baird and Brett Riley in Lyall Williamson's BMW Motorsport New Zealand team for the national two-litre touring car championship. Richards was delighted. It was an impressive operation. There were new cars, a flash transporter, and he had the chance to learn a lot from experienced operators. It worked out well. He was eventually promoted to lead driver, and was twice New Zealand champion in a BMW, and he formed a strong working relationship with team manager Martin Collins.

They continued their association at TKR where

There were new cars, a flash transporter, and he had the chance to learn a lot from experienced operators.

1985, and 35 titles later, including two New Zealand championships, he ventured into Mini Sevens where he was third in the national series. In the sixth form at Nelson's Waimea College he was offered the Canterbury Racing School's Formula Ford drive in the Nissan-Mobil meetings at Wellington and Pukekohe. His debut, at the age of 16, on the streets of Wellington on a Friday afternoon had a rather harrowing build-up. That day he had sat an exam, and he arrived in Wellington to find the traffic at a standstill. He nervously threw on his driving suit in the car taking him to the waterfront, and recalled his experience of the narrow track in a new car as rather daunting.

The following year Richards was head boy at Waimea, and a number of his seventh-form colleagues were going to university. For Richards, though, there was only one option. He had always wanted to be a racing driver, and having had a taste he wanted more. Richards later earned a business management diploma at Nelson Polytechnic. It has assisted him

Richards secured a third two-litre title in a Nissan Primera. Before his V8 debut at Bathurst in 2000 with TKR, he twice contested the two-litre super tourer version of the Bathurst 1000 km in the late 1990s, the first time with Riley and the second time with Barrie Thomlinson, only to drop out with engine failure on both occasions.

Richards, an immensely likeable, affable person, experienced huge highs and lows in 2005, having survived a life-threatening crash mid-season, and by the end having been one place away from winning Bathurst — easily the most important event on the programme. By the end of the year he was a much better driver for it, and in a team rich in potential, he is poised to become a genuine championship contender.

Jason Richards and Jamie Whincup had their best result in Supercars at Bathurst in 2005. They are seen here on their way to second place after filling third spot the previous round at Sandown.

SIMON WILLS

It All Turned Sour

Getty Images

Simon Wills

Born: Auckland, 3 October 1976
Championship debut: Round 12, Queensland 500, 1999
Starts: 53
Pole positions: nil (best: 3rd, round 8, Oran Park, 2004)
Round wins: 1 (round eight, Queensland 500, 2002)
Podium finishes: 1
Best championship finish: 20th, 2002
Bathurst record: debut 1998; 7 starts, 4 finishes; best result: 7th (2000)

Simon Wills's development into one of the hotter young properties in Australian motor racing has stalled and turned increasingly sour in the last three years as he has dropped off the V8 Supercar pace in his father Kieran Wills's seriously underfunded, Adelaide-based Team Dynamik.

Despite his father's considerable success on New Zealand racetracks, young Simon might never have been a racer had he not witnessed what he considered some unnecessary behaviour from then Auckland, and now New Zealand, team cricket coach, John Bracewell. Simon, then a third-former at Auckland's St Kentigern College, had revealed sufficient talent as an all-rounder in the Howick-Pakuranga representative side to be chosen in an Auckland development squad. But he says his delight at his selection and interest in cricket was sullied by Bracewell's behaviour. 'I didn't like the way John spoke to some of us or the language he used,' Wills recalled. 'I thought he was too hard, even telling some they were useless. As a 14-year-old I didn't enjoy it. I decided it wasn't for me. I didn't carry on with my cricket long-term at school. Dad went and bought me a go-kart.'

It was the start of a journey through single-seaters and touring cars financed by his well-heeled father, who was ambitious for Simon before he himself had any real idea of whether he wanted to make a career in motor racing. He was just 17 when he first ventured to England in 1995 to race Formula Fords. Simon's career gathered considerable momentum when he was the New Zealand Grand Prix victor in 1998 and 1999, Australian single-seater champion for two years (1999 and 2000), and Supercar development series winner the following season. He was just getting started as a Supercar regular in 2002 when he unexpectedly won the Queensland 500 km with Dave Besnard in a brief association with the Stone brothers.

Team Dynamik's venture into Supercars in 2003 started with so much expectation and enthusiasm. There were new VY Holden Commodores and new Holden Motorsport Aurora engines for Wills and Jason Richards, a modern transporter, smart gear, and the team looked well-financed and structured. However, the principal sponsor, Betta Electrical, withdrew at the eleventh hour, and Kieran Wills's business partner and car builder, Malcolm Ramsay, backed out after the first round, the Clipsal 500 km. Ramsay was disturbed by the way the team was being run, in particular by technical director Oscar Fiorinotto, who had previously been at OO Motorsport when Craig Lowndes was struggling. It didn't help either that, without sponsorship, he was required to use his own money to finance the team.

Ramsay built the team's first two VY Commodores, for Richards and Wills, at his Adelaide-based Birrana Engineering. His Birrana team had considerable success in Formula Holden single-seater racing, running some of the bigger emerging names in Australian motor sport, including Kiwis Greg Murphy and Simon Wills, as well as Jason Bright, Rick Kelly, Paul Stokell and Mark Webber, who is now racing in Formula One.

While he was with Ramsay, Wills won the Australian open-wheeler series twice, and in the following year made an immediate impact when he switched to touring cars and captured the Konica development title.

Despite the early setbacks Wills and Richards nearly won the Sandown 500 km that first year. The weather was dreadful and they were headed for an upset after starting fifth on the grid, having handled the testing conditions with remarkable composure. They would have finished at least second had not Richards tangled with the race leader, Mark Skaife, in the closing moments. The clash left the Dynamik car stuck in wet sand, and the team with nothing to show for what had been a brilliant performance by two emerging drivers. 'Jason was catching Mark, and Oscar [Fiorinotto] left

it to Jason to make the call when it was safe to make the pass,' Wills said. 'He said to Jason over the radio "just stay on the black stuff". It didn't quite pan out, which was pretty frustrating.'

Both Kiwi drivers often showed impressive speed, qualifying for numerous top 10 shootouts, and there were some encouraging results, but financial problems became increasingly apparent. Richards was among team members who were owed money, and he left the team at the end of the season in acrimonious circumstances. He took legal action, and in 2005 won a case in the South Australian District Court for back pay and other money owed. The court ordered Dynamik to pay Richards $A41,704.44 plus interest. At the same time, Kieran Wills unsuccessfully tried to sue Richards for negligence and reckless driving, after his car suffered considerable damage in racing accidents, as well as for loss of profits and sponsorship. The matter dragged on, Richards having to return to court in 2005 before the matter was finally resolved.

Despite the early setbacks Wills and Richards nearly won . . .

Fairfax Sunday Newspapers

Simon Wills had an early taste of touring car racing in this Ford Telstar, formerly raced by Paul Radisich.

In 2004 the team attracted more unfavourable publicity and brought the formula into disrepute when it was found to have tested illegally at the remote Woomera rocket range facility in South Australia. After a three-day inquiry, Dynamik was fined $A104,000, and penalised a lap for two rounds of the championship. Though Kieran Wills argued that the car, which had none of its usual signage, was being used by a third party to conduct scientific research, which had no benefits for the Supercar championship, the Confederation of Australian Motorsport said the team had breached the series rules in conducting an unauthorised test. Dynamik's actions and response were said to be naïve given that the AVESCO rules on testing were clearly laid down. It was additional to the allotted six testing days that each team is allowed in a season; it needed permission to do what it did; and, had permission been granted, it was required that any testing be

observed by a Supercars representative. Supercars chairman Tony Cochrane said the Woomera testing was unfortunate. It did the team a lot of harm. It didn't handle it as well as it should have, he said.

Highly experienced New Zealand driver Craig Baird described the Woomera incident as 'blatant cheating'. He said: 'To de-badge the car and go testing [against the rules] is no different to running around doing steroids. At that point everyone in pit lane wiped them.'

Baird estimated Kieran Wills had spent up to $A15 million on furthering his son's racing career — a sign of the harsh economic reality of motor racing. He rated Simon as a 'very good driver'. 'Simon's not got natural ability but he's done the hard yards,' Baird said.

Given the team's turbulent history it is probably no wonder that big-money, long-term sponsorships have continued to be elusive. In 2005 there were more problems when Will Davison was hired to

'Simon's not got natural ability but he's done the hard yards . . .'

Simon Wills fires up his Holden Commodore on the way to qualifying fifth at the Queensland 500 km at Ipswich in 2003. It counted for little, as he failed to finish.

The Holden Commodore of Simon Wills and Jason Richards at the Sandown 500 km in 2003 — they came very close to achieving an upset win in this event.

Dirk Klynsmith/Graphic Dak Photography

Embattled Team Dynamik owner Kieran Wills (right) flanked by technical director Oscar Fiorinotto.

make his Supercar debut only for the arrangement to lapse, much to Davison's distress. He sought redress through the courts, and the matter was settled in his favour later in the year.

During 2005, double Bathurst 1000 km winner Tony Longhurst bought both of Team Dynamik's licences, and he decided that he would partner Brazilian Max Wilson in one car at Bathurst. Simon, who had emerged largely unscathed from his serious crash in the Sunday morning warm-up in the previous round at Sandown — flying backwards over a crash barrier when the front brakes failed — was left without a drive at Bathurst. As it happened, Longhurst and Wilson were eliminated early when their car suffered damage in a mid-field melee, and part-time Kiwis Kayne Scott and Mark Porter drove the team's other car to a highly creditable 11th place.

After missing the Bathurst, Surfers Paradise and Symmons Plains rounds, Wills appeared at the season finale at Phillip Island where he finished 30th overall. A final championship position of 34th was hardly a fair reflection of his ability. 'We had good cars, and a good infrastructure, but no money,' was Simon Wills's summation of the team's woes as he sat out Bathurst. 'We never had a main sponsor. Dad's used a lot of his money. Losing our main sponsor just as

we were starting was a serious setback. We couldn't spend money on the cars' development, evolving them into faster race cars, which was needed to be competitive. The lack of a budget is where our problems have come from.'

Wills likened Dynamik's position to that of the Formula One Minardi team, whose efforts have been stifled by a lack of financial resources. He has been taken aback at the politics that one has to go through to 'get up the grid'. 'You have to get people on side all the time,' he said. 'We [Dad and I] don't go out of our way to suck up to people.' Wills said it was a pity that Malcolm Ramsay departed so early. 'It was an eye-opener to him how much money was required to run the team. He wasn't willing to contribute his own money.'

It was so unfortunate the way things had unfolded, Wills said. Despite a number of top 10 finishes, including a fourth at the Gold Coast round of 2004, and some impressive qualifying times, he had never been on the podium with Dynamik. 'All Dad wanted to do was have his own race team,' Wills said. 'He dreamed of having a V8 Supercar team, and he didn't want to close up shop, and put people out of jobs, when the going got tough. I don't think he's bitter, but just upset we haven't realised our potential when we had the cars right up there. Dad was the driving force when I was young. He probably wanted it more than I did. There was no pressure on me to succeed though. He came to England four times in that first year but he sat in the stands when I was racing.'

Wills said he was not being paid to race, saying he had declined any offers till the team had a principal sponsor. He said he was getting by as the team's signwriter, a skill he had learned in the last couple of years, and through the good grace of a couple of loyal personal sponsors. 'I've still had a lot more out of it than I expected,' Wills said. 'I never had a particular goal, I'm happy.'

Not surprisingly, he defends the decision to go to Woomera. He drove the car, and he maintains there was no attempt to do anything illegal. It had largely been seen, he said, as a chance to attract some much-needed revenue. 'We became a scapegoat.

There were a couple of other things that had gone on with other teams but we copped it,' Wills said. Dynamik turned to the Federation Internationale de l'Automobile court of appeal. A hearing was set down in Paris for early 2005 but Wills said it was decided not to pursue it because they lacked the funds to do it properly.

Amid the controversy and negative public perception the team had 'stood firm', Wills said. 'Everyone in the team knew the situation, and went about their business as usual,' he said. 'We're a close-knit bunch. We just wanted to run successfully and enjoy the sport. I'm very disappointed for Dad's sake. He's been kicked by the press. He's had to take the brunt of the criticism. He's always wanted to do the right thing. He's had good intentions.'

Kieran Wills won numerous New Zealand titles in various saloon and sports sedan categories and set a land speed record. He had a number of successful businesses, including constructing and operating rest homes and private hospital facilities, developing a nationally recognised snack food company, and moving into sports marketing. The businesses helped support his and Simon's motor racing, and provided Kieran with the capital to establish his own Supercar team. 'It was a bitter experience for me, and one I'd prefer to forget all about,' Malcolm Ramsay said. 'I got out when the rot set in, and Holden Motorsport withdrew its support early on too. The way the team was being run it was just a question of how long it would last. Things were done which were not the professional way to go about it. The team's been going nowhere. Simon's been a bit like the meat in the sandwich. He's a good driver, he deserved better. He went from hero to zero.' Ramsay said the high costs of being involved in Supercars required big sponsorship. 'It's like a bottomless pit, the costs are never ending,' he said. 'It's all out of kilter considering what the cars are.'

Greg Murphy was among those impressed by how well Team Dynamik was looking in its first Supercar season. In a column in the *Sunday Star Times* in August 2003, he wrote: 'None [of the Kiwis in Supercars] have made more of an impact this year than Simon Wills and Jason Richards in the new Team

After impressing, among others, Greg Murphy, the Team Dynamik set-up went increasingly sour.

'Simon's been a bit like the meat in the sandwich. He's a good driver, he deserved better . . .'

Dynamik. They've done a remarkable job starting from scratch. . . . It has probably cost $NZ8 million or more to set-up and run the two-car team for the first year. Team Dynamik has done it right, and had the funding to bring on board some good people with plenty of experience in V8 racing. The team is owned by a Kiwi . . . although there are several key Australians with expertise in this sport aboard.'

Once Simon Wills had had a taste for racing as a teenager, it wasn't long before he was racing an old Swift in the lower category of the New Zealand Formula Ford open-wheeler championship. By the end of that first season in the early 1990s he had displayed his competitiveness by qualifying on the front row of the grid at Pukekohe, and he was second in his category. The following summer he was challenging the leading Formula Ford drivers, Jason Richards and Shane Drake, in a newer Swift, and his father was encouraged enough to assist him to drive for the Swift works team in the British Formula Ford series in 1995 — even though Wills was still too young to know if motor racing was what he wanted to pursue in the long term.

He had three seasons racing in England, one in Formula Ford, and two in Formula Three, the latter a traditional breeding ground for Formula One drivers, during which he acquitted himself well. 'I learned so much that first year,' Wills recalled. 'As a 17-year-old I grew up pretty quickly, all the time surrounded by politics. I was runner-up for rookie of the year, and sixth overall.' After finishing 13th in the British Formula Three championship in 1997, which included twice being punted off the track by an Australian now in Formula One, Mark Webber, Wills decided it was time to shut up shop. 'I was always competitive but I didn't have the budget to beat the other guys,' he recalled. 'If I could have made Formula One, I would have. In hindsight I

was never going to make it. I had to be realistic. I told Dad it wasn't worth it financially to race there any longer. I learned a hell of a lot, and we decided to put that experience to good use in Australia. I was so raw when I first went to England. I didn't have the knowledge. It might have been easier to have had more racing first in Australia or New Zealand.'

In 1998 Kevin Murphy gave Wills a start in Formula Holden in Australia in a Reynard that proved unreliable. Things started to happen when he was signed by Ramsay. Driving a later Reynard, Wills won the series two years in a row — 1999 and 2000 — to become the Australian single-seater champion. Wills was similarly authoritative back in New Zealand, in the late 1990s collecting successive Grand Prix victories at Christchurch's Ruapuna circuit. Both times he headed off much-heralded countryman Scott Dixon — who went on to become Indy Racing League champion in the United States — and in different races beat two of his bigger Supercar rivals, Greg Murphy and Craig Lowndes.

By the time Wills had his first full-time Supercar

Simon Wills (right) is not surprisingly highly elated at his biggest moment in Supercars in 2002 when the scratch team of himself and Dave Besnard grabbed a stunning victory.

season for John Briggs Motorsport in 2002 he had already had a good taste of the formula, having made his first appearance at the Bathurst 1000 km in 1998, and having an ideal grounding by winning the development series title in 2001. He partnered David 'Skippy' Parsons in an old Gibson Motorsport Commodore VS in his Bathurst debut, and it ended disastrously for Wills at Forrest Elbow. There were no yellow flags to warn him when he came upon a number of tangled cars, and he hit one of them head on at 170 kmh. Privateer Greg Crick had his car excluded from the results for allegedly causing the incident. It was Wills's first big crash, and his injuries were severe: a cracked sternum, broken ribs and a collapsed lung, which left him struggling to breathe as he was rushed to hospital. Wills said the injuries had been worse than they might have been because his co-driver Parsons had tangled the seatbelt at the last driver change. 'As a result I moved a

team, and the absence of help. 'The team wouldn't let me develop the car. You can't stand still,' Wills said. 'It was hard to explain to 150 corporate guests at races when things weren't going well.'

The Stone brothers engaged him again for the Queensland 500 km, in place of former world motorcycle champion Wayne Gardner, to drive alongside regular Dave Besnard. It suited Wills, as he was very familiar with the Ipswich track. It was the Briggs's test venue. Besnard qualified well, and was in the top four early, Wills kept the car on the pace, and Besnard held his nerve to bring about victory. Against all predictions the scratch team had finished first, creating considerable celebration in pit lane. It ended Ford's drought of round wins, which had lasted for a year. 'I was elated. The win proved to me and quite a few other people that I was up to it after doing so well in other categories,' Wills said. 'I led the whole middle stint. I did 60 to 70 laps. I was surprised how

'I was surprised how comfortable I was leading Mark Skaife. In such a well-rounded car it made my job easy.'

lot,' he said. 'I rolled over the edge of the seat and cracked into the steering wheel, and then another three or four cars hit me.'

The following year at Bathurst, 1999, was little better. Again Wills failed to finish, this time crashing the Gibson Holden VT he shared with the Palmerston North-born John Faulkner, after he skidded on oil dropped by another car at The Cutting. His third time at Bathurst finally produced something worthwhile. Wills was signed by SBR to co-drive for Craig Baird in the Pirtek Ford AU, and in the words of Wills they 'stayed out of trouble' and finished seventh, which remains his best result in seven starts.

Wills's single-seater and Konica championships in consecutive seasons, the latter in the Holden Greg Murphy and Steven Richards drove to Bathurst victory in 1999, earned him a full start in a Briggs Cat Ford in 2002, but it didn't work out. He caused a stir in his rookie year, quitting mid-season, disappointed with the car, the inexperience of the

comfortable I was leading Mark Skaife. In such a well-rounded car it made my job easy.'

That year Wills also managed a handy 11th at Bathurst, this time partnering Jason Richards in the Team Kiwi Racing Commodore in happier times, before the debacle at Team Dynamik ruined what had been a fruitful relationship. It required a huge effort to have the car start after Richards crashed it in qualifying, and the pair were further handicapped by having to start from the rear of the grid. However, apart from the Sandown 500 km in 2003, Wills was rarely in a position to secure a second round win. The Team Dynamik Commodores were becoming increasingly tired and outdated, and he was too often firmly rooted among the also-rans.

Although Simon and Kieran were no longer involved full-time in Supercars in 2006, they helped Mark Petch. He bought the Dynamik car formerly raced by Max Wilson for a leading New Zealand V8 championship driver Kayne Scott to compete in the upgraded Fujitsu Australian development series.

CRAIG BAIRD

Unfinished Business

Photosport

Craig Baird

Born: Hamilton, 22 July 1970
Championship debut: Round 12, Queensland 500, 1999
Starts: 69
Pole positions: 1
Round wins: nil (best: 3rd, round 1, Phillip Island, 2000)
Podium finishes: 1
Best championship finish: 15th, 2000
Bathurst record: debut 1990; 11 starts, 6 finishes; best result:
    4th (V8 race 1997)

Craig Baird landed one of the better drives in V8 Supercars in 2000 when he signed for the emerging SBR. Ross and Jimmy Stone, formerly of Pukekohe, were considered two of the better engineers on pit lane, having prepared cars that had twice won the Bathurst 1000 km, and collected the Australian touring car title in 1995. The dedicated Gold Coast pair were about to embark on their third full season on their own after splitting from the team they had co-owned with Alan Jones, a past Formula One champion.

Baird came to SBR with strong credentials. He was an accomplished single-seater racer, having won the New Zealand Grand Prix on three consecutive occasions. But, like fellow Kiwi V8 drivers Paul Radisich and Greg Murphy, he tired of the hand-to-mouth existence in the financially draining open-wheelers, where sometimes there was no certainty of even completing a season, and, especially in England and the United States, the playing field was tilted decisively in favour of the teams with superior resources. He made the switch to 'tin tops' in late 1993, as much as anything because he knew the prospects of making a stable living from motor racing were much brighter there. There was a downside. It did mean conceding that he had given up on his long-held ambition of competing in Formula One. Though Baird was never quite in that league, he considered that Radisich was close

and might well have made it had he had backing similar to that given to Scott Dixon. Baird, in turn, was encouraged by being able to match Radisich in open-wheelers, even having the better of him on occasions.

It wasn't long before Baird was making an impact in touring cars in New Zealand with Lyall Williamson's slick International Motorsport BMW team. He was New Zealand champion for four years, had further good results in BMWs in South Africa, and replaced Radisich in the Ford Mondeo team in the British touring car championship. Baird had his first taste of V8s in 1997, driving for the high-profile Dick Johnson Racing. He partnered Johnson's son, Steven Johnson, and together the pair made a strong impression. They were seventh in the Sandown 500 km and fourth at the Bathurst 1000 km in a Ford Falcon EL.

Two years later, this time driving for the Stones, Baird and Jason Bright led the Queensland 500 km at Ipswich with 20 laps to go, only for their Falcon to suffer engine failure. When Bright opted to try his hand at Indy Lights single-seaters in 2000 the Stones were sufficiently impressed to offer Baird his first full-time opportunity in Supercars. It started promisingly enough when Baird drove the Pirtek Ford to first place in the second heat at the very first round at Victoria's Phillip Island circuit, and he finished third overall. The Stones were over the moon. That heat win was the Stones's first in a sprint race. But it didn't last. Baird was unable to reproduce that level of performance, so much so that he was sacked halfway through his two-year contract. There were other worthy efforts, however, including sevenths in the Bathurst 1000 km with Simon Wills and in the sprint round at Darwin's Hidden Valley, a ninth at Victoria's Winton raceway, and a strong qualifying position of sixth at the Queensland sprint round.

Baird does not mince his words when he refers to 2000 as 'a disaster', which, he says, has 'held me back in V8s ever since'. 'I got lost. You can't just jump into them. I hadn't driven V8s full-time before, and I didn't know the circuits. I came to Australia far too late [in my career],' Baird said. 'I couldn't get my head around learning to drive the car quickly enough. I didn't know how to set the car up or how to qualify it. I got down on myself. I lost my confidence. The

Stones asked me to leave. . . . I felt I owed Ross and Jimmy so much more. They'd mortgaged their houses for us to go motor racing. I felt sorry for them. I could have delivered them a lot if they'd allowed me another year. People have tended to judge me on that year. I've not been able to get the [quality] cars [to race] that Greg Murphy does.'

Though Baird was damning in his assessment of the year, it is interesting to note that his final championship position of 15th remained his best five years later. Had Baird continued at SBR, he would have been newcomer Marcos Ambrose's team-mate in 2001, and quite possibly become a star of Supercars given SBR's huge success with Ambrose and later Russell Ingall, which started to gather momentum that year.

Baird admits he found the cumbersome five-litre V8s very foreign after the more cultured single-seaters and two-litre super tourers he was used to, and he was

Baird does not mince his words when he refers to 2000 as 'a disaster', which, he says, has 'held me back in V8s ever since'.

Craig Baird in the 2000 Stone brothers' Pirtek Falcon, which he found something of a brick after the more precise machinery he was used to.

harsh in his assessment of them. 'The single-seaters were very precise, and the two-litres nimble, more sophisticated, and with a tight grip on the track,' Baird said. 'The V8s have bugger all grip, they duck and dive all over the place. It's like driving a big taxi with lots of power. They're hot and heavy, and there's bugger all electronics. You'd be hard pressed to drive a bigger monster. They're dinosaurs.'

Baird's premature departure from SBR was the second time he had lost a drive within a short space of time. He described the Mondeo as 'the worst race car I'd ever driven', and when the funding from Ford dried up unexpectedly at the end of 1998, Baird was once again out in the street. That experience soured his passion for motor racing, and was compounded by the woes of 2000, which further dampened a love for the sport he'd had since he first started karting at the tender age of four.

'I couldn't have cared if I didn't race again,' Baird recalled after the Mondeo debacle. However, he continued to excel in the New Zealand TransAm championships, so much so that when the car's owner, Alan Ferguson, took it to the United States to see how competitive it was, Baird caught the locals by surprise in running second in a round in Las Vegas in a 40-car field.

'It proved to me I was not a total wood duck,' he said. 'But I was more confused than ever about my racing future when I came back.'

His enthusiasm for the sport further evaporated in 1999 when the Stone brothers' Ford Falcon he was driving died with engine failure when leading the Queensland 500 km.

After the shattering 2000 experience Baird became a part-time driver the following year. It forced him to examine other options, and he started a furniture manufacturing business in Brisbane, specialising in lounge suites. It grew rapidly, and he still retains a strong interest in it. The long periods on the sideline left him with plenty of time to contemplate his racing career. He knew that he did not want to leave racing with his record in the

Craig Baird trying to make the best of an uncompetitive Ford Mondeo in the British touring car championship at Donington Park in 1998.

gloomy state it was when the Stones said 'goodbye'. Baird was convinced he was a much better driver than he had shown in 2000, and that given a competitive car he was every bit as good as anyone else. It was apparent, too, that as he was living in Australia the most logical way back to full-time racing was to give Supercars another try. His bruised ego received a welcome massage when he was unexpectedly offered the chance to drive for the new one-car Team Brock in 2002, a venture that sounded highly exciting. 'When it came I knew I just had to get on with it, and put all those bad experiences at Stone Brothers behind me,' Baird said. 'I had to grab the V8 by the scruff of the neck, and get the better of it.'

At SBR Baird's team-mate was Tony Longhurst, a driver good enough to twice win the Bathurst 1000 km. He considered Baird was a lot better in 2000 than the results suggested, and he recommended Baird to Team Brock owner Rod Nash. Unfortunately what looked a great set-up, and one Baird believes should now be among the most potent in the championship, withered and died within 12 months — though Brock would go on for one more year with a new team owned by Kees Weel. The potential was huge. Brock, still the biggest name in Australian motor sport, was in charge of merchandise, which was a huge seller, rivalling the hottest outfit at the time, HRT; Ron Harrop, an engineering legend, was on board; and Nash, a successful businessman and capable driver, had the capital to ensure the team was well financed.

There was a perception that Team Brock would be on a similar footing to the top Holden teams in terms of equipment. The reality was far from that, with the Holden Commodore VX Baird had to drive being off the pace. It was first driven by Nash in 2000, and in Baird's words it was 'crap', and fit only for 'privateer racing'. At Bathurst, a disappointed Brock talked about it lacking the speed to keep up with the frontrunners. Harrop, who has his own engineering business in Melbourne, was to build engines for the team, but he had little time to make an impact before the team collapsed. His expertise has since been utilised with telling effect by the increasingly effective Tasman Motorsport team.

One of Craig Baird's best moments in Supercars in the rain at Winton in 2004, when he caught his opposition off guard to brilliantly claim pole position.

'There were too many partners, and too many business plans . . .'

So why did it fall over? Brock even came out of retirement, at 57, to partner Baird at Bathurst in pursuit of a record 10th win. Handicapped by a five-minute penalty for a fuel leak and mechanical problems, they were a distant 23rd. Baird put it plainly when he said it was a case of 'too many egos getting in the way'. 'It was a total disaster,' he said. 'There were too many partners, and too many business plans. They were pulling in different directions. The idea was that it would grow into a super team. Peter became frustrated. He has a huge amount of self-belief, having achieved more than most sportsmen in Australia. He wanted to do more than sell merchandise and have his name on the side of the car.' Baird found Brock easy to deal with. 'Because of his success he would say everything on his mind,' Baird said.

Baird's results for 2002 were thoroughly forgettable. He never finished a race or a round in the top 10, his best being 13th in round two at Phillip Island. Baird's top effort was probably to qualify 10th for the Queensland 500 km, which was negated when he failed to finish. He ended up 27th in the championship. With the future of Team Brock uncertain, Baird approached his good friend at TKR, manager Martin Collins, about the chances of driving for it in 2003. The pair had had a rewarding association when Baird was driving BMWs for Lyall Williamson in the 1990s, and Baird was aware that Jason Richards was leaving TKR.

Within a day or two Baird had a letter of intent from TKR owner David John, and Baird spent another couple of years driving cars that struggled to be consistently competitive. In 2003 he was driving a Larry Perkins Holden built in 1999, and the following year a 2001 Paul Morris-built Commodore that Baird said had been 'written off three times'. Things were better in 2004. He stunned his rivals in the wind and rain in round seven at Victoria's Winton circuit when he secured his and the team's first pole position on the grid. He was 10th in the

and offering the hope of superior results in the long term. The decision to jump back to Ford after periods at two Holden teams was not made lightly. Baird had huge respect for John, who he called 'a street fighter'. He admired the way John had kept the TKR team going on a skeleton budget, against all odds. He had been offered a new contract with TKR, and would have been happy to continue had not Gore's attractive proposition come along. 'Things needed to change at TKR,' Baird said. 'Nothing had. The funds were getting drier, everything was becoming more stale. Corporate New Zealand never backed the team. It badly needed money to keep its head above water. It was a hard decision to leave. I felt sorry for David [John], and in Martin [Collins] I was walking away from one of my closest friends in motor sport, who I'd asked for a job.'

Baird's departure created some unwanted flak, though, when John announced at a team function

'The funds were getting drier, everything was becoming more stale. Corporate New Zealand never backed the team . . .'

top 10 shootout for the Queensland 500 km, and he was ninth overall in the first of two rounds at Sydney's Eastern Creek circuit. 'I've always liked driving in the wet,' said Baird of the Winton feat. 'I was still surprised though to be on pole. I knew the way we were going in practice and qualifying we could run in the top five. The car was just a jet in the wet. I had very good first and second sectors, but I almost came off in the last. I was more excited for the team than for myself. It would hopefully help their sponsorship deals, and Martin [Collins] was pretty pumped up after all the effort he had put in over the years.'

The ninth at the first of two rounds at Eastern Creek also confirmed Baird's skill in the rain. However, a final position of 27th in the championship left him dissatisfied, and ripe to be picked up when WPS boss Craig Gore started courting him. The forthright Gore offered Baird an opportunity in a better-resourced but unproven team, providing him and his family with greater security of income,

that Baird had signed for another two years and Baird had to say that he had not. He was pleased to be able to assist TKR for 2005. It included helping the partnership with Morris Motorsports, and structuring the deal for respected Kiwi engine builder Alan Draper to join the combined operation. 'I take my hat off to David,' Baird said. 'He got Paul Radisich to drive for him, and found a way to raise the money for a new car for the first time, which started to produce better results.'

In the same way Tony Longhurst helped him get a start at Team Brock, another driver put in a good word for him with Craig Gore at WPS. He was none other than ageless Melbourne-based Kiwi, Jim Richards, who had been scrapping in Australia with Baird in the Carrera Cup Porsche championship. Gore was looking for a second driver to partner the talented, but erratic, Dave Besnard, and one to help develop a new car. Despite his advancing years Gore saw Richards as ideal. Richards, however, was quick to say his full-time days in Supercars were long gone, but that, from recent experience, he considered Baird to have the necessary outlook, and an ability to win races.

Baird knew Gore was not everyone's favourite bloke. Gore is one of the most successful businessmen in Australia, and he has a reputation for wearing his heart on his sleeve. There was the perception that WPS was 'a bunch of rich guys going motor racing', and in its first season in 2004 the team became a laughing stock with the cars all too often in strife. The negative stuff was not altogether surprising. WPS is a financial services company, and chief executive Gore, though eager to learn and be fully involved in the new business, started with very little knowledge of it. He saw V8 racing as an ideal way of promoting his company, which was unusual as an overwhelming number of Supercar clients were in the automotive business. Instead of just sponsoring a team, Gore chose the far more daunting route of establishing his own team, and he invested $A15 million over three years to set it up. He bought Larry Perkins's level

one, two-car franchise — Perkins continues to race with a level two, one-car franchise and leases another — as well as old equipment from the 00 Motorsport team of Fred Gibson, and latterly Bob Forbes, which included two Ford Falcons BAs built in 2002.

In 2004 Besnard was a distant 30th in the championship, and other drivers who appeared in the second car were further back. Though the same cars were still being used in 2005, WPS was starting to earn better results after going backwards for some time. Baird's worst round was No. 8 at Sydney's Oran Park Raceway when he came away without a single point. 'A few people were sacked [in 2005] for making stupid mistakes. Craig had a bit of a cleanout,' Baird said. 'I've got new mechanics on my car, and had a new engine builder during the season. You need to trust in these guys. It's never easy starting a team from scratch. It was all a bit of a rush, and some not so good people were hired. Craig doesn't tolerate idiots, and he makes it very clear to everyone where he stands. He and I have a

Getty Images

Craig Baird's Holden leaves the ground at Eastern Creek in 2004 in what turned out to be a forgettable last round for him at Team Kiwi. An electrical fault prevented him qualifying and he failed to finish race one after starting from pit lane..

Craig Baird in his days driving BMWs for Lyall Williamson in the 1990s, an opportunity that revived his career.

lot of heart-to-heart chats. It helps I've been racing for more than 30 years. He's learning quickly, and no sponsor works harder than he does.'

It grated with Gore that Ford Motorsport has not contributed any money to the team, so much so that at the Symmons Plains round in Tasmania in 2004 Besnard displayed a windscreen strip that declared WPS received no money from Ford. He was soon black-flagged, and the team was required to cover the offending words before Besnard could resume racing. In recent years Ford has invested heavily in most of the teams running Fords, the better-performing teams particularly so.

Signs that WPS was starting to get its act together were evident at Bathurst in 2005. Even after Besnard had twice run off the track, and blown a best position of fourth, he and Baird did well enough to finish eighth, the team's first top 10 of the season. When Baird took over from Besnard, who had started the race, the car was a distant 23rd. With the Falcon displaying good speed, Baird resurrected their fortunes with an impressive long middle stint that had the car on the verge of the top 10, and well placed to capitalise on the carnage that occurred in the closing laps when Greg Murphy and Marcos Ambrose collided at Griffin's Bend at the top of Mountain Straight, blocking the track. Baird

built on Bathurst with an 11th and a 12th in the first two heats at Surfers Paradise but the ground was lost in the last two rounds, at Symmons Plains and Phillip Island, leaving a frustrated Baird languishing 23rd in the championship.

Bathurst has not been a particularly profitable place for Baird in 11 appearances since he and fellow New Zealander Brett Riley failed to finish in 1990 driving a BMW M3. In October 1997, what perhaps should have been the pinnacle of his career turned horribly sour. He and Queenslander Paul Morris were declared the winners of the AMP Bathurst 1000 km for super tourers, which that year was the official Bathurst race ahead of that run for the V8s a few weeks later. But it all fell apart when they were disqualified because Baird had driven their BMW 320i for 30 minutes longer than the three-and-a-half-hour limit. 'It was all a bit bizarre,' Baird said. 'Paul and I were on the podium, we held the trophy, we had a couple of drinks out if it. A bit later BMW took us aside and said "we've got a bit of bad news chaps". The rules were a bit ambiguous, but BMW didn't fight it. They didn't want any bad press. The second car was a BMW from the same team [New Zealander Lyall Williamson's] so the Brabham brothers [Geoff and David] were declared the winners.'

Baird was back at Bathurst the following month for the V8 race, this time partnering Dick Johnson's son Steven in a Ford Falcon. Repairs to an oil line split on lap 30 cost them several laps but they still managed to finish fourth, which remains Baird's best placing there. He has mixed feelings about that performance. While it was 'about the best I'd driven', he says he and Johnson would not be able to finish as high in today's harsher environment after losing 'four or five laps'. 'The difference between the haves and have-nots was so great then,' Baird said. 'Not many cars were competitive, and we were rookies in V8s. It was not that hard to pass all but the top few cars on Conrod Straight, but it's not like that now. I don't think I've passed anyone on Conrod for the last four years.'

Like so many drivers, Baird's early path was inevitable given his family's motor racing involvement. Baird's father, Stan, had service stations and garages, and he successfully raced a twin-cam Ford Escort before putting Craig's aspirations ahead of his own. Baird started in karts so young — he was four — that it is not surprising he remembers being 'scared' the first time he saw one. Baird assembled a formidable record in karting, being New Zealand champion seven times. He was 15 when his parents saw a Titan Ford Formula advertised, and bought it for him. Baird attended the Southwell private school in Hamilton but was not academically inclined and left at the same age. He had an after-school job at a garage, which included sweeping the floor, and on leaving school he became an apprentice motor mechanic — as had Jim Richards and Paul Radisich, among others, before him.

Baird was similarly dominant in single-seaters, developing a big reputation with his consistent performances against some pretty useful opposition. In the early days he valued the support and help of one of his father's friends, Roger Revell, and later one of New Zealand's best drivers in his day, David Oxton, acted as a mentor.

An increasingly confident Baird was New Zealand Formula Atlantic champion on several occasions, and completed a notable hat-trick of New Zealand Grand Prix victories in a Ralt, a Swift and a Reynard. He went to England one year full of hope. There was the prospect of entering Formula Three under the wing of expatriate Kiwi Dick Bennetts's West Surrey Racing team. Baird had a successful test only to have the deal offered to Bennetts collapse, and Baird was left out in the cold. He regarded it as one of his few racing regrets, believing it might have changed his career for the better. He was a worthy seventh in the British Formula 3000 championship in an uncompetitive Japanese Dome at a time when Baird could see his single-seater aspirations sliding away. There were promising moments too in the United State before Baird's reliance on prize money to keep him afloat backfired when his repair bill outstripped his income.

Though the 21st century has been a lean time for Baird, a driver who had become accustomed to

Craig Baird making an impact driving a BMW in South Africa.

Fairfax Sunday Newspapers

success, his desire to return to the glory days of the 1990s remains strong. 'I'm still as hungry for success in the V8s as I was when I started full-time in 2000,' he says simply. But Baird has mellowed from those days in the 1990s when he felt under pressure to do well, when he could be withdrawn and stroppy. He recalls some intense single-seater battles with Paul Radisich, now one of his best friends. They became so heated Baird can recall them 'grabbing each other's [racing] overalls' after one incident. Baird says he was 'a shy lad', who stuck to himself, which tended to give the impression he was a bit difficult.

Lyall Williamson remembered a shy Baird coming to see him in Auckland in 1993 about a job racing alongside Brett Riley in Williamson's new BMW team. Baird saw the prospect of a position in a magazine, and made contact with Williamson. 'Craig didn't have one dollar in his pocket, and his hair was all over the place,' Williamson said. 'He looked dreadful. He was so nervous. He ballsed up

finishes. He talks easily, and with frankness and passion, about his mixed racing fortunes, and he enjoys being regarded as a 'fairly decent bloke in pit lane'.

In April 2005 Baird was involved in a frightening crash at Pukekohe in the final of the three V8 round heats. In drizzle and fading light he was shunted from behind by the Castrol Perkins Commodore of Paul Dumbrell, and Baird's missile-like WPS Falcon hammered the infield fence, going backwards at 240 kmh. The accident, just past the start-finish line, left the huge crowd, only a few metres away, gasping in horror. There was huge relief when Baird and Dumbrell emerged shaken but otherwise okay. The incident occurred after Dumbrell had come unstuck trying to pass the Tasman Commodore of Jamie Whincup and Baird as the cars came over the hill. Whincup was in a bit of trouble when he slid off the track and ran onto the dirt. Baird slowed to avoid hitting Whincup, but Dumbrell stayed on the limit, intent on passing both Baird and

. . . shunted from behind . . . Baird's missile-like WPS Falcon hammered the infield fence, going backwards at 240 kmh.

the interview so badly. But I knew he wanted to do it, and he had the credentials. I'd not previously considered Craig because I didn't think he'd be interested in racing touring cars.'

It was a hugely successful partnership. Baird won the New Zealand touring car title four years in a row, and he takes credit for alerting Williamson to the emerging talents of another New Zealand V8 racer, Jason Richards, at that time cutting a swathe through Formula Ford. After starting out as the 'boy' in a three-car line-up, Richards went on to bring the Williamson BMW team more touring car titles. Baird raced BMWs for Williamson in Australia when the team had factory backing, and the pair retain a strong friendship and working relationship. Baird continues to cross the Tasman to drive Williamson cars in the New Zealand Porsche GT3 championship.

He is a far more rounded individual today as he reflects on a career of considerable achievement, but one he is restless to make a lot more of before he

Whincup. Dumbrell then ploughed into Baird, and Cameron McConville's Holden was also caught up in the skirmish. It resulted in Dumbrell being fined $A15,000, and losing 75 points, and he was further fined for providing false information.

With the damage to Baird's car costing around $A70,000 to repair, Craig Gore was understandably incensed, and eager to make his views known. That resulted in him being fined $NZ12,000 for using abusive language.

Baird had been concerned that if he had clipped Whincup he might, in turn, have been hit by one of the old white posts lining the inside of the track, or worse, have the car career over the wooden fence and into the helicopters parked nearby. 'I had a duty of care when I could see the potential for disaster,' Baird said. 'I slowed to avoid hitting Jamie [Whincup] but Paul [Dumbrell] didn't. I checked to see how Paul was, and we ended up shaking hands. The data showed I wasn't in the wrong.' Baird's actions toward Dumbrell were not a reflection of how he was feeling at the time, when he had a few choice words to say about Dumbrell's stupidity.

Baird and his wife Louise live on Queensland's Gold Coast with their children, Brieanna and Luca. 'Bairdo', as he is universally referred to on pit lane, loves the lifestyle, and the idyllic weather allows him to pursue one of his passions — having a perfect lawn, which he likes to mow every two or three days.

The progress made by WPS and Baird at Bathurst and Surfers Paradise in 2005 counted for nothing in Baird's case early the following year when he became a casualty of an amalgamation between Craig Gore's WPS operation and that of the longer-running Mark Larkham.

Baird and fellow WPS driver Dave Besnard were chopped in favour of one of Larkham's drivers, Jason Bargwanna, and Max Wilson, just when the prospect of a new BF Falcon offered Baird the promise of something better.

Once again Baird was without a full-time V8 drive though he expected to appear as a co-driver at Sandown and Bathurst. A disappointed Baird was happy to be paid out for the second year of his WPS contract, and concentrate instead on a fresh opportunity driving for Tony Quinn's team in the Porsche Carrera Cup.

As Baird reflects in his mid-30s on a career that promised so much, only to stall, there is a powerful feeling of unfinished business. Since having been given a chance at the Stones before he was ready, he says: 'I've not been in a competitive V8 car. . . . It's a shame. In different circumstances I could have had a 10-year career with the Stones. I don't blame anyone but myself.'

He remains adamant, however, that he is the equal of proven Kiwi drivers Greg Murphy and Paul Radisich, despite their results, particularly Murphy's, being much better. 'If you put the three of us in the same car on the same day there wouldn't be much difference between us. Murph would struggle too in my [WPS] car.'

Craig Baird keeping his WPS Ford nice and tidy at Pukekohe in 2005. The weekend ended rather frighteningly though when his car was shunted into the track's inside railing at 240 kmh.

THE WAY AHEAD

New Zealand's long-term prospects of continuing to host a round in Australia's V8 Supercars series were shrouded in uncertainty at the end of 2005. The only certainty was that, despite the serious reservations of Supercars company chairman Tony Cochrane, the shabby Pukekohe facility would be the venue for two more years after the previous five-year contract expired in April 2005. A big question mark hangs over New Zealand's options after 2007, with the planned new track at Hampton Downs, on State Highway 1, a little south of Auckland's Bombay Hills, once seen as perhaps the most likely venue to replace Pukekohe.

Other suggestions have included a possible street race in Hamilton, using upgraded facilities at Taupo or Manfeild, or setting up at Auckland's Whenuapai airbase. The indomitable Cochrane favours a street race, and remains 'very confident' that it will become a reality — even after the debacle surrounding the much-hyped Auckland street race

years from 2006. Banks, in particular, seemed to think it was a fait accompli, that the excitement, economic benefits and worldwide publicity for Auckland would outweigh concerns about noise, traffic and inconvenience to businesses.

As the protracted consent process became bogged down the pair lost their swagger, and it was a bitter pill for them to swallow when the street race never came into the light. New Zealand's many motor racing fans, some of whom had lent their weight to submissions in favour of the race, were naturally devastated. The proposed 2.6 km track, which was centred on Victoria Park, just off the Auckland motorway and a short distance from the harbour bridge, was seen by some as a flawed concept given its potential to create traffic chaos. The three independent commissioners appointed by the city council — David McGregor, Ross Gee and Gordon Macfarlane — certainly saw it that way, though in their evaluation they recognised that a street race

The indomitable Cochrane favours a street race, and remains 'very confident' that it will become a reality . . .

proposal, which was defeated in 2004 in a blaze of publicity by what Cochrane regarded as New Zealand's draconian Resource Management Act. A bid by the Wellington City Council to revive its street race also came to grief when it did not have the time to gain the necessary resource consent for a start in 2006.

However, Cochrane continues to base his optimism on the outstanding success of the existing V8 street races in Adelaide and Surfers Paradise each year — two of the favourite rounds in the series — and the superior potential they offer sponsors and corporates through exposure to greater numbers of spectators. The Clipsal 500 km in Adelaide has repeatedly won tourism awards, as well as those for motor racing, for the quality of the festival that surrounds it. In May of 2004, before resource consent had been obtained, Cochrane and the then Auckland mayor, John Banks, prematurely announced that the Queen City had secured the street race for seven

would be popular, exciting and 'generate significant positive economic benefits for some sectors of the community' in Auckland.

At the time, Cochrane commented that as a result of that disaster and the bogey of resource consent, New Zealand was in danger of becoming a sporting backwater and was increasingly unlikely to be a Supercar destination. A year later he was over his disappointment and was philosophical when he said: 'In hindsight the proposal was flawed. It was probably ridiculous to be trying to have a race in that part of the city. We [V8 Supercars] were guided by the people who said it could happen. I feel sorry for all those who tried. They became part of a political juggernaut.'

The decision left Cochrane having to eat a dollop of humble pie. After he had condemned the Pukekohe amenities, Supercars' only option to ease

A panoramic view of the start of a Supercar heat at Pukekohe.

the considerable pressure to keep a New Zealand round was to negotiate a new deal with the circuit owners, the Counties Racing Club — though, as Cochrane said, the series had now 'outgrown Pukekohe' after it had 'served us well'.

With a decision for 2008 probably not required till halfway through 2007, Cochrane remained 'totally convinced' New Zealand would find a long-term venue to replace Pukekohe which would secure its future in the formula. 'It's going to require a lot of hard work for two years behind the scenes to do it,' he said.

Auckland-based promoter Dean Calvert was pretty keen to make it happen in Wellington, as illustrated by the name of his new company, Capital Streetrace Management Ltd. However, given the negative reaction that tended to overshadow what started as a highly positive attempt in 2005, and the belated need for resource consent, the odds were against him. Wellington's prospects looked rosy in 2005 with the proposed track through the central business district already having the necessary consent. But at the eleventh hour the city council suddenly

realised the circuit was not compatible with its plans to plant a boulevard of pohutukawa trees.

Another circuit had to be found, and the new one, around the Wellington Stadium, went outside the sector that was covered by resource consent. With the deadline for advising Supercars of its position upon it, and suddenly lacking resource consent, the council had no option but to back off, and suddenly Pukekohe was back in favour.

Wellington city councillors were generally in favour of the V8s on the original circuit. However, with the council's financial position having deteriorated, public opinion swinging against them, and the costs of staging a round, certainly initially, well above the level the council would normally regard as prudent for a sound business investment, support has wavered and is unlikely to be revived.

Calvert represented the world's biggest sports management company, IMG, when it partnered the Auckland City Council to try and bring about the street race there. The Auckland result, which cost the partners around $NZ700,000 each, and IMG's inability to do any better alongside the Wellington

Many of the thousands of fans who attend Pukekohe take the opportunity to get 'up close and personal' with their heroes and favourite teams with a walk along pit lane.

City Council a few months later, contributed to IMG's decision to close its New Zealand office, and run any activities from Australia.

Undaunted, Calvert formed his new company, whose offices overlook Victoria Park. It won the rights to promote Pukekohe for two years, after Calvert had been involved in a similar role with IMG for the previous five years.

Cochrane talked of a Hamilton street race, and Manfeild, near Palmerston North, and Taupo have been consistently sidelined because they are too far away from big population numbers and lack the structures to properly cater for the crowds who would attend. Whenuapai might only come into the equation if all other options were exhausted.

A Manawatu consortium made a quality presentation to host Supercars at Manfeild from 2006 only to lose out to the superior possibilities offered by an Auckland street race. The rejection understandably

sucked some of the momentum and enthusiasm out of well-developed plans, which included promises of the finance necessary to rejuvenate Manfeild's tired facilities — which was a pity.

Happily, by the end of 2005 work on Manfeild's long-awaited improvements was gathering momentum. The argument that Manfeild is too far away from the necessary population base to be a viable option flies in the face of what occurs in Australia, and is almost an insult to the passion of the New Zealand fans. Bathurst, which has a population of around 35,000, is more than three hours' drive from Sydney, and lacks the facilities to accommodate all those who venture there every year, but it does not stop spectators turning up in generally increasing numbers. There were 166,840 over the four days in 2005, though the weather was unfavourable on the Saturday and Sunday. That number was down about 6000 on the record attendance in 2004.

Cochrane remained 'totally convinced' New Zealand would find a long-term venue to replace Pukekohe . . .

Getty Images

Promoter Dean Calvert (left), Auckland mayor John Banks (centre) and Supercars chairman Tony Cochrane are all smiles in May 2004 when they announce Auckland is to have a street race. The smiles evaporated months later when the decision was over-turned.

Getty Images

Hard-pressed promoter Dean Calvert making a presentation in 2004 in support of the Auckland street race.

Many of those attending races accept that they will have to stay in neighbouring towns, some more than an hour away. Manfeild is just a few kilometres away from Palmerston North (population 78,000), and is less than two hours by car from Wellington, and such is New Zealanders' love for the V8s that they will willingly travel from anywhere in the country to be there.

The Hampton Downs project is an ambitious one, with a motor racing track forming just a part of it. Classic racing car enthusiasts Tony Roberts and Chris Watson are the directors of Hampton Downs Motorsport Park, a 156 hectare property, which will include a 3.7 km track, 14 lifestyle blocks, 80 apartments, 12 industrial units, and a restaurant. Roberts, the managing director, says the property is less than an hour from downtown Auckland, two km away from the Meremere drag racing facility, and just a few kilometres south of Pukekohe. He said he already had agreements for the sale of various properties amounting to more than $NZ30 million. Though there will be corporate suites built above well-appointed pits, there will be no grandstands.

Instead spectators will sit on aluminium seats on grassy banks, and an initial resource consent application will be for a crowd limit of 20,000, insufficient for the numbers who would want to watch the V8s, and just a drop in the bucket compared with the potential of more than a hundred thousand a day for a street race. To increase the numbers at Hampton Downs would require further consent. Late in 2005, Roberts and Watson were trying to form a heads of agreement with Transit New Zealand, which, if successful, would help ensure the consent. Roberts, who recently bought a 1969 McLaren M10A single-seater, said the venture had received huge support and he was confident that the consent would be secured. Building the track and facilities would then start immediately, he said, and he expected construction to take 18 months.

Calvert and the Auckland City Council's manager of recreation and community services, Cameron Parr, lamented the failure of the street race proposal, both harbouring the belief it would have done great things for Auckland, with the many positives outweighing the negatives. On the back of the success in Adelaide and Surfers Paradise, Calvert approached the city council, and Tourism Auckland could see 'the wonderful effect on a city of something like this'. Calvert considered the consent process was tough on the applicants. 'They do all the work, and pay for it,' he said. 'The people appealing just have to cast doubt, and the applicants can't rebut it till the end, when the damage is probably done.'

He also believed the timing was not good, with the proposal being aired shortly before the local elections. Candidates who disagreed with the street race tended to get better exposure than normally, he said.

Parr said it would have been 'fantastic for Auckland, creating huge economic benefits'. 'It would have brought the city a minimum economic benefit each of the seven years of $NZ20 million, and put Auckland on the international stage with the race being shown on television in more than a hundred countries,' Parr said. 'It would have been all over in three days, and it was only really on the Friday that the traffic was a big issue. A lot of people were prepared to use other methods of transport to help us get over it.'

He considered that the bid fell down because seven months was too little time to provide all the information necessary to satisfy the commissioners, especially as there were a number of negative elements to be considered. The partners had looked at three or four possible inner-city circuits, Parr said. The only one that met the criteria was around Victoria Park, with Fanshawe Street having a straight of the required length and width. It saddened Parr that while Australia had a 'can do' attitude, in New Zealand it often tended to be a 'can't do' approach.

New Zealand's No. 1 Supercar driver, Greg Murphy, said the Resource Management Act did nothing for the country's reputation in Australia. 'The decision to can the street race was very embarrassing,' he said. 'It made us sound like a bunch of wusses. It was a most ridiculous form of over-democracy.' He maintained that the government should step in to ensure that 'one of the biggest events in New Zealand annually' had a settled future, just as it had when it provided financial support for continued participation in yachting's America's Cup, and when it backed the New Zealand Rugby Union's bid to secure the 2011 World Cup.

Murphy was similarly unimpressed with Cochrane's threats to drop New Zealand when the proposed street races did not eventuate. 'It's ridiculous that New Zealand shouldn't have a V8 round because Tony doesn't like Pukekohe,' he said. 'Tony can be a bully boy. I've had my run-ins with him. The Pukekohe track's too short and the facilities are average, but it has served us well for five years.'

Even though Supercars' future in New Zealand remains undecided, and a lot of the existing facilities are modest, the national scene has hardly been more vibrant in terms of the calibre of the fields and sponsorship interest. Though having a driver back in Formula One after a lengthy absence appears less likely, with Scott Dixon's single-seater career in the United States having lost some of its momentum, drivers in other open-wheeler categories are showing a lot of promise — in particular, former world karting champion Wade Cunningham, with victory in the United States Infiniti Pro Series, and

Getty Images

Jason Richards (left) and Greg Murphy talking up their chances at a press conference at Sky City before the Pukekohe round in 2005.

Matt Halliday and Jonny Reid in the New Zealand team in the new A1 international series.

At home the New Zealand V8 touring car championship is attracting many of the leading domestic drivers to a spectacular series that successfully mimics its far more expensive Supercars big brother and is even attracting drivers from Australia; the slick Toyota single-seater series has revived interest in open-wheelers; and the Porsche races have become so competitive that quality New Zealanders Jim Richards, Craig Baird, Fabian Coulthard and Halliday have flown in for rounds.

It would be a calamity if there was no V8 round in New Zealand from 2008, given the success and involvement in the series of so many New Zealanders, and the volume of interest. Tony Cochrane's mention of Hamilton as a possible street race venue emerged as a much firmer option in February 2006. It transpired that the persistent Dean Calvert had diverted his attention towards Hamilton after the city's mayor, Michael Redman, saw the potential of Supercars despite the failed bids of Auckland and Wellington. There was greater optimism this time that the necessary resource consent would be granted.

Bibliography

Ambrose, M., with Callander, S. *The Devil Racer*, GEP Books, Docklands, Victoria, 2004.

Becht, R. *Champions of Speed*, Moa Beckett, Auckland, 1993.

Brock, B. *Peter Brock: Living with a Legend*, Pan Macmillan Australia, Sydney, 2004.

Clarke, A., Horsburgh, M. & Wensley, S., (eds). *V8 Supercar Yearbook*, SAM Media, Fortitude Valley, Queensland, 2004.

Murphy, G., with Owen, P. *Murph's Law: The Autobiography*, Phantom House, 2004.

Myhre, S. *50 Years On Track: A History of Motorsport in New Zealand*, Hodder Moa Beckett, Auckland, 2002.

Naismith, B. *The Jim Richards Story*, Gary Sparke & Associates, Glen Waverley, Victoria, 1986.

Normoyle, S. *The Great Race, Vols 22 & 23*, Chevron Publishing, Hornsby, NSW, 2002, 2003.

Tuckey, W. *The Sound and the Fury: 100 Years of Motorsport in Australia*, Focus Publishing, Bondi Junction, NSW, 2004.

Wilson, S. *Australia Motor Racing Yearbook 1986–87*, Berghouse Publishing, Killara, NSW, 1987.

A number of Australian motor racing publications, particularly *V8X Supercar Magazine* and *Motorsport News*, and media guides and race programmes were also valuable sources of information.